D1551813

TRANSFORMING LITERACY: CHANGING LIVES THROUGH READING AND WRITING

INNOVATION AND LEADERSHIP IN ENGLISH LANGUAGE
TEACHING   VOLUME 3

TRANSFORMING LITERACY: CHANGING LIVES THROUGH READING AND WRITING

ROBERT P. WAXLER

University of Massachusetts at Dartmouth

MAUREEN P. HALL

University of Massachusetts at Dartmouth

United Kingdom – North America – Japan
India – Malaysia – China

Emerald Group Publishing Limited
Howard House, Wagon Lane, Bingley BD16 1WA, UK

First edition 2011

British Library Cataloguing in Publication Data
A catalogue record for this book is available from the British Library

ISBN: 978-0-85724-627-1
ISSN: 2041-272X (Series)

Emerald Group Publishing
Limited, Howard House,
Environmental Management
System has been certified by
ISOQAR to ISO 14001:2004
standards

Awarded in recognition of
Emerald's production
department's adherence to
quality systems and processes
when preparing scholarly
journals for print

INVESTOR IN PEOPLE

DEDICATED TO:

Linda Waxler

Patricia Anne Gormley Hall

CONTENTS

ACKNOWLEDGEMENTS

Transforming Literacy: Changing Lives Through Reading and Writing developed from our love of literature and learning and from our deep commitment to the belief that literary narrative (stories) and life inevitably mingle together without end. To say that is to admit that we cannot name all the people, all the experiences, or all of the texts that have influenced us; but, as you read this book, we hope you will hear some of the many voices, explicit and implicit, that have inspired us and so helped to shape it. For us, books are always alive, asking to be read, and the world is always a learning environment generously inviting human beings on a quest to know something more about themselves. Human beings have a natural desire to learn, and we are grateful to all those who helped us on our way.

We especially want to acknowledge the thousands of people who have participated in the Changing Lives Through Literature (CLTL) program, started in 1991 in Massachusetts as an alternative sentencing experiment and which, over the last 20 years, has expanded throughout the United States and the United Kingdom. That program stands as a wonderful testament to the power of literature to transform lives and is central to our thinking in this book.

We also want to thank all the college students at the University of Massachusetts at Dartmouth and the high school students and teachers at the New Bedford West Side Alternative School and the Fall River Resiliency School who taught us so much, especially while were writing this book. Our experiences with them in the classroom were deep and valuable moments, never to be forgotten.

Martha C. Pennington, our editor, also deserves special recognition for her encouragement and dedication. Her extraordinary and detailed suggestions, as well as her commitment and sensitivity, guided us through every challenge we encountered in this project, and we will always be grateful to her for lending us her support and sharing her wisdom.

Finally, we thank our colleagues and other educators, writers and lovers of literature and learning, and, of course, our family and friends—all those who still believe that the best education is always an adventurous journey, a quest to discover the questions that lead to the meaning of that which cannot be fully grasped, the mystery of human life itself.

– Robert P. Waxler
Maureen P. Hall

PREFACE

In *Transforming Literacy: Changing Lives Through Reading and Writing*, we argue for the value and relevance of reading in the education of citizens for the 21st century. Our case is built on a foundation of our reading and understanding of literary works, combined with educational and scientific literature related to reading, writing, and learning more generally; our own beliefs, stemming from long experience of university and K-12 classrooms; and a number of educational research projects in which we have been engaged that have involved students in different types of circumstances, including future teachers as well as at-risk children and adults.

If you follow our argument carefully, you will realize that when we talk about literature, we are not talking about the books silently sitting on the shelf, but something alive, something that calls to the reader, something that can excite the imagination and something that, once actively engaged, can stir the human heart. Literature in our view is very much like a mystery story, but it is better than most mystery stories because its richly textured language is always filled with surprises, endless secrets each time the reader returns to it, experiencing the language anew as that language permeates the reader's skin, penetrating the flesh into the bloodstream. For the reader, there are always hidden clues, secrets to be uncovered, as he or she moves from page to page. When one secret is revealed, another appears, and the reader is eager to turn the page and find out what happens next. Good writers always do that—they stir desire: they make you want to know what is on the next page, move forward, unravel the mystery as it is created through the reading experience—even as they also make you want to slow down as you read, to savor the words and the images and memories which they call up. That kind of reading experience does not end when the book ends. It continues to call to you, inviting you to read the narrative again, to discuss it with others, to move deeper into yourself, to extend yourself out to others. For us, that is the activity of reading as we understand it, and it is also the activity of learning, the adventure of education.

The 20th century will be remembered for its significant progress in science and technology, for its advancements in medicine and in its understanding of the biology and chemistry of the body. But we doubt that human beings have learned much of importance about the mysteries of the human heart, about compassion or community, about vulnerability or humility, about the meaning of that Socratic dictum to "know thyself." For us, that Socratic dictum defines genuine human desire, the desire to learn about what it means to be human. In a world that privileges celebrity rather than genuine heroes, images rather than substance, manipulation and power rather than dignity and love, speed rather than contemplation, we find little to celebrate and much to be concerned about. In such a world, human beings lose their way, pursue false idols, and begin to hallucinate. We believe that the classroom is the best place to reinvigorate the quest for the human, and that language and literature, intelligent and passionate discussion, story and self-reflection are the central means to that end. That belief is what this book is about.

We invite you to join us in our *Transforming Literacy* journey, and we hope that you find something of interest and of value in our book, whether it reinforces or changes your view. Most of all, we hope that our book will lead to further conversation about the important matter of the place of literacy in our lives, our civilization, and the education of our children and citizens.

CHAPTER ONE

THE READING AND WRITING CLASSROOM AS THE NEW NEIGHBORHOOD

In *Not For Profit: Why Democracy Needs the Humanities* (Nussbaum, 2010), Martha C. Nussbaum, arguably the most distinguished philosopher in the United States today, points out that there is a long and progressive tradition in education that needs to be rejuvenated. That tradition ranges from Socrates in ancient Greece to a number of scholars in other countries: Jean Jacques Rousseau in France; the Swiss educator, Johann Pestalozzi; the German educator, Friedrich Froebe; the American Transcendentalist, Bronson Alcott; and the Indian artist, Rabindranath Tagore—to name just some of the more important figures. It is a tradition rooted in the belief that the goal of education is to create a compassionate community of concerned human beings, a democracy that celebrates human beings as ends in themselves, not as means to some other end such as profits or winning. This is a tradition grounded in a fundamental belief that human beings desire to learn and to create meaning in the world. That sense of desire gives them purpose and direction. Such a tradition celebrates education as an end in itself, not as a means to an end, and so it attempts to preserve the dignity of each individual and, at the same time, the value of human community. It is a tradition that privileges "wisdom" over "smartness," the depth of compassionate under-standing and the patience of critical judgment over the cleverness of manipulation and the speed of production for quick effects. It favors unique human beings rather than commodities.

Nussbaum's context and argument are similar to ours and offers focus for emphasizing the power of education for creating a democratic community and the importance of language and literature, stories and conversation, in the 21st-century classroom. Students and teachers interacting in the space of a classroom should be engaged in the ongoing creation of a learning environment, an extraordinary place that stretches their possibilities, that offers hope and acknowledgment, an imaginative space that inspires them to recognize the depths of themselves and their interdependency on others. Our argument, put boldly, is that a primary focus on language and narrative best accomplishes this noble goal.

How do we dare make such a claim when literature seems increasingly pushed to the margins of our society, and when students often seem to have lost interest in reading significant—or any—novels and poetry? We have written this book to offer our answer to this question and to defend our position against those respected critics who disagree. For us, language and sustained narrative are linked together, located at the heart of human identity and community, and in a world riddled with confusion and chaos, human identity and community seem constantly in crisis. In such a world, we believe, literature emerges as our best hope. We will have much to say about this as we proceed, but listen to Mark Johnson, a moral philosopher and cognitive scientist, who helps introduce the point:

> Narrative supplies and reveals the themes by which we seek to unify the temporal, historical dimension of our existence, and without which our lives would be a meaningless jumble of disconnected events.... . Only narrative encompasses both the temporality and the purposive organization at the general level at which we pursue overarching unity and meaning for our lives. (Johnson, 1987, pp. 170–171)

The point here is that meaning is made through narrative, and human beings need meaning to survive and thrive. Human beings desire to learn and to understand themselves, and they need narrative to achieve this goal. As the French novelist Nancy Huston says: "Narrative gives our life a dimension of meaning utterly unknown to animals. Thus, from now on, ... human Meaning [sic] is distinct from animal meaning in that it is built up out of narratives, stories, fictions" (Huston, 2008, p. 15). The interaction human beings have with narratives is at the core of our desire to learn. Narrative provides a means of developing the self and also a deepened understanding of others.

To educate along these lines is potentially a way of educating for a "humane, people-sensitive democracy," as Nussbaum (2010, p. 25) suggests. But this is no easy task. From birth, each person struggles internally with the contending forces natural to every individual: fear, greed, and narcissistic aggression, on the one side, and compassion and respect for others, on the other side. This internal clash, mirroring the external clash of civilizations, begins at birth with universal feelings of helplessness, vulnerability, and primitive shame, disgust at our own bodily wastes, and other fear- and guilt-induced human responses. Sensing mortality and finitude from the beginning of life, that human beings are ultimately powerless against so many things, we all become anxious; both fear and shame become palpable and real. As Nussbaum (2010) explains it: "Out of this anxiety and shame emerges an urgent desire for completeness and fullness that never completely departs.... And this desire to transcend the shame of incompleteness leads to much instability and moral danger" (p. 31). As we explore in the following chapters, we believe that this insight about desire, the human need from birth to wrestle with and acknowledge our vulnerability, to embrace it in ourselves and in others, to give it meaning, is crucial to creating self and democracy. The confrontation with our vulnerability determines what we learn and the way we learn. It helps explain the desire to learn. How best to deal with it?

THE PROBLEM IS IN THE RESPONSE

What seems to be the conventional way humans have responded to this inevitable sense of human vulnerability? In her book, Nussbaum (2010) maps the dominant consequences and behaviors of societies and individuals who have refused to acknowledge this fact of human vulnerability. Rather than accepting human limitations, people usually have treated human vulnerability (often called "human weakness") as something to avoid, something to fear and to hate. The results of this kind of resistance are clear. Attempting to distance that fundamental part of human identity, which is a central element of being human, people try to throw it off, become blind to it: they engage in abjection, that is, they disassociate themselves from it, make it the "other," refusing to confront who they really are as sentient beings. The consequences of such acts of denial often create toxic results: scapegoating and bullying; stigmatization, stereotyping, and prejudice against minorities, gays, and women; rigid hierarchies and aggressive domination; irrational rage, harmful shame, and other negative behaviors and beliefs. In essence, when people distance themselves from their own vulnerability, they push it onto others, refusing to accept it in themselves, often preferring to project it on to the "other"—even attempting, at times, to crush it.

For Nussbaum, every learning environment, stretching from the classroom spaces out to families and neighborhoods, can help move people through such fear and hate, and thus restore some semblance of humanity to the society as a whole. In the classroom, human beings can learn practical competence, that they are able and free within limits to create their own meaning and direction; but they can also learn something else: they can become cognizant of the universality of human vulnerability (the stranger lurking within the depths of the self) and, through that awareness, learn to create a more mindful and authentic self. By understanding shared human vulnerability, in other words, people can learn to build empathy and compassion towards themselves and others. They can begin to achieve what Socrates claimed as the essential goal of education: knowing the self. As Nussbaum (2010) puts it: "Our very inadequacy can become the basis of our hope of a decent community" (p. 34). This is our argument, too. Especially in a learning environment energized by reading, writing, and discussion, human beings can develop a sort of "emotional contagion." Teachers can excite students to exercise their daring imaginations, teach them to negotiate meaning together in community with others, and so celebrate their common humanity. All human beings are vulnerable from the beginning; understanding that can make humans sociable, as individuals turn to humanity for comfort, communication, and connection.

STARTING OUT: THE BEGINNINGS OF CHANGING LIVES THROUGH LITERATURE

It is just this kind of thinking that inspired us to try a unique partnership between college students and high school students. We conducted an experiment in an alternative public school setting—a place of vulnerability and high anxiety. To help create the design of the experiment, we used the Changing Lives Through Literature (CLTL) program (Waxler & Trounstine, 1999) as one of the primary models, and that program, too, remains central to our thinking about the future of education.

The CLTL program, started in 1991, is an alternative sentencing program for criminal offenders, some of the most vulnerable and marginalized people in our society. The first group of offenders consisted of 8 men who collectively had 148 convictions before entering the program. Instead of going back to jail, these men were sentenced to a college classroom. The program was designed to address "turnstile justice," the toxic cycle of committing a crime, going to jail, being released, and repeating the same negative cycle over and over. The books chosen for reading and discussion were ones that resonated with the issues the men were wrestling with, books like *The Old Man and the Sea* (Hemingway, 1952), *Of Mice and Men* (Steinbeck, 1937), *Sea Wolf* (London, 1963), and *Deliverance* (Dickey, 1970)—books that evoked themes of male identity, violence, and the relationship between the individual and the established order.

CLTL began at the University of Massachusetts at Dartmouth, and can now be found in 12 states in the United States and in England. It began as a program for adult men, expanded to adult women and recently juvenile offenders as well. Through the reading and the discussion of good literature, the program has clearly changed lives. As John Sylvia, one of the first criminal offenders to successfully complete the program, puts it: "This program was a changing point in my life. There were books that I couldn't put down. They kept me interested in the positive aspects of life."

Statistics also seem to confirm the success. One early longitudinal study, for example, determined that offenders who had gone through the CLTL program had a recidivism rate of about 18 percent compared to another group of offenders with similar criminal histories who had not gone through the program and had a recidivism rate of approximately 45 percent during the same period. (This study and others can be found on the home page for CLTL at the University of Massachusetts at Dartmouth, http://cltl.umassd.edu.)

Much has been written about this program (see *Finding A Voice*, Trounstine & Waxler, 2004; *Changing Lives Through Literature*, Waxler & Trounstine, 1999; Waxler, 2008), but allow us here, at the beginning of this book, to make some general points about its educational value for us.

Although started as an experiment to offer criminal offenders an alternative to jail, CLTL was motivated by a sustained belief that readers can be moved by stories as they map their own life stories onto the stories they read. Once moved, those readers then also want to talk about the stories with others, to explore them, to respond to their complexity, and to locate themselves through the stories and the group discussion. In other words, what the CLTL program taught us was that the engagement with a single story offers stability, at least for a moment; more importantly, it offers an expanded sense of duration in that moment, a deep flow of temporal movement. Such an encounter stirs desire: it excites the experience of life itself. Wrestling with the text, in other words, in a safe place like a classroom, protects and immunizes the human being from impending mortality, from the whisper of death itself.

That is what, we are convinced, literature can do and that the CLTL program demonstrates. Such attention to a story opens up and exposes the ongoing flow of mental activity; it makes readers self-reflective, and so psychologically available for further inquiry. Through reading and conversation, CLTL indicates, human beings make sense of the world, and they can become excited about their own thinking.

For us, then, CLTL suggested the following:

(a) The raw experience of human life—a life *story*—is a journey from birth to death, a journey with an emotional arc which can be envisioned as a narrative.
(b) This journey, a person's life story, always intermingles with the stories of others and with fictional stories, thus helping human beings create a sense of identity through time and also helping them to create meaning and location for their lives.
(c) Human language—the *word*—especially when shaped into narrative, is likely the most crucial development in giving the body purpose and direction on this life journey. Through narrative, human beings become self-reflective and appreciate the deep complexity of the human experience.
(d) Conversation about a story deepens the reading experience and widens the reader's understanding of the complexity of human life and of the meaning and importance of human community. Such conversation can inspire a rejuvenated sense of self and offer a glimpse of genuine democracy.

In the CLTL program, the stories seem to read the readers as much as the readers read the stories—an observation confirmed by neuroscientists who maintain that the flow of language actually can change the brain, just as the neural circuits in the brain can change the story of a human life. One night in the CLTL program, for example, one of the men in the midst of a discussion about Jack London's famous sea captain, Wolf Larsen, from his novel *Sea Wolf*, declared: "I used to be Wolf Larsen. I thought I could manipulate everyone. I was stupid then." That moment of linguistic surprise and communal exchange around the seminar table was not an idle response to words on a printed page, but rather an opening, an utterance about future possibilities, a recognition that human beings do not have to be caught in an endless repetitive cycle, a torturous present without a future or a past. It was an announcement that this man had seen himself, what he had been, and that he could move ahead. He wanted others to know that, too. Language and stories help make us all human agents as we locate ourselves in the world.

We have observed at the best moments in the CLTL classroom what we believe is crucial to the educational process: students reading the same story but each reading that story differently; a series of shifting voices first rising from the story itself, and then continuing through the multiplicity of classroom discussion—an ongoing and expanding conversation, in other words, that offers surprise and insight along the way as the voices mingle into new possibilities and create new surprises, just as they also resist something unnamed, something that cannot be fully grasped, something that nevertheless calls to us, to our shared vulnerability and finitude.

Human beings find themselves through language in just this way. They locate themselves in the world through such richly textured exchanges and negotiations, glimpsing the complexity of human life. There is a focus on the development of self through interactions with texts and with other human beings; through that kind of interaction, a space opens for teaching and learning where all voices are privileged. Through such a process, strangers become friends, and friends learn about their own uniqueness as they create a living human community in the space of the classroom.

On another evening in the CLTL classroom, a student wanted to talk about his singular encounter with Santiago, the fisherman in Hemingway's *The Old Man and the Sea*. There he was, the student explained, walking down Union Street, the main street in New Bedford, Massachusetts, struggling to resist the temptation to return to his old neighborhood and the drug habit he had been battling for several months. He came to the corner of that old neighborhood off of the main street and could just about hear the voices of his gang then, as he felt a sudden pull urging him to make the turn around that corner. But then, as this CLTL participant recounts, something else happened. He began to hear another voice, the voice of the old fisherman, Santiago, a voice echoing through his body, reminding him about what the old man had suffered through, what the old man had heroically endured. The fictional character was alive for the student at that crucial moment, an inspiration, a stranger become a friend, a voice encouraging him to go on, telling him that he was not alone, that he too could endure. It is not an exaggeration to say that a story, a literary narrative, had caught this student's attention, had given him focus, and perhaps had saved his life that day. For this CLTL participant, language, in the form of a great story, had thrown him bounding into the future with purpose and direction.

That student had not only made a stranger (Santiago) into a friend, but he had engaged in what is, at times, referred to as "deep reading," an activity in opposition to the speed of contemporary life. *Deep reading*, and the subsequent conversation related to that reading, allowed him to get focused, to pay attention to the beat of the human heart, and to locate himself, first embodied in the classroom with others, and then embodied in the larger environment of the neighborhood, the world as he knew it.

Since the inception of CLTL in 1991, over 5,000 offenders have gone through the program, and many judges and other court officials say the program has also made a significant difference in their own lives. One judge, for example, has said that participation in the CLTL program has been the joy of his judgeship. Court officers, including probation personnel, consistently declare that CLTL reading and discussion have changed the way they perceive and interpret their everyday world. The criminal offenders also seem to agree.

Take Jeff, for example. He was a young man in his early twenties, a serious drug dealer, who, by his own admission, could make $4000 a week on the streets. He had only an eighth grade education, but he was smart, and he loved the rhythm and excitement of the neighborhood culture. His father had spent half his life in the toughest prison in Massachusetts, and Jeff might very well have been headed in the same direction. But after a couple of CLTL sessions, Jeff seemed to be beginning to change. "I love challenging your interpretations around this table, Professor," he said. "I find it as exciting as anything out on streets." Jeff might have had a "photographic mind." He was able to cite passages from the novels that most readers could not easily recall. But it was his enthusiasm for the reading and the challenge of the discussion that energized all of us. Later, he added that he was not sure what was going to happen to him, but he had begun to read to his young daughter, something he had never thought about doing before. It is not clear where Jeff is today, but it is clear that Jeff glimpsed how exciting reading and thinking could be, more exciting than the mean streets that he knew so well.

And there was Joe. One day he came into the session a few minutes late. He looked disheveled and out of sorts. "Sorry," he said, "but I had an emergency." It really was one: his apartment had caught on fire and almost everything in it was destroyed. It sounded like a total disaster. But he had the book for the night with him—Norman Mailer's *An American Dream* (Mailer, 1965) "I couldn't save much from that fire," he declared, "but I ran back in to get the book. I really enjoyed reading it." He was ready to talk about it, too.

Or the night that Jack wanted to tell all of us about his experience in a local bar during the week. We gave him a chance before the official discussion got started. Jack had been at a bar and someone had come up to his table, apparently angry about something, and the intruder started shouting, according to Jack. "Ordinarily, I would have lost it then," Jack said. "I would have gotten out of my chair and punched the guy." But Jack didn't do that—and this was the point of his story. Instead, Jack stayed in his chair and thought about the Raymond Carver story we had discussed a couple of weeks earlier. "Those characters in the Carver story got drunk and acted on their rage," Jack explained. "That's the way I would have acted, too, until I got into this reading stuff. I didn't get out of my chair at the bar, just talked to the guy, calmed him down."

These are living examples of what reading and discussion can do, and they offer glimpses of what successful education can look like following the CLTL approach. For us, these examples offer testimony about the power of literature to change lives; the examples, drawn from the Changing Lives Through Literature project, begin to suggest what significance reading and discussion can provide within the learning environment.

AN EDUCATIONAL EXPERIMENT

It was the success of this CLTL alternative sentencing program that triggered a call to Waxler in August 2006 from Bernie Sullivan at the local Sheriff's Office to see if there was any interest in helping to build a partnership between the University of Massachusetts at Dartmouth and West Side School, an alternative junior and senior high school in the New Bedford public school system. Mr. Sullivan suggested using CLTL as the adhesive for that relationship; if CLTL had worked with criminals, it should also work for middle and high schoolers, especially those at risk. And the students at West Side School were all at high risk. They were the most vulnerable students in the city's public school system. Many had been thrown out of the "regular" middle schools or high school; most were poor, some were no longer living at home, and others had become gang members.

That experiment turned into an educational project that, along with the CLTL program, brought together many of the central concerns expressed throughout this book and that has in a fundamental way helped us to arrive at many of the ideas related to our defense of literature and to our sense of the importance of education for democracy. The school project helped us to further explore issues that are especially significant to us. These are: (1) the central importance of linguistic narrative; (2) the significance of reading, writing, and purposeful discussion in the classroom; (3) the need for the classroom to be an imaginative space—what we term a "new neighbor-hood"; and (4) the belief in education as a way of enhancing democracy and so creating both individual identity and compassionate community.

Our educational experiment focused on the importance of literature and language, and this too is important to emphasize from the beginning. Although we know that much of what we will say in this book can be applied to the humanities and the arts in general, we remain convinced that the singularity of literature is intricately connected to democracy and the future of education precisely because the diminished capacity of the "reading brain" threatens democracy itself. Maryanne Wolf reminds us of this when she explains what "the reading brain" is capable of, and, by implication, what is at stake when "the reading brain" becomes jeopardized:

> The development of reading ... has two parts. First, the ideal acquisition of reading is based on the development of an amazing panoply of phonological, semantic, syntactic, morphological, pragmatic, conceptual, social, affective, articulatory and motor systems, and the ability of these systems to become integrated and synchronized into increasingly fluent comprehension. Second, as reading develops, each of these abilities is facilitated further by this development. Knowing 'what's in a word' helps you read it better; reading a word depends on your understanding of its place in the continuum of knowledge. (Wolf, 2007, p. 223)

Like Maryanne Wolf, we especially value reading and believe that deep reading (see Chapter Two) has the unique capacity to teach human beings how best to create a narrative self; how best to build competence and confidence by shaping—not avoiding—human vulnerability; and, when coupled with focused conversation, how best to create a community for learning, a neighborhood where students and teachers can negotiate meaning and create knowledge together. For us, reading and writing in this "new neighborhood" addresses the deficiencies inherent in the education system. Rabindranath Tagore describes the current problem this way in his *Creative Unity*:

> By squeezing human beings in the grip of an inelastic system, one forcibly holding them fixed, we have ignored the laws of life and growth. We have forced living souls into a permanent passivity, making them incapable of moulding their own intrinsic design, and of mastering their own destiny. (Tagore, 1988, pp. 138–139)

Our *new neighborhood* is designed to address this kind of issue by promoting active growth and nurturing the spirit of freedom in the learners who are the "residents" of this new place. This neighborhood calls for students' active participation and development of self. Reading, in and of itself, represents an amazing, wondrous, and creative human accomplishment; it is an event that points the way to developing good citizenship and creating an opening for true equality.

For our educational experiment, we chose a classroom where we could focus on literature. It was filled with a diverse group of students with differing educational and financial statuses, with differing ethnic and family backgrounds, and without a common or shared knowledge base. We knew that this kind of classroom was comprised of high-risk students, the most vulnerable by most accounts, but we were also convinced that this kind of diversity could create angles of perception that would emphasize both the multidimensional quality of contemporary culture, and, at the same time, provide just the kind of foundation for learning through a shared reading experience which could lead those students to a deeper sense of self and community. If successful, the classroom could become a place where students wanted to come, a new neighborhood where they would enjoy what they were doing and so feel deep satisfaction.

For us, literature could help students locate themselves, and through good discussion, provide opportunities for them to create community with others who are also working on finding an imaginative and safe place to inhabit. From our experience with CLTL, we knew that stories offer an exciting entry into the thrill of finding the self. If we could get students engaged in reading stories, we knew that those stories could excite their minds, too. Those stories could become more thrilling than the television screen or the mean streets. That was part of the challenge, as our CLTL friend, Jeff, had indicated: to make the classroom a place more interesting and more exciting than the action on the street or the television screen.

As we considered the challenge, we also realized that we wanted to help learners understand that there is a significant difference between educating human beings in the skills of the procedural self and educating them in the wisdom of ethics and human values. As Chris Hedges puts it:

> For Socrates, all virtues were forms of knowledge. To train someone to manage an account for Goldman Sachs is to educate him or her in a skill. To train them to debate stoic, existential, theological, and humanist ways of grappling with reality is to educate them in values and morals. A culture that does not grasp the vital interplay between morality and power, which mistakes management techniques for wisdom, which fails to understand that the measure of civilization is its compassion, not its speed or ability to consume, condemns itself to death. (Hedges, 2009, p. 103)

Stories teach us how to read our lives, and they can teach us what Socrates knew well: that for every answer there is another question. That ongoing process of questioning is the process that enables the quest for wisdom and the shaping of the narrative self. Classrooms can rejuvenate this possibility; they can become the new neighborhood for the pursuit of compassion and truth. If human beings are willing to take the risk, classrooms can give students the confidence and desire to become lifelong learners, vulnerable and compassionate in their pursuit of human wisdom.

Many critics have insisted that schools must be better managed, that classrooms need more control (Glasser, 1985), that teachers need to teach the technical skills of efficiency and the uses of the latest electronic devices. We disagree. As Nussbaum (2010) suggests, the primary concern in education should be what it always has been: the growth of that which cannot be measured—human possibility and imagination, human compassion and understanding. This kind of growth applies to teachers as well as students, to everyone in fact. Good education and teaching is, as Jon Kabat-Zinn says, "mining the resources that are present in learners, cultivating intimacy with them, and allowing them to engage in their own learning, as opposed to having the arrogance of thinking we are the ones that make them learn" (Kabat-Zinn, 2005, p. 12). Education is a lifelong journey, just as reading and discussing good stories is a journey that can be lifelong. Human beings become learners as individuals and together with others.

In the changing world where all borders are on the verge of collapse, where the private and public spheres collide, where there is no time for self-reflection, where so few people share the same memory or history, where humans have increasingly accepted the role of nodes in a network, "the skills we need more than any others," as Zygmunt Bauman puts it, "are the skills of interactions with others—of conducting a dialogue, of negotiating, of gaining mutual understanding, and of managing or resolving the conflicts inevitable in every instance of shared life" (Bauman, 2008, p. 190). We wanted our school project to help point us in the direction of helping to create opportunities where humanizing interactions were paramount and where people learned to be mindful of themselves and others. We believed the power of language and narrative could create a kind of resonance, which connected all stakeholders in a shared learning environment.

A PROJECT TO CONNECT HEAD AND HEART THROUGH READING

The conversation with Sullivan at the jail soon expanded to the principal at West Side School, Dr. Deborah Sorrentino, and we began to explore possibilities, including utilizing some of the resources of the Education Department at our university. We zeroed in on an introductory Education course which focused on preservice teachers and promoted the department's strong belief in cognitive-affective learning theory, a good fit with the CLTL notion that engagement with language and literature does not separate emotions from cognition but offers a full and complex human experience. As Owen-Smith (2004), a leader in this area of theory suggests, the "brain does not separate emotions from cognitions" (p. 1). Unless attention is given to the interest, motivational levels, and attitudes of students, as Owen-Smith indicates, learning is always fleeting and temporary. Without activating both cognitive and affective dimensions of human consciousness, learning does not endure. For us, using good literature to stimulate the love of thinking and the excitement of learning made good sense: literature and learning should appeal both to the head and the heart.

THE SCHOOL CONTEXT

Since West Side was a school where students went after they had been expelled from the mainstream New Bedford Junior High School or the New Bedford Senior High School, it was, in essence, a school of last resort which was saddled with the predictable stereotypes and problems related to that dubious status. It might have been considered safer than other schools in New Bedford because it was the only school with a metal detector at the door, as the joke goes; but it was clearly a challenging place to create educational opportunity and to test our belief in literature and the value and importance of building a new neighborhood. Many of the teachers in the classroom at West Side were extraordinarily compassionate and dedicated, but the job was not easy and could often be frustrating. At-risk adolescents populated this school; many students were not only gang members but were exposed to violence on a regular basis. Many of these students not only struggled with poverty and discrimination, but at times seemed focused mainly on survival. For some, it was a heroic effort simply to get up in the morning, face a gang member waiting at the door, and then try to get beyond the pull and the dangers of their own neighborhoods and streets to come to the classroom.

It was in this context that the Urban Literacy Group (ULG), as we called it, came together, under the belief that if CLTL had demonstrated that literature and discussion could move criminal offenders in a new direction, then perhaps similar work could help the middle and high schoolers at West Side. In the CLTL sessions, many offenders had rarely read a book, but they had nonetheless grown excited about literature. These offenders would often explain that they had never realized, before CLTL, that they could think. A good number of offenders who had fallen off the education track had returned to it as a result of the CLTL program, going on for a high school equivalency diploma (GED), or even community college and university schooling.

CLTL had shown us that as the plot of a good story unfolds for a reader, so too does the identity of the reader unfold, making reading and discussion exciting and self-reflective, arousing desire and giving a new sense of possibility and direction. This can be true for anyone:

> We all have our stories and we all have the opportunity to make a story from the raw experience of our life…. Story evokes story, builds community, because it offers us the opportunity to locate ourselves in the world, among other stories. (Waxler, 2007, p. 128)

Literature could help students locate themselves and, through good discussion, provide opportunities for them to create a new place, a new neighborhood with others, as we envisioned it, who were also working on finding safe places to inhabit in their worlds. For us, the West Side experiment seemed like an ideal way of continuing the great experiment in American public education. We wanted to make our classroom an imaginative and exciting space, a place which could connect "the experiences of vulnerability and surprise to curiosity and wonder, rather than to crippling anxiety" (Nussbaum, 2010, p. 101). Such a place, as Nussbaum explains, is very much like the kind of place that the psychoanalyst Donald Winnicot thought of as "potential space" (Winnicot, 1986), where people remain open to each other—a playful space that could contribute to the shaping of democratic citizenship because it allows for the sense of threat and risk to give way to curiosity about the other. As Nussbaum reminds us: "Democratic equality brings vulnerability" (Nussbaum, 2010, p. 100) because it teaches people "to be capable of living with others without control" (*ibid.*, p. 101). That was the kind of classroom we wanted for our experiment: a space that would free up the imagination, allow for self-reflection, and encourage learners to interact with each other—in other words, a *new neighborhood* for learners to explore unknown territory, to confront the stranger in themselves.

We decided to use the anthology of short stories, *Changing Lives Through Literature* (Waxler & Trounstine, 1999), as we began the project at West Side. The first story we read was "Greasy Lake" by T. Coraghessan Boyle (Boyle, 1999), a story popular in the CLTL program in part because it offers high adventure as well as significant depth for discussion (and a story that we will discuss in detail in Chapter Two).

"Greasy Lake" is a story that almost everyone can connect to, most readers agreeing that it is their story as well. The seventh and eighth graders at West Side were no exception, mapping their stories onto Boyle's story, identifying with the need for excitement, the hunt for a hangout, a possible party, and the dangers always lurking just beneath the surface—"about a mile down Route 88" (as Boyle, echoing singer Bruce Springsteen, puts it). The next story from the anthology, "Where Are You Going, Where Have You Been" by Joyce Carol Oates (Oates, 1999), worked equally well, generating a lively conversation, especially when the class explored some of the emotional tension in the 15-year-old Connie as she is drawn to the fascinating and deadly predator, Arnold Friend (see Chapter Three for full discussion of this story).

A FUNDAMENTAL PROBLEM OBSERVED EARLY ON

The readings and the discussions clearly excited many of the students at West Side. As one 13-year-old put it, reflecting on how he used to struggle to stay awake during his literature class: "I was mad tired. But now I'm not sleeping. I'm paying attention." CLTL had taught us that a good story, coupled with good discussion, serves as a site of desire that can arouse excitement. Stories could wake up even these West Side students, who were often exhausted by the tragic trials and tribulations of their everyday struggle to survive. Early on, we saw that these stories and discussions could take students to a new place, a neighborhood of sorts, that gives them an opportunity to retell their own stories through the stories they read—or at least to gain a glimpse of another place, a place where each student can contribute to the ongoing creation of culture through language and imagination. Language and literature stirred up the students' desire at West Side early on, got them moving, and gave them a new direction. There was hope in that, and it pointed to the ongoing dream of education as part of the great American experiment in democracy.

But just as we noticed how language and literature could wake these students up and allow them to glimpse another world beyond the boundaries of their current negative situation, we also noticed a counterforce, a pull back to the old place, their old neighborhood. Despite the desire to read, there was always an unresolved tension in the classroom. On the one side, students grew excited about the literature; they wanted to join the conversation and move their lives in a new direction. On the other side was the drag of resistance, the voice telling them that education was not cool, that the gangs and the gang leaders, and the action and the rhythm of the adventurous streets, offered them all the excitement and recognition they needed.

CREATING THE NEW NEIGHBORHOOD

This was the challenge that needed to be met at West Side: how best to begin to create a new neighborhood for these at-risk students, one that would draw these vulnerable middle and high schoolers away from the gangs and the misery of their home neighborhoods and take them somewhere else—an embodied space that would stimulate them to imagine and to dream about new possibilities. How could we get students to listen to the voices coming from books and their fellow students rather than the voices of their old gang members? It is not really a new problem, of course; it reminds us of one of bell hooks' favorite stories:

> Here is one of my favorite stories, a story that teaches and helps me. This is my version; there are many ways this story can be told. A student seeking to understand better the process of self-actualization goes to the teacher and says, "I often suffer from a split mind, lack of congruence between what I think, say, and do. How can I end this suffering?" The teacher tells the student that the potential for this split is happening inside everyone. For inside all of is there is a "sick self and a self struggling to be well and they are in conflict." When the student asks the teacher which self is winning the conflict, the teacher replies, "whichever self you feed." (hooks, 2010, p. 52)

Human beings can choose which road they want to travel, but that choice is not always easy, especially for those most vulnerable and without voice or a sense of direction. Our challenge was to give them sustenance and to stir the desire to join one neighborhood and not another.

Together with Bernie Sullivan and Dr. Sorrentino, we soon created a more comprehensive plan to further enrich and contextualize our experiment. A double literacy block was built into the middle schoolers' and high schoolers' schedules. Dr. Sorrentino facilitated a schedule for our Urban Literacy Program to meet three times a week in the afternoons. Sorrentino also chose three willing West Side teachers to be involved. It was decided that we would come in several times over the course of the fall semester to facilitate some of the CLTL discussions, and we would also come to West Side for a common planning time with the three teachers.

Reading and discussing good stories made up the core of the program, but our group knew that this would not be enough. As an added element, college students enrolled in the introductory Education course at the University were required, as a service learning project, to engage with the middle schoolers at West Side. Reading Robert Fried's *The Passionate Learner* (Fried, 2001) and Parker Palmer's *The Courage to Teach* (Palmer, 1998), the college students wrestled with issues related to adolescent students who were affectively disengaged with schooling, allowing the college students to integrate their experiences at West Side with educational theory and to begin to consider how best to build a neighborhood for education in their future classrooms. Each college student in the introductory Education course spent 15 hours tutoring one middle school student at West Side and documented the experience through a semester-long case study. The results were enlightening for us and for the students. As one college student described the experience:

> I have been attending the literacy program almost every week, and it has been a very enjoyable and interesting experience for me. I was able to see how the teachers have very

unique ways to discipline the most difficult students in the classroom. I feel most of these kids have unbelievable potential deep down; they just need guidance to prove it.

Another college student observed:

Basically, my ideas about education came from this field experience we had. Even though it was a difficult group of students to work with, and it was frustrating at times that I felt like I was not really getting anywhere with my student, I think I learned more than I would have, had I been working in a rural richer school setting. I feel like I actually probably learned more from my student and the students in his class, than they did from me tutoring them.

At the same time, research was conducted with the help of the college students collecting data on the process of preservice teachers working with these challenging middle schools students at West Side. The encounter with at-risk adolescents intensified the early teaching experience and tested the ability of these preservice teachers to struggle to build genuine educational neighborhoods:

Most people who want to become teachers have had only wonderful teaching and learning experiences. They have never struggled with school or worked with students who are cognitively or affectively challenged. (Hall, 2005, p. 8)

Such challenging opportunities offered the college students a significant entry into the teaching profession, allowing them to consider the depth of their own commitment to teaching and to the struggle to build a community that bridges cognitive and affective learning. Through these opportunities, the college students were beginning to create a valued and valuable narrative about their teaching lives.

PROFESSIONAL DEVELOPMENT AND PARKER PALMER

In CLTL, criminal offenders, sitting with professors and judges around a table, exchange ideas and share their frustrations, ideas, and feelings through the stories they are discussing. At the best moments, every mask being worn, every role being played, is dropped, and what participants hear and understand together is the full complexity of the human heart. It is a glimpse of a better world, the building of a new place to be: what we mean by a "new neighborhood."

With a similar goal in mind, we conducted some professional development for the teachers at West Side focused on differentiated instruction and building community, hoping to affectively engage those at the school as a learning neighborhood. In 2007–2008, with funds from a public service grant (Chancellor's Public Service Grant at the University of Massachusetts at Dartmouth), we provided all West Side teachers with a copy of Parker Palmer's *The Courage to Teach* (Palmer, 1998). In his book, Palmer (1998) talks about how teaching itself requires heart and how teachers "lose heart, in part, because teaching is a daily exercise in vulnerability.... As we try to connect ourselves and our subjects with our students, we make ourselves vulnerable to indifference, judgment, ridicule" (p. 17). These issues were relevant to both the West Side teachers and the college students, and it was helpful to share this common text.

Because the transformation we hoped to bring about involved both cognitive and affective kinds of learning, we also worked to create activities that drew in the larger community of stakeholders in these students' futures. They too had to become part of the story. These stakeholders include but are not limited to the school students themselves; their teachers, administrators, and legal guardians; the university students who were preservice teachers; and community members. We hosted a series of urban literacy dinners at West Side that included many of these stakeholders. These were community events which provided opportunities for people to learn more about what the ULG was trying to do and to celebrate some of the positive yet incremental changes observed in both students' attitudes and their literacy skills.

Other events contributed to the journey we were on and to the narrative we were collectively creating. We brought people together in new ways. The preservice teachers came to West Side, for example, during the semester as participants in a CLTL discussion which we facilitated, and the West Side students came to the college campus, experiencing it as a future learning environment for them. The preservice teachers saw the alternative school as a dynamic place, a possible future teaching and learning neighborhood for them, and in a different way, the alternative school students saw their future possibilities as well.

At the beginning of the spring semester, the University of Massachusetts at Dartmouth hosted its fifth annual Martin Luther King, Jr., breakfast. West Side students, teachers, and the school principal were invited to campus for this event. It was especially significant because the keynote speaker was Salome Thomas-El, a renowned educator from Philadelphia, Pennsylvania, who had worked successfully with urban adolescents and who had written a book about his experiences, titled *I Choose to Stay* (Thomas-El, 2004).

Early the following week, building on the education students' feedback from the previous semester, we held a field trip to the University campus for the West Side students. This provided opportunities for some self-selection of tutors and tutees for the second semester project. The field trip included a wide array of events. First, West Side students and teachers were given a tour of the campus. Next, students met with two student affairs professionals for an informational and motivational session. After this, the West Side students were shown a computer presentation by a Computer Science professor and his graduate students. And for the last session, West Side students had lunch with the new group of preservice teachers in the Chancellor's Board of Trustees Room. This meeting between preservice teachers and West Side students provided a further opportunity for beginning to build a community of learners across various contexts, and for the "residents" of the new neighborhood to interact and get acquainted with each other.

After the lunch meeting with West Side students, we held an informal discussion with the college Education students (the preservice teachers), inquiring about what kinds of perceptions they had of the West Side students. The preservice teachers commented that many of the West Side students seemed to believe that they could not go to college. The preservice teachers wanted to help change the West Side students' minds on this, making it one of their common goals for the semester. Believing that good teachers see possibilities in students that students themselves cannot always see, we viewed this as a valuable lesson both for the college students and for the West Side students. As role models, tutors, and future educators, the University of Massachusetts at Dartmouth students could provide the same kind of social and cognitive sustenance that a practicing teacher could provide, and they could help change the beliefs of the West Side students as well.

THE CREATION OF SUPPORTIVE SPACES
FOR LITERACY

In order to achieve cognitive and affective change, as Parker Palmer and others have suggested, both teachers and students must take risks, and this means being willing to open themselves to others and become vulnerable. West Side students had to allow themselves to be helped and to help themselves, and the college students had to make themselves available and open to the students they tutored, as teachers and professors must also admit their own limitations and anxieties in bidding for trust and connection. If educators are to build new social and learning neighborhoods, they must be honest with themselves and others, critical when appropriate, but with the honesty and respect of a vulnerable heart.

At the center of the CLTL program, and our educational work in general, is this acknowledgement of vulnerability, this sense that what creates community is the human heart and the risk human beings must be willing to take in order to open their heart in an effort to create a genuine bonded and democratic community. Teachers at West Side were at risk, and so, in a different way, were the West Side students. So too were the college students just entering the preservice experience. In such a situation, the acknowledgment of one's vulnerability becomes a central characteristic of the learning experience, a strength not a weakness—especially if the goal is a compassionate and understanding community.

After the college students read Parker Palmer's *The Courage to Teach* and interacted with the West Side students, we asked them to write about their own experience with these students in the context of Palmer's work. Then the college students' writing, their vulnerability and open self-reflection, was shared with the West Side teachers, allowing these teachers, to read, in a sense, their own vulnerability through the words of the college students. In this way, those teachers got a fresh look at their own roles and a glimpse at other possibilities. One of the teachers commented: "It was interesting to get feedback from an outside perspective. In this case the information came from preservice teachers. It allowed me to assess my strengths and weaknesses as a teacher." Another teacher's reaction is also telling: "It was refreshing to have input from an outside point of view. It helps you to reevaluate yourself as a teacher especially in an alternative setting."

WE ARE ALL READERS

Reading and writing, involving discussion and self-reflection through language, expands one's understanding of human identity, the self in relation to the world. Alberto Manguel, in *A History of Reading* (Manguel, 1997), underlines the centrality of reading to human life when he observes: "We all read ourselves and the world around us in order to glimpse what and where we are. We read to understand, or to begin to understand. Reading, almost as much as breathing, is our essential function" (p. 7). The West Side teachers read themselves through the writing of the college students; the college students read themselves through their experiences with the West Side students; and all this was helped along by the writing of Parker Palmer, whose work helped to enrich and contextualize those experiences.

In the same sense, the middle schoolers read stories that connected with their own lives. They explored connections through conversation in the classroom, arousing their desire to know and to learn, and creating the beginning of a new place for them to find themselves. Such a process contributes to the creation of a democratic narrative in at least two ways: (1) it helps encourage empathy and a recognition of mutual vulnerability; (2) it fosters self-reflection and so helps deepen the understanding of the narrative self and its interdependence with others.

That kind of process and experience, we believe, is especially important right now for adolescents, perhaps the most vulnerable of students in public schools, and so most in need of support and recognition of mutual vulnerability. As Moje (2002) has suggested, the nexus between students' day-to-day realities and the academic discourses they encounter in school needs to be the focus of increased research in adolescent literacy. Such an approach aligns well with the critical pedagogy of Freire and Macedo (1987), who note: "Reading does not consist merely of decoding the written word or language; rather it is preceded by and intertwined with knowledge of the world" (p. 29). In our view, reading helps to arouse desire in the human heart and to transform that desire into the possibilities of a new environment of genuine human concern, a context that acknowledges vulnerability, that struggles against stereotypes, and that gives students a sense of dignity and agency. Reading and discussing literature evokes the ethical imagination, the sense that we all are vulnerable, that we all share a common human heart.

One of the reasons we believe engagement with literature is so important is because it allows students the opportunity to wrestle with difficult issues, many of which they encounter on the street and elsewhere in their everyday lives. Literature that engages is simultaneously safe and disturbing. The classroom environment, the neighborhood, created around and through reading literature, provides a safe place to have intelligent conversations about disturbing matters. Through such conversation, students begin to empathize and connect the different discourses and spaces they inhabit both inside and outside of school.

Nussbaum (2010) lists many of the goals that schools should pursue in the quest for good citizens and a healthy democracy:

- Develop students' capacity to see the world from the viewpoint of other people, particularly those whom their society tends to portray as lesser, as "mere objects."
- Teach attitudes towards human weakness and helplessness that suggest that weakness is not shameful and the need for others not unmanly; teach children not to be ashamed of need and incompleteness but to see these as occasions for cooperation and reciprocity.

- Develop the capacity for genuine concern for others, both near and distant.
- Undermine the tendency to shrink from minorities of various kinds in disgust, thinking of them as "lower" and "contaminating."
- Teach real and true things about other groups (racial, religious, and sexual minorities; people with disabilities), so as to counter stereotypes and the disgust that often goes with them.
- Promote accountability by treating each child as a responsible agent.
- Vigorously promote critical thinking, the skill and courage it requires to raise a dissenting voice. (pp. 45–46)

These are values that we embrace and that we believe are best achieved through reading and discussion of literature in a classroom.

NAVIGATING NEW NEIGHBORHOODS

When the West Side experiment was still in the early stage, it was clear to us that the students' stories and the teachers' stories—their life stories—were mirrored in the stories we were reading, and that suggests to us the universal nature of all good literature as well as one way of achieving the educational goals set out by Nussbaum. Through these stories, college students were learning along with the West Side students and their teachers that the human condition is always complex and difficult, and so defies simplistic responses or limiting stereotypes. The need to break through rigid stereotypes and to recognize the complexity of human experience, to acknowledge human vulnerability and the mystery of mortality itself, is, for us, crucial to the meaning of human learning. Good literature evokes the ethical imagination, which doesn't teach restricted moral codes or reinforce stereotypes, but does allow people to recognize and investigate the complexities of the human condition. It was our job to try to make sure that the complex and vulnerable human voice was heard in the classroom, and that the voices of the individual students were both recognized and appreciated. The challenge was not to create a new stereotype, a new rigidity in the classroom, but to embrace the flow of the experience, the depth of the complexity, and to demonstrate, by example, that this experience was more exciting, these voices more interesting, than the call of the gang leader, the voices of the street.

CLTL DISCUSSION STRATEGIES FOR EVERYONE

The bulk of the pedagogical strategies employed in the CLTL program were the ones we drew on in the West Side experiment. Many of those CLTL strategies and approaches can be found in *Success Stories* (Waxler, 1997), and our detailed discussion of two stories often used in the CLTL sessions, found in Chapters Two and Three of this book, should offer guidance on those strategies. Let it suffice for the moment to emphasize that such strategies and approaches include not only the importance of reading itself, but also the discussion of that reading. Such discussion elucidates the power of conversation for students as they "experience that we have choices, and an understanding that human experiences are complex and ambiguous" (Waxler, 1997, p. 12). Without assigning prescriptive moral codes of behavior, CLTL questioning strategies privilege readers and allow them safe entry into the "storyscape." Students vicariously experience the thrill provided by good literature and the power of a shared discussion with others because that process helps create their own narrative self. They are on a journey that encourages them to explore their own vulnerability and to shape it. Good narratives do not provide answers, but they do offer ongoing questions, and it is this sense of a quest for meaning that allows human beings, young and old, students and teachers, to create and shape their life story, that journey from birth to death.

In addition, by investigating the choices and decisions that characters in the texts make, students and teachers not only begin to investigate their own choices but may also be transported to a new place—what we are calling a "new neighborhood" to emphasize that it is a communal space. They begin to inhabit new spaces as the stories they read unfold and as they talk about those stories. The classroom can then provide an alternate lens for them, a new way of translating and seeing the elements of literature in relation to their own lives. The students and teachers engaged in such learning help make the meaning of the text, and as they do so, they help make the meaning of the new neighborhood before them.

Too often only advanced students get the chance to read and discuss good adult literature, and the disengaged are easily neglected or forgotten. Such neglect comes at a considerable price. As Anne Cunningham and Keith Stanovich remind us:

> We should provide all children, regardless of their achievement levels, with as many reading experiences as possible. Indeed, this becomes doubly imperative for precisely those children whose verbal abilities are most in need of bolstering, for it is the very act of reading that can build those capacities…. [W]e often despair of changing our students' abilities, but there is at least one partially malleable habit that will itself develop abilities—reading! (Cunningham & Stanovich, 2001, p. 147)

In the CLTL program, the reading levels of the stories are often far above the reading levels of the students, but, through reading in context and through the discussions growing out of the reading, students gained sufficient understanding of the characters and the plot to contribute to a meaningful dialogue. In fact, after reading a few stories, the participants often seemed to gain confidence and increase their level and depth of reading significantly. It seems to be a foregone conclusion that the best way to improve reading skills and change attitudes about reading is to read—but, we would argue, not just any kind of text. High-quality literature evokes high interest, stirs deep desire, and helps all of us feel the depth of our human heart and the feelings and connection to others that it engenders.

CONCLUDING THOUGHTS ON THE NEW NEIGHBORHOOD

This book argues that literature can move us, and it is the best literature that moves us deeply. Whether we are talking about an attitudinal, motivational, or biological change, our work at West Side aimed to bring about transformation in the participants. We wanted to give students and teachers a view of a new environment, a place full of new perspectives and new visions. Not only did we want them to engage cognitively with the reading and discussion of good literature, we also wanted them to become motivated to invest in their futures, to see that their life story was a narrative that they could reflect on and help to create. As Shakespeare (1937) suggested, literature can give us all a habitation and a name, one that remains deep in our memory and that dwells forever in our imagination.

By reading, thinking about, and discussing stories and poetry, the high schoolers were given an opportunity to transport themselves through narrative texts and locate themselves in a new place, and to use their imagination and the engagement with language to reinvent themselves. In the broadest terms, we saw the West Side classroom as a place of hope, as part of the ongoing educational experiment of Western and specifically American democracy, where human beings desire to learn, to read good stories, to create their own stories and their own lives. Human beings are vulnerable, but they all deserve dignity and a voice that will empower them to full participation in political and social life. From the Changing Lives Through Literature program, we had been convinced of the central importance of literature, how literature could help human beings find a voice and locate themselves as citizens within a community. We believed that literature, in fact, was the best tool we had to bring people closer together and to foster respect. In the West Side classroom, we saw these concepts begin to play themselves out, and it helped make us believers in the ongoing possibility of humane, democratic education built on the significance of literature. Literature could inspire people to tell their own stories and to overcome their isolation and their fear. It could serve as a bridge to wisdom, deep feelings, and deep connection to others.

CHAPTER TWO

DEEP READING AND THE SPACE OF THE CLASSROOM

The West Side experiment helped us to formulate our strong belief anchoring this book that natural language and linguistic narrative (i.e., story) are central to human identity and purpose and that language and story should remain the primary focus for educational development and pedagogical activity in the 21st-century classroom. This belief is not simply an unfounded bias. It is grounded in our understanding of democratic education and philosophical tradition, the meaning of the liberal arts in general, and in the cutting-edge research of contemporary science, especially in the area of the brain. At the core of our belief is the knowledge and practice of that innovative program, started in 1991, called Changing Lives Through Literature (CLTL; Waxler & Trounstine, 1999), a program that embraces the kind of educational purpose that Thomas Merton had in mind when he wrote:

> Education's purpose is to show a person how to define himself authentically and spontaneously in relation to his world, not to impose a prefabricated definition of the world, still less an arbitrary definition of the individual himself. (Merton, 1979, p. 3)

To explore further our perspective on the importance of literary narrative in the learning environment, we want in this chapter to move through the following topics: first, a brief discussion about technology as one of the chief challenges to literacy in the 21st century (a topic which we will take up more fully in Chapter Six); second, a detailed and somewhat lengthy meditation on deep reading, with some attention to how language operates and what happens when people read; and finally, a focus on the elements inherent in the best kind of classroom environments for promoting deep reading (a topic which we will explore in more detail in Chapter Three), along with practical examples from the literature classroom which help to illustrate deep reading in action.

CHALLENGES TO LITERACY AND SOCIETY IN THE 21ST CENTURY

Much has been made about the growing sense of "a global community," as if human beings are expanding consciousness and deepening their knowledge of others through new technological devices; yet increasing numbers of human beings today seem to experience feelings of extreme isolation and alienation, detaching themselves from others and avoiding direct human interaction. There are many reasons for this apparent contradiction, but we want to suggest that despite people's assumption that electronic devices help human beings to connect to each other, those devices often intensify feelings of isolation and alienation. Such devices create the illusion of connection, but actually often keep people separated and at a distance. Instead of contributing to a genuine human interchange, these electronic devices lack the depth of a fully embodied face-to-face live encounter.

When people interact through a screen, for example, that interaction seems to us cold, lacking the warmth that comes through direct human presence—the flesh and the body—close enough to touch. Having hundreds of friends on Facebook and a full inbox of text and e-mail messages does not necessarily build authentic community or grant people the authentic experience of embodied and heartfelt connections with others. In fact, the rushed and hurried connections made through screens often increase rigidity and fear, encouraging a dehumanized sense of distance between human beings, a sense of distance which only serves to intensify stereotypes and prejudices.

For us, the face-to-face living encounter inherent in the flow of conversation with others about a shared literary text is much more generative for creative narrative connections and community with others than any encounter with or through a machine. Through face-to-face live encounters, human beings open themselves to the possibility of creating their narrative self in relation to the other narratives being simultaneously created around them.

Gemma Corradi Fiumara, an Italian philosopher and psychoanalyst, makes just such an argument in *The Metaphoric Process* (Fiumara, 1995) when she emphasizes the importance of narrative and its role in overcoming feelings of detachment and fear, dislocation and chaos:

> As developing humans absorb narratives they get ideas about how they may create links within potentially chaotic situations. Meaningful stories contribute to maturing persons' attempts to engage with interactive life and to perceive some order in the disparate

attachments they create. Through linguistic narratives human beings interact, reconstructing their own stories and building a coherent sense of identity. The developing subject who is deprived of narratives is apt to have to adopt strategies to avoid a reality which he cannot interpret and cope with. (Fiumara, 1995, p. 90)

For Fiumara, without human attachment at a personal and organic level, individuals feel an "absence," an isolation, an inarticulate moment in their relation to the world. They cannot deeply connect, through their bodies, out to the world. As a result, they cannot articulate what they are experiencing. They have no story of their own. They feel isolated, dispossessed. Such isolation creates blind spots in the self, and such blind spots create bias and fear of the unknown, which, in turn, affect the way people behave towards themselves and towards others. Participation in narrative, by contrast, helps people move through such a divide and acts like a kind of intelligent energy, a shaping force that pulls them back to self and others, and bonds them to the interactivity in the human world. When life seems chaotic and meaningless, narrative—the engagement with it and with others—can provide paths towards meaning, the essential human quest and a core need.

WHAT IS DEEP READING AND WHY IS IT IMPORTANT?

We believe that people must participate in deep reading to activate the power of narrative and that the classroom is an important place where this capability called deep reading should be exercised. Sven Birkerts gets the credit for coining the term "deep reading" (Birkerts, 1994), as we want to use it here. In Birkerts' (1994) view: "Reading, because we control it, is adaptable to our needs and rhythms. We are free to indulge our subjective associative impulse; the term I coin for this is deep reading: the slow and meditative possession of a book" (p. 38).

For us, deep reading is about slowing down, but it is also about creating your own pace and environment for thinking. It is about gaining focus while working within a context; and it is about moving forward and shaping a future. It is about freedom and about creativity, and about the depth of the imagination as well. That we not only participate in, but help to create, the reading experience is a reminder that deep reading can play a significant role in making a free and democratic society.

It is crucial to understand that the exercise of deep reading is best accomplished through ongoing exposure to narrative stories (rather than other kinds of texts), especially when we are talking about reading in terms of the learning environment today. What we read as well as how we read is important. Steven Johnson's recent article, "Yes, People Still Read, but Now it is Social" (Johnson, 2010), for example, explores the changing nature of our reading activities in the Information Age, and by implication how people use their time and live their lives. As Johnson (2010) reminds us, a day filled with Twitter, Facebook, and texting, "doesn't require our full powers of concentration" (p. 1). Such activity does not require full thinking, full awareness, or full presence. It might not be thoughtless, but it is limited and limiting. It fails to offer the opportunity for full expression of individual talents, for the flourishing of the whole person. By contrast, deep reading requires human beings to call upon and develop attentional skills, to be thoughtful and fully aware. It teaches humans to be thankful for, and to celebrate, their full capabilities. It makes people, in other words, feel good about being fully human.

Deep reading does not necessarily offer solutions to practical problems, but it holds possibilities for helping people make meaning and journey towards full understanding of self, helping individuals evolve a complex and linguistically based life story, an articulated identity. Deep readers constantly move from the story being read to their own self, and they create meaning in the gaps which they experience in that movement. Such activity opens up interpretative possibilities that stimulate the imagination, generate hope, and help people to create and understand their own identity and their connection to the environment which surrounds them. Unlike the "surface" reading of Twitter, Facebook, and other new technologies, reading stories *deeply* compels human beings to focus intensely on, and to think about the complexity and the inconsistencies of the life experience, the *human mystery* (we like that old-fashioned term) which is always filled with wonder and surprise.

Ernest Hemingway claimed that all stories end in death (Hemingway, 1952), and in that sense every story an individual reads contains and expresses the ultimate human mystery, that which is unknown, what is often referred to as "the other." Reading deeply allows human beings to wrestle with this other, the essence of their mortality, and, by grappling with that other, the reader triggers the quest for the understanding of self. This is why we say that deep reading is a journey, an adventure into the vulnerability of the human experience. As the German critic, Monika Fludernik, has suggested: "A good narrative story deals with the unfamiliar, 'the other' that is also 'us,' that is, the reader. Thus, when the reader engages with the depth of the story, he or she journeys towards the secret of him/herself" (Fludernik, 2007, p. 262).

Derek Attridge makes a similar point, though from a different angle, in *The Singularity of Literature* (Attridge, 2004). He argues that the act of reading, when done well, is always risky because the reader must enter deeply into the narrative and break through the rigid systems and stereotypes, the defense mechanisms that ordinarily distance and protect humans from the unfamiliar and potentially frightening territory that those depths offer. For Attridge, when reading deeply, the reader encounters the depth of the other, the unfamiliar dimension of the self. Such an experience opens the reader up to novel experiences and perspectives which challenge the rigid and familiar systems of culture and daily existence. These glimpses of new territory, often uncovering a person's biases and blind spots, can be unsettling, but they also offer new pathways for personal growth. As Attridge (2004) explains: "What we experience in responding to the artwork [including literature]... is not a generalized obligation but a call coming from the work itself" (p. 12) towards understanding its "otherness." Such reading demands attentiveness to the text, a commitment to its "otherness"—its unique perspectives—that which "calls" to the reader to explore and learn in novel situations. That other, found through the language of an author and the characters of a novel, refuses to be appropriated or domesticated, resists the familiar world of the reader, and so pushes the reader to change. Through such a dynamic between the reader and the text, new meaning develops. It is just this kind of encounter that allows human beings to learn. To read deeply, in other words, is to learn about the unknown dimensions of ourselves and the world.

Deep reading also allows people an "insider's view" on issues that may be restricted by traditional boundaries and social conventions, yet are part of being human. For example, careful readers could learn through deep reading of a narrative what the socially acceptable limits of mainstream perception might be, the stereotypes that often govern and control mainstream life, while they also glimpse, and even anticipate, what the overflow of human desires might lead to if they dare cross that border of convention and restraint and enter into unfamiliar territory. As Waxler (2010) puts it in *Courage to Walk*:

> How can those warmed by the fire understand those who are cold? How can those who are healthy understand those who are ill? How can those who are powerful understand those who are powerless—unless we take the time to listen carefully to each other's stories; unless we risk that border crossing? (Waxler, 2010, p. 105)

To acknowledge the stereotype and then to move beyond that rigid boundary by opening human consciousness to the flow of expanding possibilities defines both the deep reading experience, in particular, and the learning experience, in general.

A SCENE FROM *FRANKENSTEIN*

A good example of what we have in mind, and one worth considering for classroom discussion, comes from a crucial scene in the classic novel, *Frankenstein* (Shelley, 1967). Dr. Frankenstein has already created "the Monster," and he has abandoned it, left it to its own devices. The Monster is vulnerable and alone as he observes the DeLacey family living in a small cottage in the midst of the natural environment. Watching this family for several weeks, the Monster eventually begins to learn human language and begins to learn to read. His reading excites self-reflection as the Monster begins to think about his relationship to other human beings and his own identity:

> As I read however I applied much personally to my own feelings and condition. I found myself similar yet at the same time strangely unlike to the beings concerning whom I read and to whose conversation I was a listener. I sympathized with and partly understood them, but I was unformed in mind....Who was I? What was I? Whence did I come? What was my destination? These questions continually recurred, but I was unable to solve them. (Shelley, 1967, p. 113)

Stirred by language and reading, the Monster desires to know and understand; he seeks his identity and a sense of belonging. He eventually decides to risk knocking on the door of the cottage, hoping for acceptance and conversation with the family that has essentially introduced him to the meaning of his humanity. The Monster waits until only the old man, DeLacey, is in the cottage, and the old man answers the Monster's knock on the door.

"Enter," said De Lacey, "and I will try in what manner I can to relieve your wants; but unfortunately, my children are from home, and I am blind, I am afraid I shall find it difficult to procure food for you" (Shelley, 1967, p. 117). But as the Monster makes clear, it not food that he seeks, but warmth and family that he hopes for. The old man is generous as the two enter into a lively and heartfelt conversation, the flow of language itself creating the human interchange. It is difficult for the reader not to empathize with the Monster at this point in the story and not to feel the sense of generosity of which humans are capable. As the old man puts it: "... the hearts of men, when unprejudiced by any obvious self-interest, are full of brotherly love and charity. Rely, therefore, on your hopes; and if these friends are good and amiable, do not despair" (Shelley, 1967, p. 118).

But then the younger members of the family return to the cottage, and without taking time to speak, they act on the prejudice of their conventional perceptions. Without discussion, they attack the Monster, dashing him to the ground, driving him back to his lonely hovel. The reader sees the limitations of the characters as they respond from the rigidity of their preconceived positions, the boundary of acceptability, and feels a moment of shame at these human actions born of fear, coupled with sadness and sympathy for the Monster. In reading this way, the deep readers not only recognize the stereotype, but also can move beyond it, expand their consciousness to see a different perspective, and glimpse new possibilities for how to think and how to live with others.

In the broadest terms, the dynamic of deep reading can be described in the following way: it is a dialectic of the self and the other, of the familiar and the unfamiliar, and it is an embodied experience that, when done well, also gives the reader context and direction beyond the act of reading. The reader shuttles between his or her own identity and the identity of the other found in the narrative, making comparisons and contrasts, and, in so doing, moves beyond the familiar, the stereotypes, and so learns more about the self and the world. As Dustin and Ziegler (2005) describe this embodied process: "We engage things in our bodies, senses, and memories, and that in and of itself puts us in touch with the deepest layer of meaning" (Dustin & Ziegler, 2005, p. 157).

DEEP READING IS NOT MERE ENTERTAINMENT

You might still be asking: what is it about deep reading that makes it so different from other kinds of reading? Why do we claim its central importance for the future of education in the 21st century? Does it really matter so much *what* we read and *how* we read? At the risk of some repetition, let us try to examine these questions further.

Consider Alberto Manguel's description of his own embodied experience the first time he ever read. For him, it was like "acquiring an entirely new sense, so that now certain things no longer consisted merely of what my eyes could see, my ears could hear, my tongue could taste, my nose could smell, my fingers could feel" (Manguel, 1997, p. 6). Such an experience allowed his "whole body to decipher, translate, give voice to, read" (Manguel,

1997, p. 6). He had been transported and could read words for the first time by himself, without another reader helping him along:

> And yet, all of a sudden, I knew what they were; I heard them in my head, they metamorphosed from black lines and white spaces into a solid, sonorous, meaningful reality. I had done all this by myself. No one had performed the magic for me. I and the shapes were alone together, revealing ourselves in a silently respectful dialogue. Since I could turn bare lines into living reality, I was all-powerful. I could read. (Manguel, 1997, p. 6)

"I heard them in my head," Manguel says, as he magically transformed the world outside into the world inside—inside his own head, his own brain—transforming the black lines and white spaces on the printed page into meaning, mastering the shadows and shapes calling to him, entering into a dialogue, a conversation with words given to him as gifts by another. Thus, Manguel evocatively describes the magical moments involved in the reading process. Such a magical transformation could happen each time humans read. Manguel's sense-making in and through language allows him to experience the awe of the reading process. It serves as a model for the kind of gift deep reading can offer all students. For Manguel, the process of reading taught him the wonder of thinking, and he was then thankful. Filled with thoughtfulness, he was suddenly grateful for being alive. It is this sense of wonder that we especially celebrate and that convinces us that reading can change lives.

That is reading as we understand it, the beginning of a social contract, as Manguel (1997) also explains, a covenant between the individual self and the world that nurtures thoughtfulness and caring. Words on a page are gifts from others, creating a communal threshold and a sacred location for making sense and making meaning. Words on a page can come alive and invite the reader to participate in an ongoing conversation; those words have already been set in motion by others before the reader arrives and joins the conversation. It is as if both the reader's mind and body—head and heart—are set in motion by the words on the page, and the words give direction by evoking the reader's past and taking the reader into the future, tempting the reader with revelation about the world and his or her relationship to it. As Manguel suggests, black marks and white spaces on the page can be transformed into something magical and living. That transformation creates a space that can be considered a threshold (rather than a gap), a threshold connecting a reader to a community, inviting the reader to choose a story and to create his or her own tale amidst the stories already told and gathered there. This is an important part of the learning process, the process and the journey located at the heart of deep reading.

Through reading, Manguel (1997) suggests, people glimpse what and where they are, enabling the reader "to acquire a text not simply by perusing the words but by actually making them part of the reader's self" (p. 58). Thus does reading become a part of one's history, and so of one's future; of one's thinking, and so of one's actions.

Although it may not be entirely true to say that we are what we read, reading is always a social process, even when a person is reading alone. Deep reading is an activity allowing people to find themselves through a common language, words set before a human being by other human beings. When people read, they bring themselves, their language, their voices to the black marks and white spaces on the page, wrestle meaning from them, and recontextualize themselves in relation to them. As Freire and Macedo (1987) point out, "reading always involves critical perception, interpretation, and rewriting of what is said" (p. 36), and this rewriting, too, creates a path to help people figure out who they are and who they are becoming.

This is why deep reading is not mere entertainment, at least not the kind of deep reading we have in mind, and why deep reading should be a central requirement of 21st-century education. As the ancient poets insisted, literature can delight and can teach, and nothing has changed over the centuries in that regard. Literature calls the reader to the experiential fullness of the self in relation to the world. Students increasingly seem to diminish that self these days by living in and through what Hedges (2009) calls the "empire of illusion." That "empire of illusion" is made up of pseudo-events, which too often are accepted as knowledge, but which are actually disembodied events that create illusions of well-being and make people objects of those who control the images. Examples of pseudo-events might include a press conference with Tiger Woods, an interview with Brad Pitt, or a family on a so-called reality television show. These events do not happen by natural occurrence but are planned or incited. They are merely manipulation of images, crass creations of celebrity without substance or depth. Pseudo-events are only considered "real" after they are viewed through advertisement, television, news, or other types of media. Deep reading, in contrast to such pseudo-events, keeps us authentically engaged with the beat of the human heart and so remains our best hope for compassion and an understanding of the complexity of human experience.

We would also argue that pseudo-events rob human beings of imagination, while deep reading exercises and strengthens the human imagination. Pseudo-events are imagined for us, but deep readers imagine what they read. This too marks a significant difference between reading a narrative text and watching visual images dance across a screen. The richly textured language of good

Is teaching pseudo-events? a

literature, filled with ambiguity, always opens itself to the reader, calls to the reader, encouraging interpretation and demanding that the reader participate in the making of its ongoing meaning. Deep reading is interactive: it awakens and evokes the reader's voice, and it insists on the involvement of the whole body and mind. We make meaning as whole persons immersed in the *embodied* nature of language. By contrast, the visual images of a screen culture such as that of television and the Internet flatten the viewer out, as Birkerts (1994) has argued, imprisoning the person in the mere sensation of the speeding moment, leaving no room for that person to discover thought, or to find a personal voice, or to uncover a sense of place—a home—as a response to the experience. As one CLTL student once put it: "Reading books has at least released me from the endless boredom of watching television." He had discovered how boring it really is to be on the receiving end of rapid-fire images lacking the challenge of narrative language that urges a deep human response. Unlike watching television or engaging in the other illusions of entertainment and pseudo-events, deep reading is not an *escape*, but a *discovery*. Deep reading provides a way of discovering how we are all connected to the world and to our own evolving stories. Reading deeply, we find our own plots and stories unfolding through the language and voice of others.

THE SIGNIFICANCE OF LANGUAGE AND THE POWER OF NARRATIVE

You might agree that story (narrative) is important, but you might still ask: why is natural language so important? Don't human beings have stories on television and in the movies, on YouTube and in other formats? Why are we privileging language over images? Our emphasis is not only on story but also on the importance of language (what we sometimes call "linguistic narrative"). We want to explain that more fully now. Language and human identity are richly tied together.

How best to understand this connection? For us, language implies human activity and movement: language gives the body purpose and direction. Language counters the silence of the world. To put it somewhat poetically and bluntly, a body without language is dumb and thus devoid of humanity. It is in this sense a body without a crucial human component—more like a corpse than a living human being. When human beings grapple with language, they are in pursuit of meaning. They desire to learn who they are. That is why we believe that language and learning are richly connected and that linguistic narrative should be central to all learning environments. In fact, we would suggest that language is very much like a good teacher.

Just as a good teacher interacts with students in a classroom, language circulates and cultivates human understanding and meaning; it creates a sense of competency and helps individuals working together to support each other and create a shared community. And like a good teacher, language can help shape and celebrate the fullness of human identity, by allowing humans to express their feelings and emotions, their fears as well as their hopes. Human interchange through language creates communicative acts, allows for ongoing communal vision and expansion, and fosters insights and the discovery of meaning. Such activity augments the human imagination and its possibilities. This is the kind of education we favor.

Our approach to language and story throughout this book also favors those who think about language as a living force, as an organic activity rather than a set of rules or a computational proof. As Terence Deacon says: "Languages are more like living organisms than mathematical proofs, so we should study them the way we study organism structures, not as a set of rules" (Deacon, 1998, p. 110). Human beings are symbol-making animals, but as Jaron Lanier, a leading cognitive scientist, is quick to point out, what distinguishes the word in natural language from a command in a computer program is "the unfathomable penumbra, the mystery, of meaning" (Lanier, 2010, p. 10). Language as an activity evokes that human mystery (there's that term again!) and makes human beings think. Just as the flow of time is often thought to provide the underlying continuity of human experience in the world, language, particularly as shaped into narrative, offers a glimpse of that mystery and a sense of the continuity. It does not offer solutions, but it calls for further conversation about the meaning of human life. For us, this kind of quest, this journey to know the self, to discover that mystery of meaning, is essential for making human beings human and so is also essential for the 21st-century classroom. On such a quest, we are all teachers and learners implicated in language, communicating with our temporal and vulnerable selves and the selves of others.

ON LANGUAGE AND LEARNING AS WE UNDERSTAND IT

From birth, the individual enters a world of language and stories and sets out on a journey to discover his or her own story, to become *a person*, to know the self. Both language and meaning are in the world (not just inside the individual mind), and human beings are part of that world, that meaning and that language. This is not to say that the world is only text, but it does mean that what we call "world" is always linguistic in terms of human engagement in the world. As Gary Madison puts it:

> Words are not signs. Exactly what they are is something that cannot (literally) be said. Words are what they do, which is to enable us to be the kind of beings we are, that is, beings who live not only in an environment but in a world. (Madison, 1996, p. 86)

Language, as we see it, is not simply a sign system of graphic or articulatory elements, but a mode of understanding. If human beings are to understand themselves, they must understand the world as shaped by language, and they must imaginatively and courageously engage in that world through language.

Language itself provides the medium or conduit for activating the imagination and for understanding both self and others. Language is our home, as the German philosopher Martin Heidegger suggested in 1947 in his "Letter on Humanism," where he argued:

> Language is the house of Being. In its home man dwells. Those who think and those who create with words are the guardians of this home. (Heidegger, 1947, p. i)

Language, as scaffolding for understanding, is not to be considered a shelter for protection, but a way to think and a place to grow. Humans dwell in language because language creates a place for us, a dwelling. As Hans Georg Gadamer (1975), following his teacher, Heidegger, declares:

> Language is not just one of man's possessions in the world, but on it depends the fact that man has a world at all... Language has no independent life apart from the world that comes to language within it. Not only is the world 'world' only insofar as it comes into language, but language, too, has its real being only in the fact that the world is presented in it. (Gadamer, 1975, p. 82)

In other words, language both creates and embodies the human world. It is our way to knowledge and understanding and becomes our home in the sense that human beings learn the truth of the world and of themselves through language. Language is our best teacher. John Stewart, in *Beyond the Symbol Model* (Stewart, 1996), says something similar: "Understanding is the human way of being, and language is our way of understanding" (p. 44). Our world, as Stewart puts it, is the very meaning of language operationalized.

Graham Harman makes reference (Harman, 2007) to a lecture of Heidegger's in 1950 and this helps make our point here. In that lecture (as cited in Harman, 2007), Heidegger quotes "A Winter Evening" by the Austrian poet George Trakl. Harman (2007) translates the poem this way:

When the snow falls at the pane,
Evening bells will long resound—
The table set for many guests
In a well-provided house.
Some, along their wandering,
Follow dark roads to the gate.
Cooling juices from the earth
Will feed the golden tree of grace.
Silent drifter steps inside,
A painful threshold turned to stone,
There, in purest brightness shine,
On the table, bread and wine. (p. 144)

Harman (2007) then comments:

Trakl's poem speaks of numerous alluring things: snow bell, window, pain threshold, falling, and resounding. By naming these entities, the poem is not just giving titles to things that are already found present-at-hand. Instead, it calls these things before us for the first time. The presence of these things in the poem is something much deeper than the presence of the physical bells or snowflakes lying before us. If I were to see a snow covered bell in my front yard, I might simply represent it as a set of visible qualities. But if a bell is named in the poem, it is summoned before me in a presence that is simultaneously an absence. (p. 145)

This "presence that is simultaneously an absence" is created *by language* in the reader's mind and imagination. This creative power can evoke not only individual memories but whole worlds connected to the things named. Humankind exists in and through language; language is our home. Language calls to us as a gift, inviting us, as human beings, to enter the conversation, to respond.

THE LANGUAGE OF NARRATIVE VS. THE LANGUAGE OF DISEMBODIED PROSE

Why are we so insistent on the central importance of language and the power of story in terms of the future of education? Our answer is in part because narrative language carries with it a rich complexity not duplicated in more abstract forms of language. Narrative language offers the sensuous feel of the world, on the one hand, and, on the other hand, the thoughtfulness—even the quality of thankfulness—which humans experience in that world illuminated through language. Language makes the reader self-reflective because it makes the reader feel the world, and experience its complexity and fullness. Narrative language is embodied language, meaning that it is felt on the pulse of the reader as a fully human experience. What role the imagination plays in all this we will take up in more detail later, but we are here reminded of a quotation from Shakespeare's Act 1 of "Midsummer Night's Dream":

And as imagination bodies forth
The forms of things unknown, the poet's pen
Turns them to shapes and gives to airy nothing
A local habitation and a name. (Shakespeare, 1937, p. 185)

The difference between the language of a narrative story and the language of some other types of prose is, in one sense, the difference between embodied and disembodied writing. Narrative language is the most complex and richest language that we as human beings have, appealing to the senses as well as the mind, and so it always deserves slow and careful attention. The language of narrative can help us to experience as well as understand the issues which are relevant to self-discovery and what it means to be human. Unlike other kinds of expository prose, fictional language appears to enhance empathy, social ability, ethical thinking (not moral judgment), and perhaps the kind of thankfulness and gratitude in the world which come from an understanding of our place in it. The language of narrative calls for deep and focused reading, setting itself in important opposition to the violent speed of most electronic devices and in opposition to online social networks, which seem to counter the attentive, meditative spirit and the potential sense of wonderment engendered in narrative.

Writers have been making the argument about the power of narrative texts at least since the time of Ancient Greece, but recent experimental studies have confirmed the positive relationship between narrative fiction and people's ability to better understand themselves and others. For example, Raymond Mar, Keith Oatley, Jacob Hirsh, Jennifer dela Paz, and Jordan Peterson conducted several experiments and concluded that comprehending characters in narrative fiction appears to parallel the comprehension of peers in the actual world, while the comprehension of expository nonfiction shares no such parallels with everyday comprehension (Mar, Oatley, Hirsh, dela Paz, & Peterson, 2006). Others, like Jèmeljan Hakemulder, have done even more extensive empirical studies using similar laboratory methods to try to measure the meaning and implications of reading. In one study, Hakemulder (2000) asked two groups to read either an essay or a story, both texts addressing the subject of the position of women in fundamentalist cultures. Hakemulder concluded:

> Results showed that only the text with characters in it—the story—caused the expected effects on beliefs about Algerian women. The relevant information of the text being basically the same, it can be concluded that the presence of a character in one of the two texts ... had an effect on beliefs. (Hakemulder, 2000, p. 155)

Although our point might be somewhat overgeneralized, it is worth emphasizing here the fundamental difference we are concerned with: the language of narrative texts in its richly textured complexity offers a reading experience significantly different from other types of expository prose (whether it be the bureaucratic prose of the law, a research report, or the language of electronic devices or environments such as Twitter or Facebook). By contrast, significant fiction encourages just such a deeply embodied reading experience.

A SCENE FROM *THE BLUEST EYE*

Take the novel, *The Bluest Eye* by Toni Morrison (Morrison, 1970), as an example. As readers of that novel, we follow Cholly Breedlove's tormented journey from the day he was born, thrown in a garbage heap by his mother, herself abandoned by his father. Cholly is a black man who sees himself as "ugly," a man on the lowest rung of the proverbial ladder of the American dream. About three-fourths of the way through the story, we spot Cholly staggering home, reeling drunk on a Saturday afternoon. He sees his daughter washing dishes in the kitchen, and he brutally attacks and rapes her.

There's no excuse for Cholly's behavior and no absolute justification for what he has done. Yet, precisely because Morrison has taken us as readers through the long and tortured history of this man and the complex intricacies of his story from birth to this violent moment, we cannot dismiss him, either. We cannot easily throw him aside or distance ourselves completely from him. As readers, we have lived his experience. If Cholly now appears to be a monster, he is, nevertheless, human. He is not a stereotype, but a man, and Morrison makes sure readers realize this. Through her richly poetic narrative, Morrison makes clear that Cholly Breedlove is a complicated mixture of hatred and tenderness, of lust and love, of guilt and pity. Watching his daughter Pecola washing dishes in the kitchen triggers Cholly's violence, but it also evokes in the reader a deeper sense of Cholly, a past that includes his first love, his dreams, his glimpse of family and community. As Cholly sees Pecola, we as readers are positioned to see not only what he sees, but what he feels—his past as well as his present, his journey, and the depth of his life. The sight of Pecola "filled him with a wondering softness. Not the usual lust to part tight legs with his own, but a tenderness, a protectiveness" (Morrison, 1970, p. 159).

Reading Morrison's words with care, we realize the possibility that, if we walked in Cholly's shoes, his rage could be ours. He is an angry man, but he is also vulnerable. We cannot forgive him, but suddenly we feel compassion for Cholly nonetheless. It is interesting to note that judges participating in our CLTL program often responded in a similar way. Cholly's story compels them, they say, to see offenders appearing before their bench from a new perspective. Each offender has a richly complex story, the judges agree. Such complexity makes judgment difficult, but it deepens their sense of purpose. Such a reminder of the human complexity of experience itself raises questions about the perplexing relationship between mercy and justice, between compassion and judgment.

In this context, the stark language of the law may regulate judgment, but that kind of abstract language, we suggest, always needs literature to play against it and to deepen it. Literature can provide human depth for the law, a rejuvenated way to view situations and people's lives. Thus, deep reading opens new doors and makes new visions possible. Entering the depth of Cholly's life, in other words, is a risky journey, one that can make the job of a judge more difficult, but also more rewarding and humane. What we are saying about the role of the judge here is equally applicable to all readers— teachers and students, parents and children, and anyone determined to build a truly humane and interlinked society.

NARRATIVE LANGUAGE AND THE HUMAN HEART

To push further our distinction between the language of narrative and the language of more abstract expository texts, we want to suggest that narrative language keeps the human heart close at hand. In addition, although it often stirs emotions, the language of narrative calls for compassion in a way that the language of the law, for instance, often does not. Narrative language can enhance justice, but it seems to favor mercy over justice, questioning over sentencing, and open possibilities over closed judgment and strict discipline. By contrast, the language of the law, some have argued, can provoke its own violence. The law is founded on its own transgressions. Robert Cover's observation in *Narrative, Violence, and the Law*—"Judges deal pain and death... . In this way they are different from poets, from artists" (Cover, 1995, p. 216)—makes the point, although in an admittedly confrontational manner. Cover's point resonates with James Gilligan's equally radical point that "the attempt to achieve justice and maintain justice, or to undo or prevent injustice, is the one and only universal cause of violence" (Gilligan, 1996, p. 12). Narrative language, as we have suggested, privileges dialogue, not argument, opening the reader to the flow of the process of learning and understanding. It is a language of questions rather than answers; it favors caring and self-reflection rather than a discourse about what is "due" and what is "owed."

Cover's (1995) point is that the language of the law, like much bureaucratic language, separates and excludes because it attempts to empty language of all "emotional contagion." Such language easily becomes a language of power and manipulation, and thus often puts an end to debate or conversation. Unlike narrative language, the language of the law insists on endings and closure. To quote Cover (1995) again: "A judge articulates her understanding of a text, and as a result, somebody loses his freedom, his property, his children, even his life" (p. 203). In this context, the enactment of law connects to the violence of the state, an attempt at discipline that can thwart learning and human growth.

To extend this contrast between the language of narrative and the language of the law (a metaphor for our main argument about language and learning), we want to emphasize that literature does something different from what the law does: it is not about taking power or having control over others. Instead, story begets story, creates community, expands possibilities, and arouses desire for conversation. It does not give us rules of behavior or impose judgments that lead to any particular instrumental end. Listen to Cholly, it says. Don't automatically condemn him. His story might be yours, too. The message is this: remain open to the possibilities. Hear the voice of your brother. In terms of the learning community, the classroom itself, there are important lessons to ponder.

If narrative story invites a recognition of the complexity of human life, it opens human beings to their own vulnerability and to self-reflection. Unlike the language of most expository writing, literature does not demand judgment or decision about right or wrong, good or bad, but invites readers to question, to doubt. It takes readers on a quest to question themselves and the world. By necessity, authority figures, at times, must reduce that overflowing complexity and questioning that is the human condition to a manageable level, simplifying the narrative flow, fixing it in some kind of hierarchical order. The judge, for example, when called on, must judge with authority. In a democracy, as in a classroom, we need the law, of course; but we also need stories if we desire the expansion of democracy. In fact, for us, the best way to judge the success of a learning community is by "how inclusive it is—not by how many voices it has excluded, but by how many are engaged ... by how many can speak out as productive citizens" (Waxler, 2008, p. 680). Engagement with literature can enhance the qualities of a functioning democratic community. In CLTL, judges, offenders, parole officers, and professors all meet on level ground; all voices are audible to the others. Similarly, the classroom community we envision is one where shared reading and discussion is open to all those involved.

People read stories and they create them as they read, making a home for themselves as they join the conversation of the world. As Mark Turner puts it in *The Literary Mind*: "Knowing how to inhabit stories is the essential requirement of mature life" (Turner, 1996, p. 134). Through reading, people break free from the commonplace of their existing lives, as Turner suggests, from the linear and local perspective of ordinary existence. Readers emerge through reading from a single vision into the complexity of a multifaceted human experience; this emergence is only one of the benefits of deep reading—a benefit that is enhanced within a reading community with others.

THE DARING AND IMAGINATIVE ENCOUNTER

The complex journey that we are calling deep reading is not an easy and secure activity. It is a multidimensional movement of the imagination (feeling and thought, the heart and the head) through the language of the narrative text. The navigating involved, the journey itself, provides an exploration into the self. It can be dangerous, always ongoing, never finished—like thinking, like the beat of the human heart. As the plot unfolds, characters come alive, draw themselves into the reader's consciousness and frame of reference and become connected to the reader. This can be psychologically risky because the reader may become uncomfortable with what he or she learns about the self and others through this journey. The danger comes through the live encounter with characters in the stories and in discussions with other readers. These encounters always expose people's vulnerabilities at the same time as they hold possibilities for rich rewards of meaning-making. Deep reading is rewarding but risky business.

Santiago, the old man in Ernest Hemingway's novel, *The Old Man and The Sea* (Hemingway, 1952), a story of fishing in the deep water off of Cuba;

Atticus Finch, the idealistic lawyer in Harper Lee's *To Kill a Mockingbird* (Lee, 1960), a tale of justice in the deep depression of segregated Alabama; Wolf Larsen, the Darwinian captain in Jack London's *The Sea Wolf* (London, 1963) a sea story of survival in the deep abyss of ocean consciousness: these are examples of characters who are part of narratives that deserve deep reading. Whether a reader discovers these characters for the first time or revisits them in a second read after an absence, they are, every time, magical presences—all of them embodied in the flesh, whispering to each reader about endurance and courage, telling each of us something about our frailty and heroism as mortal human beings. Wrapped in narrative, these characters serve as models that can help us to understand what it means to be fully human.

LANGUAGE AND TEACHING

Our discussion of deep reading of narrative and the importance of language leads us inevitably back to education and the classroom. If the learning environment is a place of deep reading, a neighborhood, or home, created by and through language, it must also be a place for the imagination.

Language and teaching are human activities which are unique, in part, because they are imaginative actions that excite ongoing questing, reminding people of the continuous flow of the human, and so temporal, journey. As we have been insisting, literary narratives, in particular, offer a primary way to evoke such excitement by harnessing intention and encouraging self-reflection through time. When human beings engage in narrative, they are engaged in a dynamic that involves much more than just the "consumption" of content—links are made to one's previous knowledge and new connections are also forged. Such activity helps inspire human agency and builds competency, and it contributes to a strong sense of equality and justice. Narrative calls to the individual and the community to understand and to know what it means to be human. And this call is exactly what teaching and education are all about.

The use of narrative language and the activity of teaching are both to be taken seriously for this reason. They are ethical acts always occurring in social space and always providing an opportunity to interpret and expand human community. This is precisely the reason that, for us, reading, writing, and conversation about literary texts are the most important elements of the 21st-century classroom. Such engagement with language has traditionally been considered the cornerstone of the best education and a mark of civilized life itself. To lose that core experience is to weaken human understanding of ourselves and to intensify alienation and fragmentation.

THE CLASSROOM AS EMBODIED SPACE

The kind of learning through language and narrative that we are emphasizing is something that happens in and through the sensuous body. It is a journey into and through the senses which eventually reaches beyond the individual into the community, the collective body. We will develop much more fully our vision of the imaginative classroom space, the learning environment as a new neighborhood in the next chapter, but here we want to suggest that just as deep readers, in their interactions with a text, must be responsible to the literary work, likewise students and teachers must be responsible for each other, as bodies and minds in motion creating a shared learning environment. This responsibility for self and others is at the heart of a shared community, and so should be at the heart of the educational process and the classroom. As we have indicated, narrative language can provide the primary way to achieve such high-minded goals. Literary narrative offers up both the imaginative possibilities to move beyond the familiar and the known and simultaneously offers a glimpse of human vulnerability, the mystery and strangeness of the mortal self. In terms of the classroom, this means, among other things, that teachers and students must join together in the classroom and create a communal space where it is "safe" to be vulnerable through asking a question or trying out a new idea. The classroom becomes a space of hospitality and generous spirit in which to interact—a neighborhood, or home, evoked through language.

By reading and writing, by sharing each other's stories, by taking risks within this flexible classroom space, students and teachers can explore their own selves and their connection to others. They are bodies in a learning space, learning together. They can gain a better understanding of their shared fears and hopes, the power of their imaginations, and the virtue of their vulnerabilities within the classroom space. For us, these are important goals for the future of education and the 21st-century. They favor writers and readers in the sense that all human beings are writers and readers, creative individuals who have significant imaginative abilities and who are vulnerable and capable of compassion, especially when engaged with language.

It is disturbing to read Kutz and Roskelly's (1991) accurate description of the fragmented and disconnected landscape of many contemporary classrooms:

> Vocabulary is separated from reading, punctuation is separated from sentences, sentences from paragraphs, creativity from analysis.... The study of language becomes entirely removed from the uses of language in and outside class. And it's the separation of the skills of literacy from their embodiments in literature and in talk that encourages students to divorce what they do in one class from another class and divorce what they do as learners from what they do as people. (p. 219)

Clearly, reading, discussing, and writing about literature call for an integrated approach in which students begin to see connections between seemingly disparate activities or ideas. The desired pedagogy is a unified pedagogy with literature at its heart, fueled by the imagination, and with the understanding that reading and writing are flip sides of the educational coin.

For us, active and engaged writing is the flip side of reading. Writing, too, needs to be explored and understood as an embodied learning experience in the classroom environment. We write our own stories as we read the stories of others, and we read others' stories as we write our own narratives. People naturally "map" their own life stories onto what they are reading, and this ongoing act of self-reflection when writing is also a kind of "reading." As individuals, human beings create themselves in this way; and together, they can also create the communal space they dwell in. Teachers and students can enact a similar creative process in and through the classroom. Why doesn't this happen more often?

Nina Holzer frames the issue this way, in *A Walk between Heaven and Earth* (Holzer, 1994), where she states:

> The reason so many people block themselves from writing, from creating, is that they are not here. They have a head full of blueprints for the goal, they have elaborate outlines of how to get there, but they have never taken a conscious walk from their bedroom to their bathroom. They want to create but they know nothing of their own creative process. (p. 5)

The creative act of reading and writing requires a quiet, divergent, and playful imagining of reality. Such an imagining emerges only when the participant is fully present, focused, and free from distractions. Knowledge comes through embodied participation in the process of making, and nothing can replace one's actual experience of this singular creative process.

Developing sensory awareness is an integral component of this kind of learning process, and again, reading and writing are central to this process. Through the practice of writing and reading, human beings can develop sensory awareness, a particular kind of concentration. Eventually, if they stay with it, they will be able to control their concentration, turning the mind outward to the world and inward to their own creative engagement with language, eventually making connections between their prior experiences and the object of their current focus. As Donald Murray, in *Learning by Teaching* (Murray, 1982), states, "as we encourage our students through the composing process they discover that writing is not thought recorded after the fact, but thinking itself—humanity's disciplined, unique way of making meaning" (p. 53). Speaking and listening must also be considered in a similar context. Dialogue and conversation, speaking and listening, the flow of the auditory imagination through the classroom gives that classroom enriched life, purpose, and direction. We will have more to say about all this in the next chapter, but we want to emphasize here that the voices put to work in these interactive moments are crucial to the ongoing creation of a human classroom and community. As Bakhtin (1984) puts it:

> Life by its very nature is dialogic. To live means to participate in dialogue: to ask questions, to heed, to respond, to agree, and so forth. In this dialogue, a person participates wholly and throughout his whole life, with his eyes, lips, hands, soul, spirit, and with his whole body and deeds. (Bakhtin, 1984, p. 293)

To enter into dialogue is to encounter an embodied learning experience. The classroom should be a symphony of voices, each voice heard in its fullness, the breath and language expressing a person's "whole body and deeds." Again, our point is that the live encounter, face-to-face interactions through language, makes education meaningful. It creates the imaginative adventure of human life. It creates a fresh and hospitable space for the ongoing quest for human knowledge.

Knowledge begets seeking, which begets more knowledge, and education scaffolds this seeking, which ultimately involves development of the self and one's personal possibilities in dialogue with all things worldly. For us, the classroom, like a literary narrative, is a space to gain "deep understanding" of self and others, a hospitable space, a home for teachers and students to discover themselves—what we earlier called a "new neighborhood." (See Chapter Three for development and expansion of the idea of the classroom as imaginative space for the journey.)

ACTIVATING DEEP READING AND CREATING THE CLASSROOM AS NEIGHBORHOOD

We have developed an educational module, one specifically designed for teachers, to begin to see how deep reading can be activated through narrative and how discussion (dialogue) about that reading can help to create the kind of learning environment (the "new neighborhood") as we have been describing it. Twelve teachers from a rural village school in India participated in these educational sessions. These teachers taught various grade levels from grade one to grade eight. The idea behind the sessions was to first provide the actual experience of deep reading for them as learners and then to have them reflect on these experiences through a teaching lens. The rationale for this approach was that the teachers would need to personally experience this kind of learning before they could provide the same kind of learning experiences for their own students. All teachers should be active learners.

These teacher educational sessions utilized two different Robert Frost poems, "Dust of Snow" (Frost, 1969a, p. 221) and "One Step Backward Taken" (Frost, 1969c, p. 376). (In subsequent chapters, we will use additional Frost poems and other literary examples.) The teachers were called upon to first help create the literal narrative of the poem and then to "map" or make specific connections between their own life stories and the deeper implications and meaning, as they experienced them, in the narrative. Through that process, they could begin to discover how a shared reading experience—everyone reading the same poem and agreeing on the surface meaning of the narrative—could at the same time evoke singular, unique responses related to individual experiences. The sessions also provided a metacognitive or debriefing component, conducted a day after the deep reading experiences for each poem. Having these metacognitive sessions a day after each deep reading experience allowed teachers the necessary time to reflect on and further explore what they had learned and also to consider new ways to use narratives and the activity of deep reading in their own classrooms.

The learning goals for each poem were made clear to the teachers: essentially to understand the surface meaning of the poem, and then to engage in a meaning-making process that would allow the deeper implications of the poem to emerge as well as a better understanding of the dynamics of deep reading. Each teacher was first given a paper copy of "Dust of Snow" (emphasizing the tactile quality of the experience) and the poem was also projected onto a large screen in the classroom (emphasizing the visual quality of the experience).

Frost's "Dust of Snow" (Frost, 1969a, p. 221) is a short, eight-line poem about the speaker out walking, in or near the woods. Suddenly a dust of snow falls from a hemlock tree and lands on him. The speaker recognizes that the falling of the snow was caused by the slight movement of a crow in the tree. That recognition seems to lighten the speaker's mood. He embraces this small event, and it changes the quality of his day.

After reading the poem twice aloud (emphasizing the auditory quality of the experience), the surface meaning was explored, concluding with common agreement that the narrator in the poem is out walking and a crow either lands on or flies away from a snow-covered tree. In this way, the crow causes snow to fall on the narrator. As a result, a small amount of snow changes the narrator's experience of the day and the mood is lightened.

Once the teachers had agreed on this sense of the poem, they were then given a few minutes to respond to the following prompt: *think of an experience in your life when some unexpected and positive thing happened and explain how it changed the quality of your experience.* The responses were wide-ranging and expansive, but each teacher found an experience from his or her own life that echoed the experience in the poem. One teacher talked about how she had grown up in the city, but had married someone from this small village and so had come back with him to it. She had been unsure about how she would adjust to the dramatic change in lifestyle, but her "Dust of Snow" moment, or the cause of her lightened mood, was the discovery of the joy she had found in her small village school. Another teacher told about the time he was required to take a test in a nearby city, but he wasn't able to book a train ticket so as to make it to the test site on time. In despair, he suddenly found out that his friend was driving to the city that same day and could provide a ride. Finding transportation on such short notice lifted his mood from anxiety to relief and happiness; an unexpected occurrence had affected the quality or mood of his day.

For "One Step Backward Taken," the learning goals and the process were exactly the same. Each teacher was given a paper copy of "One Step Backward Taken" (Frost, 1969c) and the poem was also projected onto a large screen in the classroom.

Frost's "One Step Backward Taken" (Frost, 1969c, p. 376) is a 14-line poem about a landslide or a mudslide, describing what is happening in this natural disaster. The narrator appears in line eight ("I felt my standpoint shaken") and then begins to explain how after taking one step backward, he or she was saved from the danger. Nature's savage wind and rain subsides at the end and the narrator is dried by the sun and made safe.

After reading the poem twice aloud, the surface meaning of the poem was discussed. Teachers were then given a few minutes to respond to the following prompt: *think of an event in your life when you made a decision to take a step back from something ("One Step Backward Taken") and describe how you believe this stepping back saved you from some kind of danger or negative experience.* Again, the teachers' responses were wide-ranging. One teacher talked about how she had to miss school one day because her pet dog had run away from her home. Stepping back for her usual routine, she was missing school, but she had to do it. Her pet dog had bitten others before (including her brother). By staying home, she was able to catch the dog and bring him home before he hurt someone else. By stepping backward (as she understood it), she was able to avoid disaster and return to safety.

Another teacher talked about how he had been invited to go with friends one evening to a nearby town. But he was worried about the driver's recklessness and so decided not to join his friends. As it turned out, the police stopped the teacher's friends for bad driving. By stepping back and deciding not to go, this teacher, as he experienced it, had saved himself some trouble with the police. One other teacher said that in order to become a teacher, she had to step back from the advice of her older relatives. These relatives had advised her not to become a teacher; they did not consider the teaching profession to be the right choice for her. "Sometimes older people make problems," she said. Despite her relatives, she explained, she knew that teaching was her true calling so she stepped back from the advice of relatives and saved herself from making the wrong decision. She had, in other words, stepped back and found a safe place, saving herself from the danger of committing to something not in accord with her nature and talents. She loved learning and loved teaching others and knew that becoming a teacher was the right profession for her.

By making connections to the deeper meaning of the poem, these teachers activated the deep reading process, mapped the depths and curve of the narrative language of "One Step Backward Taken" onto their own life stories, and then listened to each other's stories, which, in turn, often inspired them to tell their own stories.

TEACHERS' METACOGNITIVE SESSIONS AFTER DEEP READING

Metacognition, or thinking about one's thinking, requires that learners see the same experience through different lenses. This process, too, helps everyone to understand the commonality of human experience, how humans can share and build a sense of community, and to simultaneously appreciate the unique and individual meaning of those common experiences. It is a way of gaining and expanding knowledge in an imaginative learning space. For this session, the discussion was focused on enabling teachers to view their deep reading experiences through the lenses of both student and teacher. The teachers reflected on how they experienced the learning for themselves as students and then on what their thoughts were from a teaching vantage point. The teachers understood that the activities were designed to help the learner understand both the surface and depth of the poem. What was new for them was the idea that they had activated deep reading by making personal meaning of the poem. The discussion highlighted the importance of using narrative as a learning tool.

When the teachers were asked what they had learned through the sessions with each poem, they again responded in a variety of ways. One teacher, for example, explained that she had learned that "what happens in one's life is good for us." She went on to say that telling personal stories in connection to a poem's meaning helps one to better understand both the poem and oneself. The principal of the school, who was also a participant in all of the teacher education sessions, shared this idea: "Teachers should share both their positive and negative experiences with students." She added that "life is a story." As an important leader in the school, she came away from the deep reading sessions with a renewed sense of how stories can be important for learning and for student development. Another teacher discussed the connection between decision-making and the idea of stepping back developed from the "One Step Backward Taken" poem. As he suggested: "Whatever decisions we make in life, we should take them confidently." These sessions modeled how teachers can use narrative or story to help students understand a particular narrative, and, in turn, understand their own life stories in connection with that narrative. It also helped them to experience and understand the importance of dialogue (conversation) in the learning process. These teacher education examples provide a view on how language serves as a conduit for making meaning of narrative itself, of one's own life story and identity, and of one's connection (teacher or student) with others in the learning environment.

DEEP READING AND ITS IMPLICATIONS FOR THE CLASSROOM

The reading of a literary narrative is crucial; but the conversation about the narrative is at least as important, if not more so, than the reading of the text itself. We want to expand on this point.

The use of language is a cultural and social practice, and in this sense, the classroom, like a cohesive neighborhood community, can be considered a kind of "shared sociolinguistic scaffolding." As the neuroscientist Alva Noe puts it: "Linguistic knowledge depends on our active engagement with our surroundings" (Noe, 2009, p. 91). In this interactive and welcoming space, students and teachers can be involved in an engaged and imaginative pedagogy that allows all voices to be heard and all perspectives to be considered. It is the flow of the conversation that extends and develops the deep reading of the story, and it is in the classroom space that the various voices can mingle and gain purpose and focus. "Brain, body, and world form a process of dynamic interaction. That is where we find ourselves" (Noe, 2009, p. 95). Language and engagement are intertwined, and it is that dynamic intermingling that helps to expand consciousness. An imaginative classroom space that invites all participants into the dialogue becomes an *enchanted space* where participants' thinking—their brains—can actually be changed.

Conversation energizes the classroom space, offering the possibility for the development of a democratic and redemptive neighborhood of learners within formal education. As bell hooks (2010) says: "Many students often feel that they have no voice, that they have nothing to say that is worthy of being heard. This is why conversation becomes such a vital intervention, for it not only makes room for every voice, it also presupposes that all the voices can be heard" (p. 45). Likewise, Mary Rose O'Reilley, in *The Garden at Night* (O'Reilley, 2005) poses important questions about the quality of the classroom environment: "What kind of attention do you, the teacher, pay? What is the relationship between the quality of your attention and your need to control the situation?" (O'Reilley, 2005, p. 6). Teaching is not a one-way imparting of knowledge. We insist on this: teaching is a journey towards meaning, and the mode of travel in the classroom is a responsive and living conversation between and among teacher and students.

The relationship between language, narrative, and learning is beyond debate, and, again we want to make clear that although this is not a new argument, it is crucial to the future of education in the 21st century. Many commentators on education have made parts of the argument for us, although not perhaps this crucial link. Kutz and Roskelly (1991), for example, have urged that a teacher must consider the quality of relationships within his or her teaching and learning space in order to build a community for learning:

> We see teaching and learning as active, which means that teacher and learner, reader and writer, *act* rather than react in the classroom. We see a relationship between teachers and learners as individuals and as part of culture and believe that classrooms build and expand ways of knowing by using the relationship between individual and community and culture. (p. 11)

Like Kutz and Roskelly, we emphasize the social dynamics of the classroom and how these dynamics aid in the creation of community. By promoting these social interactions, teachers can foster students' abilities to actively participate with one another, which can create community in this learning space as well as make links to the larger community. Milner and Milner (1999) reinforce the idea that the classroom should support dialogic interaction between the teacher and his or her individual students. As we have suggested throughout this chapter, reading and discussing literature works to this end. It emphasizes the classroom as a linguistic space which draws out the relationship between the brain, the body, and language shaped by a narrative text that promotes human identity and active creation of a community.

Kutz and Roskelly (1991) also conceptualize learning as active. As a critical component of creating community in the classroom, they emphasize an open flow of communication between and among students and teacher, which may increase and expand "ways of knowing." The relationship between teacher and student, as individuals who are communicating their experiences and their met and unmet needs, expands the ways of knowing and the possibilities of growth for all learners.

Following the work of Freire and Macedo (1987), Kutz and Roskelly (1991) also make clear that

> language is the primary subject of study in the English classroom, [and] that "subject," and the way it is taught, usually has little connection to the ways we use language to make sense of the world. The study of language, of reading, of writing is too often seen not as a way of perceiving the world or representing ourselves to others, but as a series of technical terms or steps, to be memorized or followed. Yet the learner in the classroom makes sense both of the classroom and of the larger world through language. That learning is a continuous process, one that pulls thinking and naming together with speaking, listening, writing, and reading. (Kutz & Roskelly, 1991, p. 191)

Language implies intention and helps give human beings direction and purpose. Engagement with narrative provides opportunities, through this intentional use of language, for students and teachers to both make meaning of the world and deepen their understanding of self.

ANOTHER EXTENDED CLASSROOM EXAMPLE USING "GREASY LAKE"

Let us now share another example from our work with high school students and preservice teachers to provide another glimpse of how the classroom as a new neighborhood can be activated. In this example, teachers will be able to identify some of the classroom elements and qualities of good teaching that have been discussed in the previous section. One might also keep in mind that students often believe they have no story of their own—no voice, nothing to say—at least until deep reading and conversation ignites that voice. As hooks (2010) says, conversation "not only makes room for every voice, it also presupposes that all voices can be heard" (p. 45). Language shaped by narrative can excite passion and expand the learning space, setting into motion the desire for connection and community.

To investigate some of these matters, we have used "Greasy Lake" (Boyle, 1999) for an experiment in the classroom context, asking the students seated around a table to read the story silently. We read it with them, watching to see how they are doing. It usually takes about half an hour for everyone to finish. We want the conversation to extend and expand what Boyd (2009) calls "emotional contagion," but we also believe that the conversation itself can contribute to the building of community in a sense similar to what Searle (2010) has recently claimed for language in general—that it is crucial for the construction of human civilization. As Searle (2010) puts it: "In human languages we have the capacity not only to represent reality, both how it is and how we want to make it be, but we also have the capacity to create a new reality by representing that reality as existing" (p. 86). Through our capacity for language, we create the human future by projection, in the imagination. For us, as for Searle, shared language already assumes a social contract. It enacts a common desire, moves towards a common goal, and helps to create an ethical sense of articulated obligation. When it is working well, we are engaged together in the classroom space, moving towards the goal of a community vision.

"Greasy Lake" (Boyle, 1999) is a story about three 19-year-old young men looking for adventure late one night. They drive up to the local hangout, Greasy Lake, hoping to find some last-minute excitement before they head home. Jeff, Digby, and the unnamed narrator are suburbanites in their mother's car, "wannabes," dreaming about being "bad boys." For them, a practical joke is usually excitement enough to satisfy their need to be "bad."

When they get to the lake, they lose their keys, get in a fight with "a bad greasy character," and come close to killing him and then raping his girlfriend. The three young men have, by this time, traveled far down a path on "the dark side." It is as if they have made a journey from innocence to experience, from one state of consciousness to another. For them, the adventure is frightening and exhilarating at the same time. Pumped by primal instinct, they are living their own nightmare.

When another car pulls up to the lake, the boys flee—the narrator into the lake, the other two into the woods. In the murky lake, the narrator, wrestling with his own darkness and mortality, suddenly discovers a floating corpse, a terrifying confrontation with his own condition.

Finally, the three boys re-emerge on shore, discover the keys at the light of dawn, have one final encounter with two older girls, and then head home. It has been quite a night—an adventure, and much more than which they had bargained for.

When we introduce "Greasy Lake" to our classes, each student reads the same story, but each maps his or her *own story* onto the *story read*. Each has a focus and perspective as they enter the conversation. As teachers, we readily admit that this is *our* story, too. This "mapping" is promoted and generated through the engagement with language and the activation of imagination.

In order to encourage all voices in the classroom and around the table to speak and be heard, we ask questions about the three boys first, not for any didactic purpose, but to begin the quest for complexity. Unlike a judge looking for the truth or the answer, we want to keep the questions as open as possible. We are not interrogating a witness, but beginning a quest. As teachers, we are on the same quest as the students, although we are in a different position, with a different backstory or history and a different point of view. The conversation about the story extends and expands the story; it helps to create the future and shape a common goal, an intention, within a community of those with common experience of the story. As mentioned in Chapter One, we begin with a line of questioning which includes:

- *What kind of people are these three boys?*
- *Are they really "bad"?*
- *Why do they want to be "bad"?*
- *How do they compare with the other characters (the "greaser," or hoodlum; his girlfriend; the group in the second car; the older girls at the end of the story)?*

Opening with a class discussion of these questions allows us to situate the characters, to begin to explore their differences, but also their similarities— their common desires and expectations. We are helping the group to build a common context for the storyworld within the classroom, and we'd like everyone in this neighborhood to appreciate how complex these characters are.

The responses to the questions are as various as the voices in the classroom. Some students insist, at first, that these are "bad boys," having crossed a line and transgressed or even having broken the law. Others see them as "wannabes," but basically "good boys" who have temporarily gone too far. Eventually, though, these characters are seen as the same complex human beings we all are: they could be any of us.

The opening discussion often leads to another line of inquiry, the journey itself, not only to Greasy Lake, but into the interior terrain of primal consciousness. This discussion is co-created by the group. There are no right or wrong answers, but instead an exploration, an opportunity for meaning-making. Questions that we might ask to lead into this terrain include:

- *What can we make of the narrator losing his keys?*
- *How does he feel when he starts to hit "the greaser" with his tire iron?*
- *Why does he attack the girl?*

With these questions, we begin to focus on a pattern common to many of the stories our students will read in the classroom and the stories that they (and we) have experienced in their (and our) own lives: a richly textured pattern suggesting the seduction and thrill of adventure and violence—the quest for excitement, despite fear, in the midst of boredom. Through the conversation, we begin to look at the meaning of transgression and the powerful forces unleashed with raw instinct. "It's as if these characters are on a roller coaster ride," students might say. "They are bored, seeking a thrill that they rarely have experienced before," or "it's like taking drugs," some suggest. Students offer that "they are addicted to the powerful force."

Questions we might then ask include the following:

- *Is this a power we all feel at some moment in our lives?*
- *What does such instinctual power do to the human sense of connection? To the connection with ourselves?*

As they respond and discuss the different answers to these questions, the students begin to recognize themselves, as we all do, reflected in the experiences described in "Greasy Lake." They are making a journey both into themselves and out to their fellow classmates, just as the narrator moves from the shoreline of Greasy Lake and into the water itself.

We then move into the lake with the narrator. We continue to question and, as teachers, add our own comments as we go.

- *What does the narrator feel when he first encounters the corpse in the murky lake?*
- *What is he thinking about?*

Such questions evoke a variety of further responses, reminding us of the multiple dimensions of human consciousness and the complexity of human emotions. Some typical responses are:

- *"He must be thinking he has gone too far."*
- *"He must be thinking about his own death."*
- *"He must be considering how he almost killed the guy on the shore."*
- *"He must be wondering how he ever got in this mess."*
- *"He must be thinking about what he is going to tell his parents."*

Usually, the results of this investigation into the meaning of adventure open to a recognition that we all have choices, that human experiences are complex, that the adrenaline high is dangerous but reflects a shared pattern of human behavior: it could happen to any of us. We are in this together, and we have shared this experience.

If time permits, we often pursue a final line of inquiry in this context, speculating about a future that we can now represent through shared conversation, the language binding us together:

- *How do these three friends feel as they head home?*
- *Will they return to Greasy Lake soon?*
- *Is it easier for someone considered "good" to become "bad" or for someone considered "bad" to be or become "good?"*

Some students voice their belief that the characters will not return to Greasy Lake. Others believe they will. Some insist that it is easier for those who are considered "good" to do something "bad"; others say the opposite. All agree, however, that the story is complex and filled with surprises—much like the human experience itself. We can hear the students continuing to discuss the story as they leave the classroom and move out to the corridors towards their next encounter.

CONCLUDING THOUGHTS ON DEEP READING AND THE SPACE OF THE CLASSROOM

We want to conclude this chapter by taking a moment to celebrate teachers in the context of our argument so far. To help other people define themselves authentically and spontaneously in relation to helping students understand themselves and their worlds is, for us, the primary task of a teacher, and such a purpose suggests why teaching is a noble profession. To us, the recognition of human language, the engagement with literary narrative as a consequence of that recognition, and the importance of creating an ongoing learning space are all acts of human dignity that underline one's ethical responsibilities at the core of human identity.

As human beings, we are all learners and communicators, but the same thing can also be said about most animals. Unlike other animals, though, human beings are able to recognize that they are capable of learning and communicating, and this sustained activity of self-reflection offers a difference, not just in degree but in kind, between humans and other animal species. For us, this complex sense of self-reflection, tied to the desire to learn and to communicate, makes us human. Human beings desire to know themselves and to connect to others, and, as we have argued, this happens through the intentional use of language. Teaching then becomes a noble response to a human call for a shared community. It may very well be natural to learn and to communicate, but for human beings to recognize that they are capable of learning and communicating, that they are able to speak and be spoken to, is to say something about the mortal quality of human life and its exceptional ability to be self-reflective and purposeful. Such recognition suggests that all human beings desire the shared space of education to grow and flourish, and such recognition also points to the importance of shared natural language processes in all classroom environments.

To put it differently, such acknowledgment of these unique human capabilities creates an ethical demand for people to enter into conversation and to teach. Because human beings not only desire to learn, but recognize this desire, teaching becomes a significant human activity—just as listening becomes an ethical responsibility because others have the desire to speak. Human beings meet their human responsibilities, in other words, through shared acts such as speaking and listening, teaching and learning. Such activities contribute significantly to social and cultural evolution, and they advance understanding from generation to generation.

In this context, as we pointed out in Chapter One, we are convinced that, as Socrates suggested, the primary work of human life is to come to know one's self. Human beings are driven to understand themselves and to locate themselves in and through the world they inhabit. It is this sense of both questing and questioning that makes an individual truly human, and it is this dynamic that should remain a central aim of all classroom education. Such work is dynamic and ongoing, and natural language and stories (the narratives created from natural language) are central to this ongoing process. Language and stories are empowering extensions of the human self, and as many researchers, such as Andy Clark (Clark, 1997), are beginning to conclude, language shapes the learning brain as much as the learning brain shapes language. We cannot imagine any work more important than this— what a teacher can do.

In this chapter, we have emphasized the importance of deep reading and how it is central to our vision of the classroom as a new neighborhood. We believe that before teachers can create a new neighborhood in their own classrooms, they must first have a holistic perspective on deep reading. We have offered some ideas about this perspective and some practical application. These examples are not meant to be prescriptive, as there is no exact recipe for the kind of classroom environments for promoting learning. Instead, these examples simply provide glimpses of the new neighborhood in action. Teachers may draw upon these ideas in creating their own classroom neighborhoods, but they also must find out what works for them through ongoing practice and reflection on that practice.

In the next chapter, we will show how a deepening understanding of this adventure can be developed in the classroom space, as an imaginative journey into the temporal and spatial dimensions of the educated self.

CHAPTER THREE

THE CLASSROOM ADVENTURE:
TO LEARN AND TO UNDERSTAND

In the previous chapter, we suggested that deep reading should be an important component of any significant pedagogy because it helps human beings to know themselves, as Socrates urged, and it allows them to learn something important about their relationship with others. Human beings are temporal selves, unsettled and always engaged in an adventurous pursuit of understanding; deep reading intensifies that engagement, that pursuit, and that adventure. In this chapter, we want to expand our discussion by exploring further this sense of adventure in the context of the classroom and its relationship to the human desire to learn and understand. As bell hooks (2003) says, the classroom should be "a place that is life-sustaining and mind-expanding, a place of liberating mutuality where teacher and student work together in partnership" (hooks, 2003, preface, p. xv). For us, the adventure in the classroom is very much like the adventure of deep reading. Deep reading serves as a microcosm of the classroom itself. Neither celebrates speed or quick effect, but rather depth and self-reflection. Language is at the center of both, serving to "unconceal" what is at the depths.

Language is the medium for creating the literary text, but also the distinctly human classroom. Just as people create through language and participate in the shaping of a literary text, students move through the classroom as learners seeking to know themselves. The crucial role of language in this adventure cannot be underestimated. In his *Literary Theory* (Eagleton, 2008), Terry Eagleton makes the point for us in his discussion of the German philosopher Heidegger:

> If human existence is constituted by time, it is equally made up of language. Language for Heidegger is not a mere instrument of communication, a secondary device for expressing "ideas": it is the very dimension in which life moves, that which brings the world to be in the first place. (Eagleton, 2008, p. 55)

For Heidegger, language creates that distinctly human place where reality "unconceals" itself and so gives itself up to human self-reflection.

We are not far from John Searle on this point (although Heidegger and Searle seem far apart on most issues). In *Making the Social World*, Searle (2010) reminds us of the capabilities and potentialities inherent in human language and persuasively argues that the foundation of the human self and of the institutional structures related to community is language. Language can generate a new reality as well as depict reality in its current state, and language is what generated and continues to generate the institutions of our society and the human bonds that we consider to be finite but genuine in our endeavors with others.

Language shaped into narrative is especially suited to remind human beings of their temporal identity and their location because of its richly textured appeal to the body and the soul, the flesh and the spirit, the mind and the emotions. Narrative language reminds human beings that they are vulnerable bodies with memories and desires, and so they have a past and a future. That language can remind human beings of all that is in itself remarkable. It demonstrates the kind of hope that language can foster. But it also reminds us that human beings are always in movement, from the past to the future. They are always "being towards death" as Heidegger liked to say, and on this journey, they can discover (and uncover) vast worlds of surprise and wonder. When language is used to shape narrative, it can evoke the imagination as well, and so allow people to experience the pleasure of an experience which is playful and open in its wonder and surprise. This is precisely the kind of experience that we anticipate in the classroom space as well. We shape narrative, the same way we shape the classroom, both language and the classroom being events in motion with all kinds of human possibilities. That those possibilities are ongoing and open-ended is also important. Narrative language, like the classroom we envision, always offers an opportunity for the possibilities of democracy and equality rather than an enclosed space of exclusion and separation. Language and the classroom become a kind of staging ground for a democratic space where all participants interact with each other, sharing a richly textured sense of the past as it is evoked through language and, at the same time, moving together into the future.

When the social critic Chris Hedges argues that human beings are losing the ability to differentiate between the pseudo-events of the corporate state and the authentic events of our human lives (Hedges, 2009), he too is making just this kind of point about the rich potential and power of language. As Hedges (2009) warns: "The more we sever ourselves from a literate print-based world, a world of complexity and nuance, a world of ideas, for one informed by comforting, reassuring images, fantasies, slogans, celebrities, and a lust for violence, the more we are destined to implode" (pp. 189–190). For Hedges the goal of education and democracy is individual freedom and a just and compassionate society, not the acquisition of ruthless power or personal profit. Equality and democracy are not an outgrowth of competition and market economies, but are based on self-sacrifice and compassion. We need language and stories to help us on the way.

We will have much more to say about the effects of this corporate state (and consumer culture) in subsequent chapters, but the cultural drift that Hedges warns against, a warning echoed by many other thinkers—Freire and Macedo (1987), hooks (2003), and Nussbaum (2010), to name only a few—reminds us that what is taught in the 21st century classroom and how that classroom is created is no trivial or incidental matter. The human stakes are very high; human identity as we know it may well hang in the balance.

THE CREATION OF THE CLASSROOM MUCH LIKE THE CREATION OF NARRATIVE

The creation of an effective literacy classroom is much like creating a good narrative story. Both are capable of drawing human beings into imaginative rhythms, taking them on an engaging journey, a lived-through experience, a meaningful engagement which includes the emotional and the cognitive dimensions of the embodied moment. Humans need sensuous language, the feel of the story, just as the sensuous body needs an environment in which to live and to learn. A "deep reader" moves with the curve of the emotional quality of the living language, and that makes a difference in the reader's mind, life, and experience. No abstract or condensed version of the story (think *Spark Notes* or, if you are older, *Cliff Notes*) can make that imprint on the reader. In the same sense, a classroom lacking passion and sensuous enjoyment cannot hope to quicken the quest for genuine knowledge. The philosophers call what we seek here "qualia," the depth and duration of the human spirit, *gravitas*. This quality of mind is the mark of an educated human person, a human being who is continually engaged in learning and who understands that the world itself is like a classroom. The classroom, like the world, should encourage and enhance this quality of mind, and it should invite this kind of adventure, this quest for genuine knowledge.

Denis Donoghue seems to be thinking along similar lines when, in *The Practice of Reading* (Donoghue, 2000), he argues for what he calls "aesthetic reading." Donoghue wants to return readers to the attention demanded by beauty and by the rich complexity of the literary text. His discussion of the reading experience mirrors what we believe should happen in the classroom experience as a whole. Drawing on a tradition stretching from Kant and Schiller to contemporary thinkers such as Louise Rosenblatt, Donoghue takes the position that deep reading (we could call it "deep classroom experience") is crucial to the creation and understanding of human identity and the complex experience that used to be called *human life*. Like the classroom process at its best, the reading process should evoke both cognitive and emotional interactions, drawing on what neuroscientists now claim to be functions not only of the temporal lobe but also the limbic system—the "lizard brain," as it is popularly referred to. Through this kind of reading, students do not simply hunt for facts and quick information; instead, they enter into a new experience filled with anticipation and surprise. That kind of experience also helps to define what we see as the dynamics of a genuine classroom environment—teachers and students interacting together, creating an adventure, a narrative. In this dynamic, the teachers are not working to manipulate students, not trying to persuade them, like salesmen or politicians might, not treating them as an object to be pushed to a certain judgment; instead, teachers are engaged with students in a process filled with the richly textured possibilities of creating narrative, heading towards what used to be thought of as beauty and truth. Donoghue (2000) cites Rosenblatt's (1981) views on the levels available for readers as they engage with a text:

> The actual lived-through reading process is, of course, not a word-by-word summation of meaning, but rather a process of tentative organizations of meaning, the creation of a framework into which the reader incorporates ensuing words and phrases. The notion that 'literal' reading should come first is the result of the very assumption I am challenging; that literal, or efferent, meaning has a priority.... Aesthetic reading is not efferent reading plus aesthetics elements, but a distinct kind of reading, requiring an initially different stance, a different focus of attention, a concentration of lived-through experience, on the part of the reader. (Rosenblatt, 1981, p. 24)

Rosenblatt's views on aesthetic reading, as cited by Donoghue (2000, p. 13), are relevant not only in terms of reading literature but in terms of creating the classroom experience. Donoghue gravitates to Rosenblatt's views on reading, in terms of how meaning is made and what differing levels of meaning can be made when a reader "enters" a text. When a reader first engages with a text, he or she begins to develop a framework or a temporary sense of meaning created from words and phrases. As Donoghue (2000) reviews it, Rosenblatt points out that the literal meaning of the text comes first, but then there is a deeper level of meaning to be made in connection with readers' real-life experiences. This deeper level of meaning-making requires a different kind of organizing on the part of the reader. With full concentration, the reader organizes this level of meaning-making by using his or her life experiences as a lens through which to view deeper meaning (Donoghue, 2000).

If students are only asked to find literal meaning when reading a text, students easily grow bored in this kind of classroom environment where there is little engagement and little passion, where the rational and cognitive abstractions trump the sensuous and pleasurable emotions, and where imposed judgment and enforced teaching for information masquerade as education. In such an environment, probing the depths for beauty and truth, for qualia, gives way to mere surfaces, to the manipulation of bits and pieces of information pretending to be knowledge.

The challenge is to create classrooms as learning environments that arouse and inspire students both cognitively and emotionally, and, in this sense, the challenge is to treat students and knowledge as ends in themselves—not as objects to be manipulated or stamped with the seal of teacher approval. The reading experience, when done well, can be seen as equivalent to the classroom experience, when also done well. The meaning of the space of the classroom for teaching and learning is co-created by teacher and students. Like reading, the creation of meaning within the classroom space should be celebrated as part of the adventurous quest that it is, for the pleasure it offers, a temporal pleasure which emerges first from experiencing the difficulty of the challenge, and then from the sense of accomplishment evoked by successfully working deeply through the classroom experience unfolding through time. In the same sense, working through the space of a narrative text can be difficult but also joyful and playful, a ludic act in which the reader focuses full attention on the depth and delight of the richly textured language, the depth of the human self. Whether we are talking about reading a literary text or experiencing the learning environment, learners move through, and help to create, an unfolding story. As readers and learners, they are focused and hopeful, eventually arriving at a moment of harmony, a moment that fulfills promises and expectations, a moment that provides a delightful surprise. Then they are pulled forward once again by renewed creative forces and desire, language always leading the way. Such movement enhances the possibility for the education of the whole person. Teachers act as guides or facilitators who evoke within learners the aspiration to find truth through the exercise of their faculties.

BOTH COGNITION AND EMOTION MAKE A PERSON WHOLE

The learning experience should be much like the reading experience—a living and vital experience, moving through the narrative curve of language to create a uniquely human dialectic. In fact, human beings read and write for the same reason that they desire to learn: in part, because they need to create and to communicate, and in part because they have an innate desire to exercise their imaginations, to discover their uniqueness, and to belong to something larger than themselves. They come to the classroom with the same desires and needs. As mortal human beings, sensing their imperfections and vulnerability, their capabilities and strengths, human beings feel that words shaped into stories have meaning and purpose; such language helps them to make cognitive sense of the self and the world and contributes to a feeling of human connection—a connection that should radiate throughout the classroom, activating both cognition and emotion. Such a dynamic opens the way to teaching to and from the whole person.

Alice Flaherty, a leading neuroscientist, explains in *Midnight Madness* (Flaherty, 2005) that human beings consistently move between pleasure and displeasure, approach and avoidance, the cognitive and the emotional, always seeking meaning as they go. According to Flaherty (2005), this dialectical movement can be traced in the brain itself, mapped in the interaction between the temporal lobe—where much of the linguistic system operates—and the amygdala, the limbic system, where animal instincts and emotions seem primarily to reside. As Flaherty (2005) says:

> The interaction between temporal lobe meaning and limbic meaning (conceptual meaning and emotional meaning) reflects what has been called the tension in language between the dictionary and the scream. Without the former, we would have no ability to communicate; without the latter, the need to express our needs, we would have no drive to communicate. (Flaherty, 2005, p. 220)

Others, like Zull (2002), also highlight this strong connection between cognition and emotion, the connection necessary for all deep reading and, more generally, for all deep learning.

For us, that sense of "the tension in language," as Flaherty calls it, includes an acknowledgment of the central importance of the human voice and the human imagination, the inspiration traditionally connected to the breath of human life. We view this sense of voice and breath as close to the human origins of identity, and it has certainly contributed to the shaping of culture, and, most importantly, to the creation of human community. Humans live in and through the stories they tell, and those stories reinforce the culture and simultaneously put the culture into question. Human beings can only engage in that "doubleness," both creating and questioning what they create, if they are capable of self-reflection through this process of language. To do that effectively, though, they must also find their voice and discover the depths of their imagination.

THE DISTRACTED STUDENTS

Our experience with students suggests that in our media-saturated world they are, at times, drawn to visual sensation and, as a result, lose the fundamental connection with the mystery of their own voice and imagination. Too often, they seem hypnotized by the hyper-representation of images copied from other images, images speeding like ghostly illusions, like commodities without origins, breathless. Seduced by the sensation of these images, students also ironically claim that they are bored. Why are they bored? Because they are disenchanted; they have lost their own desire and imagination. Many students, claiming boredom, seek what they think is the thrill of spectacle, but that thrill is actually a retreat. They withdraw into simplicity, into what they believe is a fast sensation but ultimately turns out to be a place of defense far removed from the truly fragile and dangerous condition of real, mortal life. When they embrace only the thrill of spectacle, people are not making the best use of their imagination and creativity. We fear that this lack of use will cause atrophy in their creative ability— analogous to what happens when people no longer exercise their "reading brain" or when they are bedridden for long periods of time.

To desire and to imagine is to complicate rather than to retreat, to appreciate the complexity of life as it is. In the classroom today, many students seem disembodied, retreating from complexity and engagement, withdrawing from the world out of fear, refusing to embrace the environment defined by their own bodies and individual voices.

The difficult challenge of the classroom is to create for students a "welcoming" return to what they are missing: the rich texture of complex lives, the complications of human desire, the struggle for the beautiful and the sublime, the symmetry and harmony of imaginative possibility, the pleasure of play, and the fragile and dangerous nature of vulnerable human life. The fresh and original language of imaginative writers, combined with the living voices of their classmates in the felt presence of a classroom space, is well-suited to this challenge of drawing students back from their disembodied states and encouraging them to activate and stretch their creative and imaginative "muscles."

Students are drawn to spectacle because they are flattened out, the unknown depth of their identity left unexplored as a result of the very spectacles they find thrilling. What spectacle lacks is the interchange in the classroom—a place where they can safely risk an exploration of their evolving identities. Unlike spectacle, deep reading and discussion are always two-way (at least) exchanges, dialogic interactions. Spectacle is a one-way event without a "live" interaction; spectacle is consumption without reflection. Art in general and literary narrative in particular can shake a person and stir up imaginative possibilities. Every story carries with it a promise as readers are drawn deeper and deeper into its rhythms, its voices, its secret places. Unlike the unanchored images floating across the surface of the computer screen or the instrumental prose of commerce and bureaucracy, the rich texture of literary narrative offers a temporal duration and spatial depth with no explicit purpose, no commercial message about consumption or commodification. Through the originality of their playful language, the best writers offer instead something that readers cannot fully grasp, possess, or control. They offer beauty to enjoy and to contemplate, the sublime to transport and inspire at the very moment of terror and transgression. That is the goal that our version of a classroom also aspires to. Such a goal demands that students and teachers alike (all of us) slow down and reflect, as well as interact, creating together a space for a pluralistic and communal learning adventure.

Students in a classroom need only journey with Coleridge's "Ancient Mariner" (Coleridge, 1969) to understand what we are suggesting. In fact, for us, "The Rime of the Ancient Mariner" embodies one version of the adventurous journey we are talking about. In that poem, Coleridge invites the reader (teachers and students) to follow the poet's imagination—from the land of wedding guests to the depths of the deep ocean, from the ordinary events at the surface of everyday life to the strange and haunting perceptions of unexplored territory (geographical and psychological, outside and inside), from the daily routine of safety on land to the extraordinary sense of lonely terror at sea, from the conscious to the unconscious, and then back "home" with all the rich experience of difference that the sublime experience offers.

The journey begins with the departure from conventional landmarks, moving deeper into new possibilities.

> Merrily did we drop
> Below the kirk, below the hill
> Below the lighthouse top (Coleridge, 1969, ll. 22–24)

For those readers willing to engage in the journey and to suspend their disbelief, they begin to awaken to their own strangeness and their own imaginative capabilities. Both the auditory and the visual imagination are stirred and intensified, appealing directly to the human senses.

> And now the Storm-Blast came, and he
> Was tyrannous and strong (ll. 41–42)
> ....
> And now there came both mist and snow,
> And it grew wondrous cold:
> And ice, mast-high, came floating by,
> As green as emerald. (Coleridge, 1969, ll. 51–54)

The engaged reader moves with the Ancient Mariner, and the rest of the crew, with the ocean breeze and the breath of imaginative life—until stopped by the Mariner's sudden announcement of his inhospitable act:

> ... with my cross-bow
> I shot the Albatross (Coleridge, 1969, ll. 81–82)

At that moment, the reader pauses, wondering whether to continue on. The journey then takes the reader still deeper into unknown territory, closer to the silence of the ocean itself, and closer to the loneliness of the mortal body devoid of human language.

> And every tongue, through utter drought,
> Was withered at the root;
> We could not speak, no more than if
> We had been choked with soot. (Coleridge, 1969, ll. 135–138)

It is as if the courageous readers, teacher and students, have arrived at the sight of their own phantom existence, perceiving a skeleton ship in the midst of the ocean (according to the external events of the poem), sensing the origins of their own sexuality and death (according to the internal psychology of the language).

> Are those her ribs through which the Sun
> Did peer as through a grate?
> And is that Woman all her crew?
> Is that a Death? And there two?
> Is Death that Woman's mate? (Coleridge, 1969, ll. 185–189)

But then, out of this moment of terror and affliction, comes a renewed moment of hope, a rejuvenated sense of imagination, as the Ancient Mariner blesses "the water snakes" (l. 273)—"A spring of love gushed from my heart" (l. 284)—and the reader (and the ship) moves forward, making a slow, but certain, reentry back to the landmarks of hospitality. Returning to land with the Mariner, the reader is now "sadder but wiser" (l. 624) for the effort. With such a journey, the engaged reader feels enchanted, compelled towards and prepared for further adventure and conversation.

Such a journey reflects the kind of classroom experience we have in mind. It can delight through understanding but also moves every student forward through shared attention and focus, thus creating and reinforcing a model for better citizens for the future. Imaginative language always says more than a reader can think, and that is a mark of both its cognitive and emotional appeal. Such direct engagement is an adventure, calling for further imagination and conversation. The multiple voices moving through a story or a classroom, in this way, make everyone responsive to the differences that demand to be heard and to the strangeness of what we might at first take to be ordinary life.

A different kind of example of a classroom journey, although with similar goals, can also be seen in a practical classroom exercise conducted in India. The poem used was Robert Frost's "The Road Not Taken" (Frost, 1969d) and the teacher created two learning goals for the students in this experience: (1) to teach the poetic device of image, and (2) to have students understand how symbol can be used in a poem and how a poem can holistically represent a symbol. In the first session, the teacher focused on helping students learn and understand the poetic device of image by using a visualization and mental practice approach. In the second session, the teacher focused on the idea of the "journey" as a symbol in the poem and as a symbol in the students' lives. (In Chapter Seven, there is a description of how we used this same Frost poem with preservice teachers and high school students in a different context and for a different purpose.)

For this particular literary exercise, the teacher wanted to have two sessions of students from the school with pairings of younger and older students for each session in order to create a democratic space for learning, one where individual students' voices were privileged. Each student would have a guide and a friend with whom to share the learning experiences. Pairing older with younger students would create opportunities for each to enrich the other's learning opportunities. Each student could then draw on his or her own internal development of language and cognition, while also developing his or her social sense of language and cognition through communicating with others.

Students were excited to work with other students who were five or six years different in age, both older and younger. The teacher was primarily interested in providing a direct experience with the language so that the students could use their imagination and life experiences to "see" an image in the poem and make connections between their own life journeys and the journey of the poem.

THE FIRST SESSION: A FOCUS ON IMAGE AND IMAGERY IN POETRY

When the teacher worked with the first group of students (second graders and eighth graders), she identified both the learning goal and the method to be used, explaining that everyone would be learning about images in poetry and doing a visualization activity as a medium for this learning.

To begin to build the desired learning space, she first asked each pair (second grader and eighth grader) to get to know a little about each other and then to report at least one thing they had each learned about the other. She gave them five minutes to talk with each other and familiarize themselves with their designated learning partners, thus creating a feeling of comfort and safety. Although the teacher was providing the scaffolding for this learning experiment, she made clear that the students would be learning from their partner as well as teaching their partners. Just as the actual poem would eventually be shaping the readers and the readers would be shaping the text by their interaction with it, the participants themselves would be shaping each other in this direct engagement with language.

After students shared information with each other about themselves, the class moved on to reading the poem. The poem was read aloud twice and the lines of the poem were projected onto a large screen in the auditorium where the activities took place. After reading the poem twice, the teacher shared a photograph of a natural forest setting to help students transport themselves into this forest where Frost's "two roads diverged." She then asked them to imagine themselves sitting in this forest. For two minutes of silence, all having eyes closed, the students visualized what it would be like to be in this forest. As they did this, the teacher, evoking the senses and the embodiment of the experience, asked: What do you see? What do you hear? What do you smell? What do you feel? After two minutes of silence, the students gently opened their eyes and reported to their partners what they had experienced, and the teacher reminded them that these responses would be shared with the larger group.

They saw birds; they pictured lush trails in the woods; they heard leaves rustling under their feet and heard birds singing; they smelled fresh air; and they touched cool grass and earth under their feet. One student excitedly proclaimed, "I see the nature of India!" Students then made connections to particular lines in the poem and how the images they visualized and imagined were connected to particular lines. In this context, they began to deepen further their understanding of how the imagination and language were connected and how their inner identity and the external world were also linked.

THE SECOND SESSION: A FOCUS ON SYMBOL AND SYMBOLIC JOURNEY IN POETRY

The second session was composed of fourth graders and ninth graders. Each fourth grader had a partner in the ninth grade. After giving students a few minutes to find out about their partners, the teacher asked them to report some of these findings. Some reported that their partners liked a certain food, had a particular hobby, or liked one subject of study more than another. This simple activity helped evoke all voices in the classroom space, making it active and participatory.

Next, the teacher explained that in this session the focus would be on learning through narrative or story. The learning goal for the poem, "The Road Not Taken," (Frost, 1969d) was to understand the poem as a metaphor for life as a journey. The poem was read twice, and the lines of the poem were projected up on a large screen for all to see and follow along. The ninth grade students explained that they knew of this poem; it appeared in their ninth grade literature collection.

Before making any links to particular students' life choices, the class discussed the situation in the poem. The teacher then called upon the ninth grade student in each pair to think of a choice or decision he or she had made in the last few months, and to explain both the choice and the "difference" (drawing on the language of the poem) this process of choosing had made in his or her life. Students then shared these examples with each other with interesting results. After sharing with her fourth grade partner, one ninth grade girl, for example, explained a choice she had made and how it had affected her—how it had made a difference. One day she didn't feel like attending school. As she was thinking about making a choice to stay home from school that day, she started to worry that she might miss her dance practice and that they might be learning new dance steps. As a result, she decided that she shouldn't miss school. She didn't want to be left behind if the other dancers were taught new dance steps. As it turned out, they did teach new dance steps that day in school. She said she was relieved afterwards that she had chosen to come to school, and that coming to school and being present to learn the new dance steps had made all the difference in her situation.

The teacher had asked the older students to brainstorm a situation where a choice or decision had affected their lives. Emphasizing that these choices and decisions were not necessarily either "good" or "bad," just choices, the teacher was emphasizing how choices, even small ones, in poetic language or in life, create meaning that always make a difference. This modeling by the ninth graders was designed to scaffold the thinking processes of the younger students. The older students shared their experiences, ones that they had "mapped" from the poem onto their own lives. In this way, meaning-making was explored and became part of an ongoing learning experience. Students found ways to connect their own life experiences with the ones that the writer had created.

This classroom journey helped demonstrate how each individual internally engages with the development of language and cognition and also develops the social domain of language and cognition through communicating with others. For us, the quality and effectiveness of the classroom learning environment provide the underpinning for an individual's growth in both the internal and social development of language and cognition, which is at the heart of all learning.

To put it in other terms, when students experience a story directly, they map their stories onto the stories they are reading. As the language of the story unfolds, the identity of the student reading the text also seems to unfold. At the same time, the students contemplate the story from a safe distance, gaining pleasure as they go. That kind of "double action," both inside and outside the story, is exactly what should happen in any learning environment.

THE SUBLIME AND THE ETHICAL IN THE CLASSROOM JOURNEY

In *Theories of Reading*, Karen Littau seems right on target when she argues that "moving the audience to rapture is a valuable end in itself" (Littau, 2006, p. 87). And, as the ancient critic Longinus puts it:

> For the sublime not only persuades, but even throws an audience into transport. The marvelous always works with more surprising force than that which barely persuades or delights. In most cases, it is wholly in our power, either to resist or yield to persuasion. But the sublime, endured with strength irresistible, strikes home, and triumphs over every hearer. (Longinus, 1973, p. 73)

Helene Cixous, a French commentator, celebrates just such reading. Cixous' (1988) reader gives himself or herself fully to a text, to "The sublimity of poetic nourishment." Describing her approach in the classroom, Cixous (1988) comments: "We work very close to the text, as close to the body of the text as possible; we work phonetically, listening to the text, as well as graphically and typographically" (Cixous, 1988, p. 148). This is the experience of the story, the sublime adventure of the classroom itself: the narrative journey accumulates and structures that experience as the students move through it, and in that reconfiguration the students are always surprised as they return to themselves and simultaneously are thrown outward to others, to further conversation with classmates, to ongoing learning about the self and the other. The reading of the literary text helps create the story of the classroom, and the story of the classroom moves the students to new adventures.

The narrative curve of the adventure with deep reading and discussion insists on surprise but also dialogical relations to affirm humanity. People need stories to stir desire, even to shock the imagination, but also to know who they are in relation to others. As Alasdair MacIntyre, the renowned philosopher of ethics, puts it: "I can only answer the question 'What am I to do?' if I can answer the prior question 'Of what story or stories do I find myself a part?'" (MacIntyre, 1981, p. 216). In the same context, Maxine Greene, an educational theorist, underlines the importance of this kind of imaginative questioning and connection:

> When it comes to the ethical imagination, one of the first things I think about is the other, our relationship to the other. A little bit, as Robert Penn Warren said, you can't really have ethics unless you can think of yourself in relation to somebody else. And then imagination makes everything possible. Imagination makes it possible to somehow, as

somebody else said, recognize the familiar in the stranger, the ability to try to see through some else's eyes, the ability to reach out. (Greene, 2007, p. 5)

Students today seem to have no story, no context, nothing to say. Perhaps they are depressed, anxious, and worried that they have lost their voice—or have never had a voice—and so they have lost their future. As Greene (2007) sees it, the classroom can foster an "ability to come close to someone else, to see through his eyes, to see the work, the preciousness of that other human being" (p. 6). Teachers in the 21st century classroom are obligated to help return students to the ethical role of stories and story-telling, which is to simultaneously create and cocreate meaning of both texts and selves. This mapping of one's story onto a piece of literature, along with understanding the meanings of the text, is what we refer to as the creating and co-creating of both texts and selves. Together, teachers and students should be making an ongoing story, the story of the classroom as an evolving new neighborhood in our sense.

Teachers and students grappling together with a literary text, with the classroom space as the reading space writ large, can create a classroom equivalent to what MacIntyre and Greene envision, and to what, in a different context, Emmanuel Levinas calls "a curvature of intersubjective space" (Levinas, 1985, p. 291). For Levinas, the other standing before you deserves full attention and acknowledgment, and when that attention and acknowledgment are given the two human beings standing before each other experience the ethical depth of human relationship. As Levinas (1985) puts it in his difficult and often puzzling language: "The way in which the Other presents himself, exceeding the Other in me, we here name face" (p. 291). For us, Levinas is suggesting that at such moments of genuine human encounter, human beings sense something beyond their ordinary self, something beyond the surface of what can be seen. They move beyond the ordinary and friendly face of the socially acceptable and suddenly find themselves in a strange place, exceeding even the boundaries of what they thought was unknown. As they look at the other (even the student before them), it is as if they have just encountered something profound and inexplicable calling to them, demanding it be acknowledged.

xLevinas' point here has an analogy in deep reading and its ethical dimension. As Fludernik (2007) and Attridge (2004) suggested about narrative (see Chapter Two), the commitment and risk of reading deeply can bring the reader into unfamiliar territory, strange and dangerous places which make the reader vulnerable. The reader finds such places strange because the reader is confronting his or her own strangeness, the other.

In a similar way, we would argue that the commitment to and acknowledgment of this other in the classroom is somewhat like imagining a student who is a stranger until that student becomes a friend or reflecting on a literary character who seems weird and unfamiliar to members of the class until they dare to open themselves to this character, to engage with the person, and to shake this person's hand. The strange character in a narrative, in other words, is like the other, and that other evokes not only its own strangeness, but the strangeness in the class itself. As the poet Wallace Stevens aptly put it in "Tea at the Palaz of Hoon" (Stevens, 1921):

> I was in the world in which I walked, and what I saw
> Or heard or felt came not but from myself:
> And there I found myself more truly and more strange. (Stevens, 1921, ll. 12–14)

On the journey of life, human beings find themselves when they encounter friends and strangers, the self and the other, but they always find them themselves, which is exactly what needs to be encouraged in the classroom. At such moments, humans move beyond themselves, acknowledging similarities and differences, familiarity and strangeness. And, with that kind of acknowledgment also comes further recognition, that human beings are unique individuals and social selves desiring to belong, a strange mixture of individual freedom and inevitable necessity. Similar to each other and yet so strange and different, one from the other, humans are bound to the other. It is a central ethical demand that each human being acknowledge that other before him or her, and listen to the voice of the other.

The ideal classroom builds capacities for responsible agency and individual flourishing along these lines. With reading and discussing literature at the forefront, the classroom environment can provide a space to help people to understand the nature of responsible human agency and self-respect in terms of the extent to which they are, as individuals, justly held accountable for their life prospects and life choices, their actions and character traits, and their relations with friends and strangers. Without interaction with the other, we believe, the best environment and community for learning is not possible. Deep reading paves the path.

DEEP READING AND DEEP LEARNING AND THE HUMAN VOICE

Our argument about deep reading and deep learning in the classroom should not quickly be dismissed as a rant by dinosaurs still walking the earth in the frenetic digital age of multiple screens. We are not ancient relics nor are we luddites advocating abolishing or breaking electronic devices. Granted some critics might insist that our position suffers from nostalgic longing and a perverse fetish for the book. We respectfully disagree. Language and its embodiment in the book are central not only to the human past but to the human future. We might not be able to recover fully the secrets of the universe or the origins of the self, but it is worth the journey to try to get as close to that mystery as possible. To discover the full presence of the self, "the unmediated voice," we might say, is increasingly impossible in world saturated with electronic media and a sense of widely fragmented selves. But we are convinced that a defense of the human is still viable. With the breakneck speed of digital transformations that threaten the loss of emphasis on literature and written language—what has for thousands of years been the most significant human value in building culture, community, and mindfulness—slowing down, going deep, and listening to the human voice make good sense to us.

The relationship between oral culture (speech and listening) and print culture (writing and reading) is relevant in this context. For centuries, thinkers from Plato to Derrida have examined and commented on this thorny relationship in terms of literacy. Although oral culture is usually considered to precede writing and reading, the interrelationship between speech and writing is clearly more complex than was earlier thought. In terms of the evolution of language, speech has had significant impact on writing, just as writing has significantly influenced speech. Because it seems to have come first, speech is often privileged over writing although the act of writing, its production and product, is often celebrated for expanding human identity and consciousness, allowing for a heightened level of self-reflection (as well as the creation of academic knowledge, libraries for learning and study, metacognitive teacher reflection, and so on). To deny the importance of speech and listening, its living presence, is analogous to denying what we insist needs to be preserved. How to preserve that sense of speech, that evocation of the human voice and the auditory imagination, is also an aspect of our challenge.

Walter Ong is an important participant in this kind of discussion. As Ong (1968) says:

> Speaking and hearing are not simple operations. Each exhibits a dialectical structure which mirrors the mysterious depths of man's psyche. As he composes his thoughts in words, a speaker or writer hears this word echoing within himself and thereby follows his own thought, as though he was another person. Conversely, a hearer or reader repeats within himself the words he hears and thereby understands them, as though he were

himself two individuals. The double and interlocking dialectic ... provides the matrix for human communication. The speaker listens while the hearer speaks. (p. 51)

Ong's description fits well with our sense of "the doubleness" created by language in terms of both creating and then questioning what is created, and our emphasis on the way language can help create and preserve the imagination and human community. His insights are also confirmed by much of the recent research on the human brain, a topic which we will explore extensively in the next chapter.

Those who advocate for "visual literacy" defend electronic media by suggesting that on-screen culture can help us recover this sense of speech, returning humans to the presence of the human voice. Ong himself, at times, seemed to be moving in this direction. Books on tape emphasize speech, for example. Video conferencing allows participants not only to see but also to hear another at a great distance. No doubt there is some truth in such comment, although the issue of "great distance" remains problematic when we consider "deep learning" as an embodied experience. Donoghue (2000) asks the important question here: "but what about the electronic media, computers and information technology? If the technology of print enforced its values but still allowed voices to be heard, surely the electronic media will be even more hospitable to voices?" (p. 121). His response to this question is telling: "The prudent answer is: not necessarily. What orality had to fear from script and print was the fate of being silenced, its values displaced. What it has to fear from the electronic media is the abjection of being tested and mocked" (Donoghue, 2000, p. 121). To be laughed at is often a fate worse than being displaced, as Donoghue indicates.

Literary narrative at its original best brings us close to the human voice: readers sense a human presence in the language, allowing an experience of authority and continuity, a glimpse, at least, of human purpose and identity. Without that human presence felt through the timbre of the human voice, human beings lose the ability to discover human connectivity. When people distance themselves from their imaginative capability to believe and to make-believe, the energizing center of the classroom space—that is, the impetus to learn—cannot hold.

The magic that young children find in stories, even in the words "Once upon a time," comes, in part, because they experience the resonance of an adult voice close by. That voice evokes their own voice as well. Recent brain research by Patricia Kuhl and her team (Kuhl, 2009) in the laboratories at the University of Washington, for example, indicates that children between 8 and 10 months old can quickly learn the fundamentals of a language when an adult speaker, face to face in the same room, talks directly with them. The children focus intently on the face of the speaker and on the language flowing towards them. By contrast, those same children put in front of a screen with an adult speaking through that electronic technology do not learn the language at all. Without the crucial human presence and interaction—evoking the basic dyad of parent and child—something extraordinarily valuable and critical to learning seems to be lost. We do not believe that it is mere nostalgia to desire the rooted and embodied experience of this type of human interchange, and we acknowledge that the purity of that voice, the origin of that presence, is heavily mediated in most situations in the present era. Yet the evolutionary process that led to the creation of language marks the making of the human being. To lose that sense of voice and human connectivity is to lose a basic value and driving force at the center of the human self. It is to put into jeopardy the communal and imaginative space of the classroom as we envision it.

THE POETICS OF THE CLASSROOM SPACE

Can we be more specific about the texture of this classroom—this imaginative space, this ongoing neighborhood of possibilities? Gaston Bachelard, a French philosopher of science, in his astonishing book, *The Poetics of Space* (Bachelard, 1994), turns his attention to what he aptly calls "a phenomenology of the imagination." Writing over 50 years ago, Bachelard can still insist that "the poetic image" has a "sonority of being"; that the poet speaks "on the threshold of being" (p. xvi). For this French philosopher, "the places in which we have experienced daydreaming reconstitute themselves in new daydreams, and it is because our memories of former dwelling-places are relived as daydreams that these dwelling-places of the past remain in us for all time" (Bachelard, 1994, p. 6). Although Bachelard does not say so, his phenomenology connects with that of Merleau-Ponty and Heidegger, and, like Ong, he too anticipates the contemporary work of today's neuroscientists, who understand the link between body, mind, and environment as well as the significance of brain plasticity.

Bachelard (1994) offers a detailed "topoanalysis," as he calls it, of the sense of place, the space of a house, for example, demonstrating how such pedestrian space can become a place of memory and imagination where the past and the future interact, a place of peace and contemplation where a feeling of trust and safety abides, a place of happiness and hope, a place of well-being. His "house" is our classroom. As Bachelard says, when humans read about a room in literature, they write that room; they excite the imagination. "The reader who is 'reading a room' leaves off reading and starts to think of some place in his own past. You would like to tell everything about your room. You would like to interest the reader in yourself, whereas you have unlocked a door to daydreaming" (p. 14). For Bachelard (1994), the imaginative image, the daydream can evoke the "feel of the tiniest latch" (p. 15), the latch of a door from childhood that still remains in your hands and your memory.

Bachelard's meditation on the imaginative space of a house calls up precisely what we believe the experience of students in the imaginative space of a classroom should feel like. The classroom space should embody dreams, become those dreams, linking the past experiences of the students to future possibilities. The kind of classroom we have in mind should unlock doors to the imagination, but it can only do that through felt experience, not so much from the expression of utilitarian facts and pedestrian methods, but through the depth of feeling that invites everyone to speak, that creates inspiration for voice, memory, and desire—a call to self-reflection and belonging.

The classroom space should be a dream place to travel, a place of ongoing questing where students and teachers transform their pedestrian selves and journey instead on paths that—to borrow from Robert Frost's (1969b) poem, "Neither Out Far Nor In Deep"—*are far out because they are in deep.* As Bachelard (1994) explains:

> How precise the familiar hill paths remain for our muscular consciousness! A poet (Caubere) has expressed all this dynamism in one single line: "Oh my roads and their cadence." When I relive dynamically the road that "climbed" the hill, I am quite sure the road itself had muscles. As I write this page, I feel freed of my duty to take a walk; I am sure of having gone out of my house. (p. 11)

The imaginative space brings us home just as it brings us to the world.

Parker Palmer knows what Bachelard is talking about. In *The Courage to Teach*, Palmer (1998) creates an alternative model for the classroom, what he terms the "community of truth." Although Palmer, a visionary educator, does not speak of the classroom as a "dream space," his space resonates with a kind of sacred quality. As he puts it: "to teach is to create a space in which the community of truth is practiced" (Palmer, 1998, p. 97). For Palmer the core mission of education is the mission of knowing, teaching, and learning, and the classroom space should inspire that mission. For him, the classroom dynamics that create that possibility always brim with energy and imagination. The space of a classroom, then, is shaped, as he puts it, by paradox, an imaginative tension that, we would argue, is mirrored in the complexity of narrative and language itself.

Palmer (1998) intends this "community of truth" to address what he perceives is needed in a teaching and learning space. Although he identifies necessary components from therapeutic, marketing, and civic models of community, he stresses that his community model is required to create a "community of truth":

> The hallmark of the community of truth is not psychological intimacy or political civility, or pragmatic accountability, though it does not exclude these virtues. The model of community reaches deeper, into ontology and epistemology, into assumptions about the nature of reality and how we know it on which all education is built. The hallmark of the community of truth is in its claim that reality is a web of communal relationships, and we can know reality only by being in community with it. (Palmer, 1998, p. 95)

Palmer offers no prescription for creating particular communities of truth because different teachers must find their own ways to create them. For him, the making of such communities must emerge from the identity and integrity of the particular teacher and the acknowledgment of the paradoxes and complexity of the living classroom space. When teachers can identify their strengths and are in community with themselves, then the right method will emerge.

For Palmer, the community of truth puts the subject (such as literature) at the center of learning and encourages an atmosphere that creates knowledge out of shared conflict, a form of mental exercise that bypasses the cliched notion that competition is merely about winning or losing. All people, including teachers, are constantly changing. As long as teachers maintain a connectedness with themselves, they will, according to Palmer, discover ways to bring all learners together in the classroom. When teachers and learners gather together in shared inquiry around a subject or a narrative, self-knowledge becomes paramount to the creation of a community of truth because each participant's identity and integrity are shared.

Palmer (1998) outlines six paradoxical tensions that are necessary in any learning space, and those paradoxes underline the kind of complexity and ongoing vitality that we, too, favor and celebrate for the 21st century classroom:

1. The space should be hospitable and charged.
2. The space should be bounded and open.

3. The space should invite the voice of the individual and the voice of the group.
4. The space should honor the "little" stories of the students and the "big" stories of the discipline and the tradition.
5. The space should support solitude and surround it with resources of community.
6. The space should welcome both silence and speech. (p. 74)

Like the poet Keats, Palmer seems to suggest here the importance of "negative capability," that intuitive ability to hold opposing views in mind without any grasping for absolute certainties. His community of truth, like Bachelard's dream space, is a dynamic place inviting learners to an ongoing adventure and interaction, a narrative journey. Part of holding these opposing views together involves a learning community where "dialectical" activities are privileged, in the good old Socratic tradition; it involves first and foremost reflection through shared discussion and exchange.

LIFE AS A JOURNEY

Is this narrative journey really central to human life, or even to the classroom? The American philosopher Philip Lewin asks the question this way: " 'Life as narrative' is this merely a metaphorical way of understanding life or is the metaphor motivated by isomorphisms between the constructive components of narrative and the enabling conditions of human life?" (Lewin, 1997). Lewin then goes on to argue that life experience is, in fact, narrative, that the metaphor ("life as narrative") suggests that like human lives, narrative consists of affective and conceptual components always desiring the shaping power of imagination. Following the philosophers Ricoeur and Heidegger, Lewin argues that "life as narrative" is an expression of the primary condition of how we live out our embeddedness within the world. Human beings are, in other words, predisposed, if not prewired, for narrative, for story, for life as a journey.

For Lewin (1997), everyday experience takes on "an affective charge" when it is "emplotted within a narrative frame," and it is through the shaping of this narrative frame that human beings create themselves. For us, this again is the classroom experience as we envision it, the journey of life itself. The "affective charge" of everyday experience positions the self in the midst of various voices interacting with the senses of the body in and through the classroom space. As Lewin puts it:

> At first I speak myself through the voices of others. The process of forming a coherent self becomes a process of sorting through the ... multiplicity of voices that co-exist first around me and then within me, until discourses that are internally persuasive emerge. (p. 4)

At its best, the classroom space resonates with those multiple voices, as learners journey through Bachelard's "dream space" or Palmer's "community of truth." It is a place brimming with language and imagination, an enchanted space of adventure offering the curve of a journey, open to the creation of individual and collective identity. The journey may be curved because it is not necessarily linear; the shape of the journey is collectively and literally shaped by the participating teacher and students. In that classroom space, learners continually exercise affective and cognitive neural circuits, sensing an ongoing connection with that space in which the body and mind move.

For us, the body is the vehicle of being in the world and in the classroom, and having a body means being involved in that expansive environment. Language gives direction and purpose to that body as it negotiates its journey. Stories populate that space as the body moves through it. That classroom space is filled with imaginative possibilities, a playful and safe place, not managed and controlled as much as encouraging and empathetic, inspiring learning. In such a context, the classroom provides openings and opportunities for engaging in learning, the kinds of possibilities that broaden notions of identity and dignify the human by emphasizing contemplative practice and imaginative inquiry. This is our version of the classroom as a community of adventurous learners.

CONVERSATION AND COMMUNITY

Many researchers help widen and support our position here. Wheatley and Whyte (2006), for example, reflecting on key points growing out of recent psychological investigations, report on how important community is to the formation of individual identity. Noting the paradox, they emphasize one overarching finding: "The identity of individual human beings is predicated, ironically enough, on belonging" (Wheatley & Whyte, 2006, p. 11). Brian Boyd extends the discussion in terms of stories (Boyd, 2009). For him, narrative "develops our capacity to see from different perspectives, and this capacity in turn arises from and aids the evolution of cooperation and the growth of human flexibility" (Boyd, 2009, p. 176). Marcia Baxter Magolda's work serves as still another example from a different angle:

> First, individual learning and knowledge claims are grounded in how individuals construct knowledge.... Learners interpret their experiences to form assumptions, reorganize those assumptions to guide meaning-making.... Second, how learners construct and use knowledge is closely tied to their sense of self.... Learners who are intensely concerned about what others think of them have difficulty authoring their own views. (Magolda, 2000, p. 1)

For us, the classroom space creates a neighborhood, a safe place to ask risky questions, that is, to quest and conquer fears about being vulnerable in front of their peers. That neighborhood is a place where people help each other learn, where strangers become friends, and friends celebrate the stranger. All such neighborhoods begin with a conversation. Quoting Wheatley and Whyte (2006) again:

> What brings a human being alive is a sense of participation in the conversation of life with others, with the great things of the world, with the trees or landscapes or skies or cityscapes, and ... this conversation is the way by which a human being comes to understand the particularity of their own gifts in the world. (p. 11)

Conversation about "the great things of the world" (for us, literary texts, in particular) shapes the people engaged in the conversation, creating an ongoing quest without end. Such conversation is not a battle to be won, but a focal point enlivening the neighborhood.

According to Wheatley and Whyte (2006), the classroom used to be the "place of radical declaration. It was the place where the frontier was actually being forged" (p. 12). Nowadays, the classroom seems often to be a place of overwrought caution, of fear, as Wheatley and Whyte put it, "the place where you cannot say many things" (p. 13). In such an atmosphere, the adventure is put into check, learning is limited to the familiar, and the boundaries of our knowledge of self and the world are drawn tight by unimaginative language.

The literary text, the self, the neighborhood, and the imagination in the flow of conversation—how best to bring them together? How best to begin "deep thinking" in the classroom? In *Ethics and Infinity* (Levinas, 1985), Emanuel Levinas suggests that thinking:

> ... probably begins through traumatisms or gropings to which one does not even know how to give a verbal form: A separation, a violent scene, a sudden consciousness of the monotony of time. It is from the reading of books—not necessarily philosophical—that

these initial shocks become questions and problems, giving one to think. (Levinas, 1985, pp. 21–22)

For Levinas, the book is of central importance in this process, opening the encounter with the other. A trauma, a shock in the classroom environment, the surprise that a good book offers, opens the way to thinking and to conversation. Humans respond to the unknown, the other, because they are part of the human community, and because they desire to know more about themselves and their connection to that community. As Levinas (1985) says: "Response or responsibility is the authentic relationship" (pp. 87–88). The desire to respond is a natural human inclination and a human responsibility. As human beings, we are all called to our larger sense of self and purpose, and it is our responsibility to respond to the other. This applies to teachers and students alike because in the democratic classroom, all voices are heard, valued, and privileged.

ANOTHER PRACTICAL EXAMPLE FROM THE CLASSROOM

In our work with urban alternative school students and college under-graduates, we planned a series of short story discussions to begin to create the kind of classroom adventure that could lead to a new sense of neighborhood. One story we used for that purpose was Joyce Carol Oates' "Where Are You Going, Where Have You Been?" (Oates, 1999), generally considered a story of temptation, a tale about the devilish Arnold Friend seducing the innocent Connie. The story is usually discussed as a cautionary tale about adolescent girls growing up in a dangerous American culture dominated by male structures and voices. We like to use this story in a different way, to explore the notion of "life as narrative" and the difficulty of creating identity in modern culture. The story can shock the reader into thinking and then into conversational response. It can create heated discussion in the classroom, and we will trace that possibility later; but first we want to look at the story in some detail, linking it to the fundamental notion that literary narrative appeals to both affect and concept, to the body, the emotions, and the mind—and so it activates the possibility for creating the imaginative space necessary for a vital and responsible classroom.

Oates (1999) opens the story thus: "Her name was Connie. She was fifteen and she had a quick nervous giggling habit of craning her neck to glance into mirrors, or checking other people's faces to make sure her own was all right" (p. 27). Connie is attractive. The reader knows it, and Connie knows it; and although she giggles when she stretches her neck to look into the mirror, suggesting that the power of her beauty is a ticklish subject for her, the image that the mirror gives back to her no doubt confirms her appeal.

Unlike her mother, who has lost her looks, and her older sister June, who is "so plain and chunky and steady"(Oates, 1999, p. 27), Connie desires a life worthy of her beauty, a life of pleasure and sensuous freedom beyond the confinement of her father's "asbestos ranchhouse" and the socially restricted role of mother and sister. Connie is, in other words, at the beginning of a narrative journey. Like so many young students, she wants to create a story for herself, but she is not sure exactly how to do that.

At times, Connie wishes her mother were dead and that she were dead, too. But that is only one side of her, and, as Oates makes clear, everything about Connie has two sides. That her mother makes her upset suggests part of her problem. How can she become "a whole woman" and at the same time the woman whom her mother has already refused to be? Can she create a story for herself that is different from her mother's, especially given the pressure of all the other stories that already exist in her society?

To make the situation even more complicated, Oates insists that girls are always in a more dangerous position than boys, and this too suggests a problem for Connie. Both boys and girls share the desire for erotic romance, but the passage into sexual adulthood is more difficult for girls than for boys, as Oates would have it, because the social order is dominated by male voices that seem to keep the voices of girls "on the other side of the border." Can a girl possibly cross this boundary? Is it possible? Oates seems to wonder, and so too does the reader.

Most readers of "Where Are You Going, Where Have You Been?" agree that Connie has "crossed over" to somewhere else at the end of the story, probably to a place where she will be raped and murdered by Arnold Friend. Oates justifies this kind of reading when she says in an interview that the story is primarily about a young girl who mistakes death for erotic romance. In *Smooth Talk* (Chopra, 1985), the film version of the story, the director Joyce Chopra finds hope, where most of us find fear, in Oates' ambiguous and complex language at the end. For Chopra, Connie not only moves out to new territory with Arnold Friend, but returns to her family apparently rejuvenated, a more mature young woman. The language of the final paragraph in the story best articulates the complexity of the issue:

> My sweet little blue-eyed girl, he said, in a half sung sigh that had nothing to do with her brown eyes but was taken up just the same by the vast sunlit reaches of the land behind

him and on all sides of him, so much land that Connie had never seen before and did not recognize except to know that she was going to it. (Oates, 1999, p. 42)

What can we say about Oates' ending here? On one level, Connie seems to disappear into Arnold Friend's version of erotic romance, a perverse fantasy that has nothing to do with Connie as flesh and blood, but everything to do with the fantasy matrix of both Connie and Arnold throughout the story, a fantasy matrix that continues to serve as Western culture's formula for erotic romance—that of courtly love. Arnold is by no means a traditional knight in shining armor, but as a decadent and absurd icon of popular culture, he has arrived to court his ideal Lady, not Connie herself. He desires the fantasy image, and he wants that fantasy image to desire him and seems to have the power and the control to make that happen. Oates makes clear that this sense of control is reinforced by common cultural structures deeply embedded in the voices and stories of childhood itself. Oates' use of fairy tales such as *Snow White*, *Cinderella*, *Sleeping Beauty*, *Rapunzel*, and *Little Red Riding Hood* clearly indicate her perspective on the dynamic and the structure of these relationships.

Arnold Friend's seduction of Connie is driven by the masculine side of the courtly love story. Connie's response, if we can call it that, is driven by the other side of that story, the fantasy which supports her own feminine identity and one way that she can create her own identity. Or, to put it in different terms, Arnold Friend is a product of the "trashy dreams" he mimics, pop culture dreams recycling the older fairy tale stories. That dynamic gives him an advantage; it allows him a strange familiarity, making him a popular culture icon, a representation of the "trashy dreams" that Connie finds fascinating. We might say that Connie desires the desire of Arnold Friend just as much as Friend desires the desire of Connie. But Arnold, as both familiar friend and strange fiend, has "two sides" just as Connie has. The difference between Connie and Arnold is the sexual difference, the impossible difference that never meets between them; Connie cannot fully "cross over" into the male story, although she might be able to find her own feminine identity in the "sunlit land" of death, nor can Arnold cross over into her story.

Throughout Connie's journey, the reader sees Connie's desire mirrored back from whatever she encounters. Her desire, fueled by pop music, shapes her perception of Arnold Friend as "half real." That Friend's desire is also fueled by "the trashy daydreams" of popular culture helps create the contemporary nightmare, but in so far as his voice and story dominate the culture, he appears as Devil and seducer, the perversion of a Christ demanding sacrifice on the altar of sex and violence, a pop culture icon, creator of the secret codes of the social order. Friend is the driver of the golden chariot which entices Connie, for example, but which also has written on its side "the numbers 33, 19, 17," which Connie cannot decipher: Numbers which not only reflect his sexual desire (69) but the ages of women he has apparently already killed—Connie, at 15, being the next maiden counted for death, prepared for sacrifice.

Oates has been accused of an obsession with feminine masochism, especially in her early work, and as a result she has often been criticized for adopting stereotypes that seem to blame the victim. It seems more accurate to say that Oates sees the feminine journey as dangerous and difficult precisely because of the structure of male-female stories and gender relationships. That is, Oates confronts a crucial question of human identity: Can Connie become a complete individual; can she become the representation of a complete woman? Can Arnold Friend become a complete person, the representation of a complete man? In the context of the story, both characters are doomed—doomed, as all human beings are, by the attempt to fully externalize human desire. The point here is that human desire cannot be fully externalized; there is always more desire than what can be said or visualized. When one tries to articulate desire fully through language, or tries to visualize it fully in an image, it will always fall short. Can the human heart ever be fully externalized? We do not believe this is possible. There will always be something left inside, something that cannot be measured, spoken, or seen: that is part of the "human mystery" which is beyond quantification or calculation. This is why desire is measureless because it cannot be fully externalized.

At the end of Oates' story, Connie is emptied out; she is robbed of herself. In a curious way, though, according to Oates, she has achieved a kind of heroism. Her emptiness is her victory as well as her defeat. By comparison, Arnold Friend is also a failure, having successfully driven the process of control to its perverse overflow, its sadistic climax. Friend is a body snatcher. It is incorrect to assume, despite his crass comments that he wants, for example, to come inside Connie's body. What Friend desires is the obliteration of her body, Edgar Allen Poe's version of the perversity of the human heart in "The Tell-Tale Heart" (Poe, 1843). As Friend puts it: "I'll have my arms around you so you won't need to try to get away and I'll show you what love is like, what it does" (Oates, 1999, p. 42). What love does in this context is to provoke violence. Because I love you, I must kill you. That seems to be Friend's motto as it was Poe's.

As we suggested earlier, the language at the end of the story is filled with ambiguity and sunlit possibilities as well as hints at mortality and death, and it is primarily through the complexity and richness of the language that the story evokes the imagination and the sense that the possibilities are open and endless. In the film version of the story, Connie goes out into the sunlit landscape with Arnold Friend and then returns home to her family a more mature and appreciative human being. This seems unlikely from our reading of the story, but it is nonetheless a possibility, one that Oates herself is willing to accept. The director primarily working with visual images had to make a choice, in a sense, but the reader working through the complexity of language is left in a different position. For the reader, discussion calls.

In one of the sessions in the alternative school classroom in December 2009, we videotaped just that kind of discussion to demonstrate one way of beginning to create the kind of classroom space we have in mind. Considering the central thematic concerns explored in this chapter, we want now to comment on some of that conversation in terms of those themes, especially:

(a) Our emphasis on the imagination as a way to create paradoxical space (the imaginative classroom);

(b) Our belief that the classroom space should inspire adventure, a frontier to help create an ongoing and shared narrative;

(c) Our commitment to the idea that both teachers and students should work together as sense-makers, creating a future through a community questing for human understanding; and

(d) Our sense that the classroom should be a place of ongoing trust and integrity, a place of respect, but also a place of risk, a neighborhood bounded (i.e., defined by boundaries) and bounding (i.e., offering connections to other spaces).

In this particular videotaped class, the teacher begins the conversation by putting the Oates story at the center; the literary text is the center of attention. To achieve initial focus, he asks students, seated in a circle, to recount details from the story they have read and experienced. The circle invites discussion and serves as a sign of equality and hospitality. It is made up of alternative school students, college students in preservice education, and the teacher himself. "So, we'll review a little of the story to get everyone involved," he says, quickly adding that his story is like "Greasy Lake" (Boyle, 1999; see previous chapter). Both stories enact a journey, familiar yet strange; they are richly textured, wide open to interpretation. Both stories call to the readers to help create the narrative, to help write the story they have read. In this classroom environment, the self-enclosed student suddenly becomes a listener, and then a speaker interacting with the voices in the story and around the circle.

Through this opening move, the human imagination is evoked to enrich the experience of the story, stirring desire to make sense of the story and to respond. As a further prompt, the teacher next asks about the characters in the story, inviting the students to empathize with the characters, to sense their complexity, and to shape a relationship with them. Focusing on Connie's character, the teacher asks: Is she a typical teenage girl? She is and she isn't. Is she egotistical? Conceited? She looks into the mirror over and over again—but she has two sides. She is, and she isn't filled with vanity. Connie is confident, but yet she isn't. She appreciates her own beauty, but she craves attention. As the students reflect on Connie, they are beginning to make sense of her complicated character and her position in the world. They are experiencing her and themselves, listening to her voice, the voice of other characters in the story, and to the voices of other students in the class. Collectively and individually, they are deepening their understanding of themselves and their classmates, where they have been and where they are going (as the title of the story indicates). Participating in the conversation, they are beginning to create an imaginative space, not quite in the literary text, not quite around the circle, but in that dream world of language itself. Each reader reads the same story, but each reading is different; each student is participating in the same flow of conversation but each from a different angle and a different depth. The classroom is alive with people making sense of their embodied experience as they converse with the story, with themselves, and with each other.

The set-up of the classroom in a circle encourages a sense of equality and that boundary expands through the voices bounding forward to the future and back to the past, creating an intense rhythm of memory and desire, deepening their adventure into the story and the self. The circle is a democratic configuration for conversation, a place where each person's voice counts and is respected and where all students take risks safely. It limits the sense of hierarchy, although it does not restrict the authority of the human voice. The circle reminds everyone that open space calls for boundaries, that the law implies its own transgression. The college students mix with alternative high school students; a teacher facilitates. Together they are forming a neighborhood, negotiating the meaning of a literary text and the shape of a community. As a group coming together, they are embarking on a journey through language, an adventure in which controversial topics demand ongoing exploration.

One of the high school students responds by talking about his feelings about the story in general and then specifically about Connie. With pent-up emotion, he claims, at the outset, that he doesn't like the story or Connie.

The teacher does not reject the student's response, but acknowledges it. "You have really been affected by this story," the teacher says.

"Let's think more about Connie," the teacher suggests. "Move closer to her actual experience." What can we say about Connie's relationship with her mother? Suddenly, one of the university students offers an extended comment:

> Connie has a difficult relationship with her mother. She thinks that when her mother was younger she was pretty. Now that her mother is older—she has kind of lost her looks. And I think the mother is kind of angry with Connie for being beautiful. June (Connie's older sister) isn't that pretty. So Connie thinks maybe it's easier for the mother to love her because Connie's mother isn't jealous of June.

The student's insight moves the discussion forward, helping everyone to mirror the character and reflect on their own relationships. Everyone has a mother, present or absent; everyone struggles with that relationship, each in their own way.

The teacher continues to prompt the discussion, intensifying and broadening its concerns. How else does Connie act? What else does she do? One high schooler responds, "Well, Connie says she is going to the movies, but then she rides in cars with older guys that she meets at a burger joint. She goes driving with older guys and parks in an alley with them." The students look around the room at each other, knowingly.

The teacher then reads from the story: "Everything about her had two sides to it" (Oates, 1999, p. 28). What does that suggest? "She dresses one way at home and then another way when she is away from home," another student says. Other students join with their voices, pointing out that Connie's behavior always seems different at home than when she is in the company of her own friends.

As the students continue to sift through the details of the story, the teacher continues to intensify the risk level of the discussion, asking the group if they think Connie's behavior can at all be considered promiscuous. Opinions are mixed. Some think that Connie may have been sexually active with the boys in the story before she encounters Arnold Friend; others think she may have kissed them, but only with a feeling of romantic innocence. One university student comments that she doesn't believe Connie is different from most other girls her age: Connie simply wants to look good and to attract the attention of older guys.

With this comment, the teacher moves the discussion from character analysis to the plot action, as if he is taking the class on the journey, allowing everyone sitting in the circle to reimagine the deepening movement and energy of the story as it grows increasingly disturbing. At home, Connie is alone, her parents having left for a barbecue. The devilish Arnold Friend pulls up in the driveway with one of his friends and comes to the door of Connie's house. What do we know about Arnold, first seen by Connie at the drive-in stand and now appearing close up in front of Connie? The students reflect, suggesting that Arnold appears, at first, to be a teenager, but then he seems much older, over 30 years old, and certainly an odd and creepy guy. Why is he there at Connie's house? Most of these students agree that he wants to control Connie, assert his power, perhaps even attack her. Arnold threatens her family, the students point out, and Connie finally agrees to go with him without being physically forced. Connie does seem to go along with Arnold voluntarily, some of the students emphasize, perhaps to save her family from harm. But she is clearly under considerable duress. Is her vulnerability a weakness or a potential strength? Is she a victim or a hero? How can we best view her and understand her? How do we understand ourselves in this context? What would you do in her difficult circumstances?

The students wrestle with the story, grappling with these sensitive and disturbing issues, agreeing, and at times, disagreeing, as they struggle to make meaning out of their personal and collective experiences. The students insist now on discussing whether or not Connie can, in any way, be held responsible for what happened to her. (Everyone assumes, with good reason, that she was probably raped and perhaps killed by Arnold.) The intensity of the discussion is heated and difficult, the students unsettled about their positions. Most insist that she is not at all to blame, that to accuse her in any way is to blame an innocent victim and that such blame is unjust and ill-conceived. How can anyone blame the victim? A few however argue that Connie needs to take some responsibility for her actions. They suggest that she might have been too curious, too eager for new experience. Many claim that she was too innocent, in any case. Some suggest that she is heroic, willing to act in order to save her family. It is a cautionary tale.

The students are engaged in passionate discussion, overflowing at times, expressing views filled with emotion, but they also respect the boundaries necessary to keep the conversation going. As the teacher reminds them:

> Everyone can have their say. This can get very, very heated and people can get very passionate. This is a topic that people take very seriously. People might know someone who has gone through this. The one thing we need to do is we need to have a very open dialogue and be very conscious of not attacking or cutting off people because they may disagree with you. We need to set that as one of the ground rules.

For us, the classroom is not a place to teach moral rules or even norms; rather it is place where each person must arrive at his or her own judgment, a moment of stability after wrestling with the complexities of human experience, a place that allows each participant to move beyond stereotypes and rigid pronouncements. The conversation about the story promotes the imaginative moment. The flow of the conversation—bounded in some ways and unbounded in others—promotes creative tension without losing control and spinning into chaos.

The story provokes controversy, but the boundaries of mutual respect inspire trust, a sense that everyone has the right to voice a considered opinion without exposure to unwarranted attack. The story remains at the center of activity; the students are focused there, energized and willing to adventure into the frontier. As a result, the conversation and the classroom become an ongoing space for adventure, for surprise and competence in sense-making. Vulnerable but trusting, these students enact an imaginative place, making it theirs, creating as they go a vision, a neighborhood for ongoing inquiry. As they head down the school halls and maybe also later out in their nonschool neighborhoods, they are still talking about "Where Are You Going, Where Have You Been?" (Oates, 1999).

CONCLUDING THOUGHTS ON THE CLASSROOM ADVENTURE

In this chapter, we have explored the space of the classroom and how it can support deep reading and deep learning. Teachers, as the main facilitators of these spaces, need to be aware of what kinds of pedagogical elements and methods work to make the classroom space more inviting and open, as well as what might prevent or hinder the kind of openness and vulnerability needed for learning. The journey into the narrative is the adventure; the thrill lies in learning to communicate with others and to understand our connections to self and the larger world. Meaning evolves on many levels as teachers and students engage in narrative texts and create new and empathic vantage points to view the human condition.

Engaging students in the classroom adventure is now more important than ever because it involves face-to-face encounters with others. We worry about how technology, under the guise of connecting people to other people through gadgets and media, can actually serve to isolate people. We view the flash of images and sensations that technology provides as something shallow and disembodied, whereas we see using one's imagination in dialogue with others about a story in the classroom space as having potential for deep meaning-making. Imagination and creativity are activated in the classroom space through the shared conversation about a story, and, just like muscles in the human body, these powers must be exercised to develop and to stay vital.

The classroom examples in this chapter from Frost's (1969) poetry and Oates' (1999) short story are meant to illustrate for our readers what the adventurous space of the classroom looks like. These examples of classroom adventures are not meant to be prescriptive, but they are meant to provide teachers with glimpses of classroom spaces where students engage directly with the literature and navigate paths to meaning for self and others. Through Robert Frost's poetry, primary and secondary level students, paired together, first encountered the literal meaning of the poem "The Road Not Taken" (Frost, 1969d) and then were given opportunities to find connections to their own life stories and experiences. The learning goals were to understand image and imagery, along with symbol and the symbolic journey. The teaching methods included visualization and story-telling, and through these modes of learning students "mapped" their own stories onto the narrative of the poem. For the example with Oates' short story, we offer analysis and then share a classroom discussion involving alternative school students and college undergraduates who were working together in our literacy program. The discussion of "Where Are You Going, Where Have You Been?" (Oates, 1999) was charged and exciting, filled with adventure and controversy, and, as a result, the alternative school students and college undergraduates interacted together as sense-makers.

CHAPTER FOUR

LITERACY, FOCUSED ATTENTION, AND CONTEMPLATIVE PRACTICE

How do we keep them focused

A central theme of this work has been that of the value of deep reading and deep learning in an imaginative and dynamic classroom space. In previous chapters, we have developed our argument in these terms, trying to build a persuasive case that reading (and writing) should be central to education in the 21st century. Some of the language we have used, and some of the ideas as well, might seem outmoded on first consideration, but we believe that what we claim is in fact supported by ongoing discoveries in areas of cutting-edge research, especially in the exciting new areas of neuroscience, evolutionary biology, and cognitive science. As V. S. Ramachandran, a prominent brain researcher at the University of California at San Diego, points out, "The advantage that scientists have today is that unlike philosophers we can now test our conjectures by directly studying the brain empirically" (Ramachandran, 2004, p. 41). New work in brain research, for example, provides physical evidence for what prominent thinkers, from Aristotle to Searle, have been saying for hundreds of years: that language is crucial to our understanding of human identity, that reading and writing are unique activities central to human culture, and that narrative texts (stories) are powerful means to transform thinking, to change lives, and to keep us human.

LEARNING THROUGH HABITATION IN THE PRESENT MOMENT

Later in this chapter, we take up with some detail the research which we believe supports our position. But it is not only the contemporary scientists who are arguing along lines similar to our own. When Jon Kabat-Zinn makes connections between learning, healing, and being ever mindful of the present moment (Kabat-Zinn, 2006), he, too, focuses on the same broad issues that we do—the way human beings find themselves in the world, a world best considered as an ongoing learning environment. For Kabat-Zinn, as for us, learning is holistic. Holistic approaches to learning privilege the integration of mind, body, and spirit. Learning is always interactive, always occurring in the depths of the present moment, always an embodied experience that can inspire self-reflection and mindfulness. That interactive dynamic between the self and the learning environment is continuous and ongoing, always "rearranging" the flow of experience. If the contemporary culture demands that human beings change, Kabat-Zinn would argue that human beings are always changing anyway—biologically, culturally, and spiritually. Contemporary science often seems to put a premium on physical changes ("molecular rearrangement"), but, in fact, human beings are always changing and have always changed. As educators, we should more readily recognize how present moment learning experiences are always grounded in our natural biological capacities. As Kabat-Zinn says:

> [the present moment] asks us to transform, to actually reconstitute ourselves, to undergo what you might think of as "molecular rearrangement" to a way of being that releases our potential to be fully human. But we are being rearranged anyway. What do you think learning is? An extremely important part is collaborating with these natural biological capacities by grounding our awareness in embodied experience. (Kabat-Zinn, 2006, p. 160)

For Kabat-Zinn, recent scientific research confirms what human beings have always known—the learning environment is an extension of the self, just as what appears outside the body is an extension of what is inside the body. Learning is always an interaction and, in this sense, an embodied experience: a dynamic process between the outside and the inside, the environment and the self. We agree with Kabat-Zinn that enduring learning happens more readily when learners are given opportunities to "inhabit," that is, deeply experience, the fullness of the present moment—what we call "present moment learning."

It is precisely this notion of interactive learning, as we have suggested in the previous chapters, which convinces us that the act of "deep reading" can lead to "deep learning." The focused interaction between the reader and the literary text has an impact on the whole person, including the mind and the body, and inspires the reader to reach out to the world which surrounds him or her, in an ongoing adventure to learn. Kabat-Zinn (2006) knows this as does Arthur Zajonc (2006a), who calls for a renewed perspective on knowing and living in contemporary education:

> I am calling for resituating it [education] within a greater vision of what knowing and living are really all about. That re-imagination of knowing will have deep consequences for education, consequences that give a prominent place to contemplative pedagogies … . Such contemplative inquiry not only yields insight (*veritas*) but also transforms the knower through his or her intimate (one could say loving) participation in the subject of one's contemplative attention. Contemplative education is transformative education. (Zajonc, 2006a, p. 1743)

In this passage, Zajonc joins with Kabat-Zinn to emphasize the importance of contemplation as a process of ongoing transformation and as a way of learning about the depth of human identity, a process that can now be confirmed by what fMRIs and PET scans tell brain researchers: when human beings root their awareness and attention in embodied experience, they are engaged in a learning moment, a moment that will be remembered because it is experienced thoroughly, that is, "thought through," passing from short-term to long-term memory circuits. Such moments affect the body, mind, and world of those individuals who experience those enduring moments. Such learning moments are deeply felt and known, arousing the flexible imagination and activating the plasticity of the brain itself, inspiring the ongoing desire of human beings to know more.

THE ANCIENT INDIAN ROOTS OF
CONTEMPLATIVE EDUCATION

In Chapter Six, we examine the challenges which digital technologies pose to literacy. This chapter, however, focuses on the antithesis of digital technologies, what Tobin Hart (Hart, 2007) refers to as our "interiority." For Hart, the challenge for education is to develop this interiority as a kind of "spaciousness on our inside to take us to the world that is before us" (Hart, 2007, p. 2). Hart sees this interior development as a balance to the exterior development of the digital technology that never stops:

> Perhaps the more information and technology there is on the outside—and certainly we are deluged these days—the more spaciousness and richness of interiority is necessary. That is, the greater the complexity and demands of the outer world, the more essential is our internal discernment, our attention to values, our ability to be present in the midst of streaming information. (Hart, 2007, p. 2)

We agree with Hart that cultivating interiority ("our ability to be present") is increasingly important, especially in the age of digital technology. But the idea of "interiority" is nothing new—it comes from the wisdom traditions of the world. When Kabat-Zinn (2006) or Zajonc (2006a) write about mindfulness or contemplation, they are drawing on similar traditions. When we refer to "present moment learning" as an umbrella term for cultivating and focusing attention in educational practices, we are drawing on these same traditions.

In fact, the roots of much of what we call "present moment learning" find their origins in ancient India (Mookerji, 1947/2003; Thurman, 2006), where the practice of education centered on developing focused awareness in individuals, and ethical service for society. As Roeser and Peck (2009) describe it:

> For more than 2,500 years, the contemplative traditions of India have developed highly sophisticated curricula and corresponding sets of practices by which the refinement of awareness, attentional training, and the ethical development of individuals can be cultivated. (p. 127)

We believe that these ideas and practices are as relevant for the 21st century classroom as they were for the ancient world. Many of the contemporary educational terms and practices, which grow out of these ancient Indian traditions, share the same goals for building students' attentional skills, refining their awareness, and helping them to develop into ethical members of the larger community and world in which they live.

CULTIVATING ATTENTION FOR TEACHING AND LEARNING

For us, deep reading can be connected to this wisdom tradition. It inspires contemplation and evokes the right questions. That is part of the reason that we have been insisting that keeping the narrative text and the celebration of verbal literacy at the center of education is critical to the health of human society.

The term "literacy" is increasingly used in a number of different senses and contexts these days, and we observe a widening focus in present-day society on what is referred to as "procedural literacy," whereby people learn the skills necessary to perform particular procedures and to manipulate devices. So-called "procedural literacy" addresses matters of how some action occurs or how some result comes into being. The sequence of actions or outcome that is the goal of "procedural literacy" emphasizes the *how* of actions and outcome, but not the *why*. "Procedural literacy" lends itself to measurement and quantification, but, in our view, it does not get to the *why* of what really matters. It misses the deep sense of human understanding and of the self. Its focus is on skills but not on wisdom, the depth of human knowledge. By contrast, the development of verbal literacy is commonly understood to mean the ability to read and write at some length and depth, with attention and understanding that leads to involvement and personal connection. Verbal literacy thus allows for and stimulates readers' imaginations while also making possible a more empathic and hence a more compassionate view of others and of the human condition. "Verbal literacy" does not simply mean learning how to read and write. For us, it means being "literary," in the sense of being attentive and engaged, being an educated human being who continually reflects on ideas and emotions, who can hold opposing ideas and emotions in mind and move forward. As John Dewey, in *The School and Society* (Dewey, 1899/2009), once put it, arguing for genuine education:

> A person who has gained the power of reflective attention, the power to hold problems, questions, before the mind, *is* in so far, intellectually speaking, educated. He has mental discipline—power *of* the mind and *for* the mind. (Dewey, 2009, p. 84)

The qualities of an educated person, as Dewey describes, include developed capabilities for reflection that come through the focused attention of mind. We believe that deep reading and deep writing in the classroom, a created space where engaged discussion with a group about a narrative is put at the center, can help students to achieve this kind of educated identity. An educated person is a wise person.

COGNITIVE-AFFECTIVE LEARNING AND CONTEMPLATIVE EDUCATION

In the mainstream tradition of higher education, learning is viewed as essentially a cognitive activity, which often leads to the manipulation of abstract ideas or the memorization of bits of information, but rarely to the wisdom of embodied knowledge. For us, the affective context of learning must be part of the classroom experience because it is part of what it means to be human and because it involves consideration of motivation and emotions. Immordino-Yang (2008) has carried out many studies demonstrating the importance of emotions in learning. The human brain does not in fact separate emotion from cognition, so that, without proper attention given to student motivation, student interest in a given subject, the best foundation for enduring learning, is unlikely to be secured (Chickering, 2006; Owen-Smith, 2004). Hall (2005) explains what teachers need to do to incorporate affect into cognitive learning in their classrooms: "To establish a connection between the affective and the cognitive, teachers need to create a space in which students can integrate what they are feeling and learning" (Hall, 2005, p. 12). To create this kind of space where students can link what they are feeling (affect) with what they are learning (cognition) is to provide a learning environment, to help build "a new neighborhood" for education, that encourages wisdom and contemplative practice.

CONTEMPLATIVE EDUCATION AND CONTEMPLATIVE PRACTICE

We support Contemplative Education, which represents the kind of education which privileges and promotes the cultivation of students' attentional capacities. Roeser and Peck (2009) offer a definition of contemplative education as "a set of pedagogical practices designed to cultivate the potentials of mindful awareness and volition in an ethical-relational context in which the values of personal growth, learning, moral living, and caring for others are also nurtured" (p. 127). Teachers who utilize contemplative practices connect with their students as whole persons, reaching their students on an emotional as well as an intellectual level. Such teaching can be pictured as an organic process which evolves in connection to the immediate and ongoing context. We see such teaching as an embodied process, an adventurous journey that can facilitate the desired "new neighborhood in the present moment" and provide teaching and learning modes which are capacious enough to hold heart and mind, thoughts and feelings. Teachers can find their own ways of facilitating contemplative practices in the classroom through deep reading and deep writing and thereby improve learning. As Hall and Archibald (2008) suggest:

> When we focus within our classrooms on contemplative practices, we attempt to develop a teaching and learning space that allows sustained reflection and focused mindfulness in the learning process. (p. 2)

Contemplative practices create an imaginative space in the classroom, a palpable space that allows students to glimpse new possibilities and to experience the connectivity of the human community. Each teacher creates his or her own unique space for teaching and learning, but he or she may also try out methods which other teachers have found successful. As with all teaching, there is always a process of trial and error. In the best kind of teaching, reflective practice follows a deliberate trial-and-error strategy in which the first trial is critiqued and then new refined attempts at teaching are retried with the refinement gained through reflection on what worked well and what didn't (the "error") in the earlier trial. For teachers, there are two kinds of reflective spaces created. The first one is made for student reflection in the classroom, and the second for the teacher when gauging the effectiveness of the reflective space that is created. Contemplative practices encompass a whole range of activities, including contemplative writing, yoga, meditation, and other activities. In our own work in the classroom, we have drawn on various aspects of contemplative practice to inform our continuing development and application of CLTL and reflective literacy. (Information about contemplative practice, including a graphic "Tree of Contemplative Practice," can be found on the Center for Contemplative Mind in Society's web site www.contemplativemind.org.)

There is no doubt that the kind of engagement with language that we have been describing throughout this book can often be considered as an act of contemplation. Deep reading and deep writing often create a meditative rhythm, for example, a contemplative experience. After reading a story, participants also often engage in dialogue, experiencing the rhythmic breath of speaking and listening, sound and silence. "Deep listening," meaning listening and dialoguing to gain a deep understanding of what is being said and of the person who is speaking, is especially noteworthy in this context. Mary Rose O'Reilley, a practitioner who writes about teaching as contemplative practice, explains the significance of deep listening in the learning environment:

> One can, I think, *listen someone into existence*, encourage a stronger self to emerge or a new talent to flourish. Good teachers listen this way, as do terrific grandfathers and similar heroes of spirit. (O'Reilley, 1998, p. 21)

What O'Reilley means is that an involved listener is able to enter the language of the other, and through this process is able to hear that other's words, the voice of the speaker's deeper self. The language of the other evokes something deep within the listener, something unknown until heard, something that allows the listener to acknowledge the other. This something that stirs a person to really hear another gives voice to humans on the quest for wisdom and knowledge.

Deep listening and the creation of the dialogic space in which humans interact and come to know one another (as discussed in Chapter Three) are two of the elements involved in teaching to and from the whole person and enacting contemplative practice as a medium for enhanced literacy learning and the continuing development of self. Palmer (1998) emphasizes this point when he discusses person-to-person dialogue, arguing that dialogue can be seen as an attempt to uncover truth. As he indicates, such discussion in the classroom can work as "the passionate and disciplined process of inquiry and dialogue itself, as the dynamic conversation of a community that keeps testing old conclusions and coming into new ones" (p. 104). This is what the core of learning should be, making the learning environment a place to uncover truths (*veritas*) through a communal dialogue.

EDUCATIONAL TERMS FOR PRESENT MOMENT LEARNING

For us, Dewey helped inspire a movement in education to improve learning by considering the learning process holistically and by emphasizing the importance of inhabiting the present moment, being attentive and engaged in the depth of what is in front of you. Although he did not use the terms "embodied experience" or "contemplative practice" for his classroom theories, many educators have drawn on Dewey and developed terms that, we believe, echo his ideas and support our own views as well. This section explores additional educational terms which connect to what we think of as "deep learning" or "present moment learning," such as, Teaching to and from the Whole Person, Holistic Education, and Integrative Education. Each of these may evoke specific and differing views in their details, but we think that in their broad concerns they resonate with Dewey's conceptions of education. They also seem consistent with recent discoveries by brain researchers and other cognitive scientists. So, let us briefly review these terms and concepts, all pointing to our developing notion that "deep learning" means appealing both to emotions and cognition, heart and head, to the development, in other words, of the whole person—that is, to what literature can do so well.

TEACHING TO AND FROM THE WHOLE PERSON

Teaching to the whole person is not a new construct but has been undervalued in the current educational climate. As Jack Miller describes that climate: "Educators are more interested in testing students than exploring how they can learn and develop as human beings" (Miller, 2007, preface, p. vii). Nevertheless, as Miller (2007) explains, although some educational leaders are only focused on preparing students "so they can compete in the global economy" (p. 3), there is a growing interest in teaching students as whole persons.

We believe that teaching to and from the whole person through deep reading and deep writing can not only remedy the current hyperfocus on testing, but can also lead to an authentic sense of global education, the kind of learning that is concerned with the full development of all human beings. By "full development," we refer to learning that values and promotes mind, body, and spirit and prepares students to be ethical and productive members of the society. Students should be encouraged to make connections between narratives from around the world and their own developing "self-narratives" in order to understand their place in the community and the world and also to gain appreciation not only for the differences between people but for what they have in common.

HOLISTIC EDUCATION

Miller (2007) speaks of "holistic education" in broad terms, making clear that "holistic education attempts to bring education into alignment with the fundamental realities of nature. Nature at its core is interrelated and dynamic" (p. 3). He explains that "the human world since the Industrial Revolution has stressed compartmentalization and standardization. The result has been fragmentation" (Miller, 2007, p. 3). Such fragmentation can be seen in life overall as well as in education, where curricula have been increasingly divided into individual subjects, modules, and bits of testable information, and have attempted to separate cognitive from affective and physical aspects of learning—science from humanities and art—and to de-emphasize the latter.

Other writers, theorists, and practitioners (Hall, 2005; hooks, 2003; Zajonc, 2006a) concur that fragmentation in education is worrisome and works against the best development of self or learning. By contrast, holistic educational practices combat this fragmentation, focusing on cognitive, aesthetic, and affective aspects—head and heart—together. Nell Noddings also speaks to the identified deficiency in education which privileges cognitive learning and ignores the affective domain:

Affect has been neglected in education and this neglect reduces the engagement of both students and teachers in their studies … . For the past 200 years, philosophers have emphasized reason over affect … . Emotion has, for the most part, been dismissed as unreliable. (Noddings, 1996, pp. 435–436)

We agree with Miller, Noddings, and others who celebrate the development of all aspects of what it means to be human. For us, deep reading and deep writing promote the best kind of learning through the integration of both thought and feeling in the learning process.

INTEGRATIVE EDUCATION

Parker J. Palmer and Arthur Zajonc, in their new book, *The Heart of Higher Education* (Palmer & Zajonc, 2010), also make the argument for renewing the integration of heart and mind in higher education. In the opening chapter, they explain that although higher education is slow to change,

> ... many individuals within the institution have kept the vision of an integrative practice alive in their hearts—using *heart* in its original sense, not just as the seat of the emotions but as that core place in the human self where all our capacities converge: intellect, senses, emotions, imagination, intuition, will, spirit, and soul. (Palmer & Zajonc, 2010, p. 20)

Integrative education seeks "forms of knowing, teaching, and learning that offer more nourishment than the thin soup served up when data and logic are the only ingredients" (Palmer & Zajonc, 2010, p. 21). Such education takes into account both inner and outer worlds and does not only value data and rationality. Palmer and Zajonc (2010) make clear that teaching and learning must be as complex as the learner. This complexity involves "human knowing, [which,] rightly understood, has paradoxical roots—mind and heart, hard data and soft intuition, individual insight and communal sifting and winnowing" (Palmer & Zajonc, 2010, p. 22). Palmer's earlier solo work, *The Courage to Teach* (Palmer, 1998) highlights many of these ideas as well, emphasizing that teaching a complex human being can never be reduced to a recipe; good teaching comes from inspiring students to experience and acknowledge the complexities of human life. It begins by igniting the spark of imagination, by allowing students to feel the adventure of the richness of life, by moving them to appreciate the multiplicity of the living self and the complexity of the environment which surrounds them and helps to shape them.

READING AS MEDITATION: GROWING CONNECTIONS

As we mentioned earlier in this chapter, the act of reading in our sense of "deep reading" and the conversation about that reading can also be thought of as connected to the practice of contemplation and meditative wisdom. What happens when the student is attentive to the narrative text (outside the skin) affects what happens inside his or her body: the outside inscribes itself on the inside just as what happens inside affects the outside. Language becomes the mediator of the sign and meaning created through the reading process, much as the skin mediates between the body and the environment. Jack Miller, in his *Holistic Curriculum* (Miller, 2007) reinforces the idea when he insists that making sense and meaning of stories holds myriad possibilities for the development of the self. As Miller argues, "[l]iterature, mythology, and story allow the self to emerge" (Miller, 2007, p. 186). Reading narrative texts and talking about them create a space for further contemplation and insight, inspiring both affective and cognitive activity that moves the student forward to self-reflection and an expanded sense of self and other.

Ideas from ancient India link contemplative practice with the reading of sacred texts. *Vedanta*, which means "unified consciousness," comes from one of the oldest and most inclusive religious philosophies in the world. The philosophic view encompassed in Vedanta, which is based on the sacred scriptures of India called *Vedas*, affirms the ideas of oneness and harmony across religions. Although Vedanta is the philosophical foundation of Hinduism, its ideas cross many boundaries, across all cultures and backgrounds. Vedanta represents a search for self-knowledge and a search for a higher power or a greater spiritual understanding.

The ideas of Vedanta can be useful, even inspiring, in secular ways. As a part of the intellectual search for self, Vedanta has particular traditions for turning words into wisdom; one tradition involves a three-step process for contemplating sacred texts. These steps are: (1) *Shravana*: Hearing, listening (or reading); (2) *Manana*: Thinking, deep reflection; and (3) *Nididhyasana*: Meditation. In ancient times, when there were only oral traditions, people would not be able to read a text; they would hear the text orally. In the modern day, this idea of *Shravana*, hearing or listening, can thus translate to reading. The second step, *Manana* becomes deep reading, when the text is starting to be digested through reflection; it means making sense or making meaning of the text. The third step, *Nididhyasana*, refers to meditating on the narrative; it is a way to integrate or internalize the ideas that have been read into the reader's world. Through this process, words turn into wisdom, and then the reader returns into the world of experience, carrying with him or her new insights gained from the encounter with the narrative, ready to further explore the complexity of human identity.

MULTIPLE SELVES FOR NAVIGATION THROUGH DEEP READING AND DEEP WRITING

V. S. Ramachandran, a leading brain researcher, argues that the self has many dimensions and the idea that a human has one identical self is an illusion. In his work with Sandra Blakeslee, titled *Phantoms in the Brain* (Ramachandran & Blakeslee, 1998), the *mnemonic self* is described as being:

> Your sense of personal identity—as a single person who endures through space and time—[it] depends on a long string of highly personal recollections: your autobiography. Organizing these memories into a coherent story is obviously vital to the construction of the self. (p. 250)

Through memory and imagination, human beings organize their multiple selves into a coherent story, as Ramachandran and Blakeslee suggest: one "writes" his or her own life. In a world where introspection is often limited, reading and discussing good literature provide opportunities for students to not only make sense of the stories they read, but also to make sense of, or "map," themselves in relation to those stories. Such activity significantly enhances introspection and depth of understanding and response.

Like recent research in neuroscience, the research about the evolution of language, that is, how the species acquires language, as well as the research on how human beings learn to read and write, also contributes to our argument here. No doubt animals have limited language skills, dramatically demonstrated, for example, by the brilliant scientist Sue Savage-Rumbaugh in experiments with the bonobo apes, Kanzi and Panbanisha (for discussion, see Kenneally, 2007, pp. 40–51). But, such research appears to indicate that animal language is rudimentary, reaching, at best, the abilities of a three- to four-year-old child. The richly textured language of the mature speaker, which includes that of narrative, developed over centuries of evolution, clearly distinguishes human beings from other species and underlines their self-reflective nature.

Human language significantly enriches human consciousness—it activates the "deep interior" of human memory and human identity, which is strikingly self-reflexive. As a result of engagement with language, human beings can perform an action and also reflect on that action in sophisticated ways not available to other species. There is a self-reflective dynamic in humans' use of language, which is also represented in the very texture of human language. As Derek Bickerton puts it: "The evidence from neurolinguistic research suggests ... that what we are conscious of is what we are able to process linguistically" (Bickerton, 1992, p. 210). Language inspires conscious reflection, the ongoing human desire to learn, in a way that, we argue, visual images do not.

Through the recent work of cognitive scientists, we now know that the brain dynamically adapts to new needs and is always influenced by experience (see, e.g., Wolf, 2007). Such a dynamic suggests that body, mind, and environment are all interactive parts of the self that cannot be separated; they can, however, be reflected on through language, the core of the human process, as we see it, to know thyself. For us, the process of language itself is also an embodied process, a human dynamic that resonates through the body and mind, as well as the surrounding world, and that also indicates a common bond among all people.

What we think of as metaphors, for example—imagistic language connected to specific meanings—are, according to brain researchers, the result of a process embodied in the cross-modal areas of the brain linked to our sensory systems, which are, in turn, connected to the larger human environment. These embodied language processes, such as the making of metaphors, define us as human and bind us together as a community, especially when new understanding or meaning-making is promoted in a community of learners. Metaphors often surprise and delight, and they also expand understanding as they bring people together through that expanded understanding. All human beings seem to delight in metaphor and often welcome the challenge of expressing concepts in fresh ways. All human beings share a similar process for creating language, including metaphors and other creative expression. To demonstrate that all humans have similar conceptualization processes related to language, V. S. Ramachandran has conducted an experiment (Ramachandran, 2004) showing that the apparently meaningless (in almost all languages) words of *bouba* and *kiki* each arouses in all human beings a universal image and sound—a spiky shape associated with *kiki* and a rounded cloud shape associated with *bouba*. The experiment demonstrates that no matter what the local meaning of the words might be, they carry similar feelings and ideas across the human sensory system of all people.

THE EMPATHETIC BRAIN AND HUMAN NARRATIVE

Our argument is not only about the importance of human language, but also about the significance of narrative, that is, story. A number of cognitive scientists have recently highlighted the importance of narrative or story in defining human nature (e.g., Immordino-Yang & Damasio, 2007).

Mark Turner claims that "the literary mind is not a separate kind of mind, it is our mind. The literary mind is the fundamental mind" (Turner, 1996, p. 1). Taking on some of the giants of linguistics (e.g., Noam Chomsky and Stephen Pinker), Turner (1996) argues against the commonly held view that grammar precedes story. He concludes his persuasive book-length study on the topic by asserting:

> The story I have offered reverses the view that language is built up from the sober to the exotic, that out of syntactic phrase structures one builds up language, that out of language one builds up narrative, that out of narrative, literary narrative is born as a special performance, and that out of literary narrative comes parable … . It works the other way around … . Story precedes grammar … . Parable is the root of the human mind. (Turner, 1996, p. 168)

Whether others will concur with Turner (contra Chomsky and Pinker), there is little reason not to believe that complex literary narrative is central to human identity and to learning per Socrates "to know thyself." Turner's quote underlines the importance of story in the evolution of the human mind; story comes first.

Alan Richardson, in *The Neural Sublime* (Richardson, 2010), makes the important point that narrative theory has recently proven to be an especially rich area for the interface of literary narrative and the sciences of mind and brain. In a fascinating section of his book, he explores what many cognitive theorists (Michael Tomasello and Josep Call being the first ones; e.g., Call & Tomasello, 1998; Tomasello & Call, 1997) now call "theory of mind," the human ability (to oversimplify his discussion) to read other people's minds (Richardson, 2010, p. 83). According to Richardson, cognitive scientists have constructed several competing models to explain this "mind-reading" ability: (1) the modular approach; (2) the evolutionary account; and (3) the simulation model. Despite differences in approach, however, most "theory of mind" researchers share common agreement that "mind-reading" is part of "a universal core human endowment that involves a quite amazing repertoire of cognitive abilities that few other animals can even approximate" (Richardson, 2010, pp. 84–85). Possessing these abilities means, according to these scientists, that most (e.g., non-autistic) human beings can not only infer the full range of mental states of other human beings (their desires, beliefs, emotions, intentions, and so on) but also, through this ability, anticipate actions derived from such cognitive and affective conditions.

To us, "theory of mind" seems a lot like old-fashioned "empathy," the imaginative ability to walk in another's shoes, both to think and to feel the experience of the other. The concept of theory of mind, or empathy, also helps explain the wonder of narrative and the importance of "deep reading." Reading a story is very much an exercise of "empathy" in just this sense: readers become the characters and participate in the story they experience. Those literary characters become part of the consciousness of the readers and, once that connection is made, readers then reflect on these characters much as ordinary citizens reflect on their encounters in daily life. Brian Boyd (Boyd, 2009) makes a similar point when he discusses recent brain research:

> Evidence has also begun to arrive that even vicarious and virtual experiences activate the mind in ways that partly mimic direct action. Witnessing or even hearing about activities can cause neurons involved in producing the action to fire. Social neuroscience has begun to discover how our minds can be affected by emotional contagion, by responding, even without registering consciously, to cues of specific actions in others. (Boyd, 2009, pp. 191–192)

Boyd's reference in this passage to "emotional contagion" not only highlights how human beings read the emotions and thoughts of others, but how important it is to consider and activate both emotions and ideas in the learning environment. In the latter sense of connecting emotions and ideas in the learning environment, we see the term "emotional contagion" as being related to what Immordino-Yang and Damasio (2007) describe as "emotional thought," a term they use to capture the overlapping "process of learning, memory, and decision-making, in both social and non-social contexts" (p. 8). For them, "emotional thought" is the conduit by which bodily sensations come into our conscious awareness. Emotions are not simply layered on top of cognition, but are intertwined with it, interacting through the widely distributed networks of the body and brain. In this sense, we might say that the human sensory system thinks. That is, the old notion of the duality of body and mind begins to give way to the idea of embodied experience as learning experience. People grow to know themselves and become educated as human beings through the narratives they create in the interaction of body, mind, and environment.

What does this say about "deep reading" in the classroom? Through "deep reading," we would say, students acquire the capacity to shape their emotions and thoughts through the narrative curve of the story experience, and through that focused sense experience, they are then also able to direct their attention to the social environment with which they interact. For us, as we will discuss at length in the next chapter, other traditional art forms and the new digital literacies, as important as they are, cannot quite replicate what literary texts offer in this regard. As Denis Dutton, in *The Art Instinct* (Dutton, 2009), remarks:

> The teller of a story has, in the nature of the story-telling art, direct access to the inner mental experience of the story's character. This access is impossible to develop in other arts—music, dance, painting, and sculpture—to anything like the extent that it is available to oral and literary narrative. (pp. 118–119)

Embodied language provides humans with interiority, connectivity, and communal understanding. Such language offers the human voice, a singular experience that leads to the kind of direct access to the inner mental experience of the story's character that Dutton refers to. That is what a classroom should be all about.

MIRROR NEURONS

We view "emotional contagion," or empathy as we understand it, as connected to the remarkable recent discussions that brain researchers have advanced concerning what they call *mirror neurons*. Some of this discussion seems highly speculative and, at times, overdetermined, but the concept of mirror neurons further strengthens the long-standing belief that literature can excite the empathetic imagination and arouse self-reflection. Mirror neurons also help to explain the "mind-reading" process that is central to theory of mind.

Mirror neurons are a "newly discovered subset of cells (that) seem to directly reflect acts performed by another in the observer's brain ... without any need for explicit reasoning about them" (Rizzolatti, Fogassi, & Vittorio, 2008, p. 13). As Marco Iacoboni explains, these are special cells, "tiny miracles," that "are at the heart of how we navigate through our lives. They bind us with each other, mentally and emotionally" (Iacoboni, 2009, p. 4). According to Iacoboni (2009), when we watch movie stars kiss on a screen, we know how they are feeling because "some of the cells firing in our brain are the same ones that fire when we kiss our lovers" (p. 4). Perhaps the firing of these neurons even inspired the beginning of human narrative, arousing the desire to create language to express these common feelings and to preserve the shared experience through time. When Brian Boyd comments on the origins of narrative, he, too, stresses the importance of shared experience in human evolution and development:

> With narrative we could, for the first time, share experience with others who could then pass on to still others what they had found most helpful for their own reasoning about

future actions. We still have to act within our own time, but with narrative we can be partially freed from the limit of the present and the self. And our ability to see connections between accounts of the past and present or future action prepared us for some of the core fascination with fiction. (Boyd, 2009, p. 166)

For us, the concept of mirror neurons deepens the meaning of Boyd's passage. Mirror neurons, we would suggest, can be aroused by narrative. By arousing the firing of mirror neurons, narrative fiction seems to call human beings to pay attention and augments the human capability to connect with social patterns and human movement. For Boyd (2009), narrative inspires minds and taps "into the swift efficiency of our understanding of agents and actions" (p. 208). Stories and characters are able to "open up and populate possibility space" (*ibid.*, p. 208). It is just that sense of "possibility space" that defines the kind of imaginative classroom we have been advocating. The concept of mirror neurons adds to our belief in narrative and its importance in the classroom.

Immordino-Yang (2008) also emphasizes the importance of mirror neurons in understanding the learning experience. Human beings learn from others through an ongoing exchange of mirror neurons, from one brain to another. In this context, human beings cannot <u>not</u> learn, just as they cannot <u>not</u> communicate. For Immordino-Yang, a neuroscientist shaped by her experiences as a former middle school teacher, students in a classroom are always automatically interacting, learning about each other and themselves. With the help of mirror neurons, human beings internalize the actions of others, and so learn not only about what is familiar to them, but what is unfamiliar. They are always part of the other. But, most importantly, they also have the extraordinary capability of shaping that interactive experience with the other in the ongoing learning process. As Immordino-Yang (2008) points out:

Although the internalization (through mirror neurons) of another's situation can be automatic, the representation of another's situation is constructed and experienced on one's own self in accordance with cognitive and emotional preferences, memory, cultural knowledge, and neuropsychological predispositions—the "smoke" around the mirrors. (p. 70)

Humans are a complex mixture of necessity and free will, nature and nurture, biology and culture. They extend beyond their own skin whether they like it or not. But human beings also have the ability to shape the meaning of their interactions, to create their own "smoke" (as Immordino-Yang puts it): they can shape their own individual narrative, their own self through language.

Narrative language can move us and others; it creates "possibility space" (as Boyd says). We would argue in this context that narrative gives meaning and provides understanding for what we all experience through the automatic exchange of mirror neurons. As Iacoboni (2009) says: "It is as if mirror neurons help us understand what we read by internally simulating the action we just read in the sentence" (p. 94). Readers simulate the action they read about in literary narratives, and then they become self-reflective about that action, defining themselves in relation to what they have experienced.

Brain research seems to confirm the value of classroom discussion of literary narratives. Human beings help to create what they read. They also apparently can speak from the depths of what they hear from other voices. Quoting Iacoboni (2009) again: "When we listen to others, our motor speech brain areas are activated as if we are talking" (p. 104). Listening to other voices is a form of talking. We deepen our own voice by hearing the voice of other human beings. When people talk together about a story in a classroom, their words and actions become a coordinated joint activity, a collective movement, headed to a concentrated and common goal.

Along the same lines that we are developing, Maryanne Wolf (Wolf, 2007) and Stanislaus Dehaene (Dehaene, 2009) see reading as a gift that has created human identity. For Dehaene (2009), reading is a cultural invention that separates human beings from all other species. As he says: "In the midst of many cultural treasures, reading is by far the finest gem—it embodies a second inheritance system that we are duty-bound to transmit to coming generations" (Dehaene, 2009, p. 324). For Dehaene (2009), the "theory of mind" should be combined with the idea of a "global neuronal workplace" where human beings "[a]ssemble, confront, recombine, and synthesize knowledge" (p. 318). Like other neuroscientists, Dehaene is reminiscent of the great poets—in this case, S. T. Coleridge, who argued that "the secondary imagination" (as he called it) was the transforming power of the human being (Coleridge, 1983). That imagination, activated by the will, which "dissolves, dissipates, in order to recreate" (Coleridge, 1983, p. 306), seems to anticipate what today we think of as "brain plasticity," the ability of human beings to rewire the brain and to create through language new possibilities for themselves and others. The ape brain can acquire a knowledge of symbols and tools; however, as Dehaene (2009, p. 315) points out, what is missing in nonhuman primates is not the capacity to learn, but the ability to invent and to transmit cultural objects. What else is missing in nonhuman primates is the ability to read and write stories. Only human beings, we would suggest, can create original stories; only human beings can build community through the power of the literary imagination.

In chapters to come, we will explore more fully some of these issues in relation to the arts and the "new literacy" and how the human brain is affected, and often distracted, by changing media. Before we do that, we want, in the remainder of this chapter, to turn briefly to a discussion of what happens to the human brain when reading and then explore more extensively the relationship between literacy and attention, with special focus on the classroom.

THE READING BRAIN

As we have stressed, the importance of the classroom is for us directly related to the reading and writing process, and that process involves the body, the mind, and the environment. These elements are inextricably connected in the learning process. As Dehaene (2009) indicates: "Learning to read involves connecting two sets of brain regions that are already present in infancy: the object recognition system and the language circuit" (p. 195). From infancy, human beings are wired to see objects in the world, and they are also wired for language. Those two "regions" in the brain need to come together if we are to develop as mature human beings, people who know themselves and their location in the world that surrounds them. Reading and writing are part of that mature development, and they include both visual and linguistic components which implicate readers' bodies and minds, as well as the environment which surrounds them. But "deep reading" includes a much more inclusive sense of human experience. Reading is not an innate human ability but an intricate process that the brain must be taught to do. Given the declining attention to reading in the present era, how long humans will continue to read is the question. Both Wolf and Dehaene are concerned.

There is no one clear pathway or process that occurs in the reading brain. The brain's plasticity is the key to reading because, as Dehaene (2009) claims, many different structures and processes must be called upon and/or recycled for a person to read. The existing structures and functions of the brain don't automatically work in order for the brain to read, but, as Dehaene (2009) points out, the "circuits" are "functional and only need to be minimally reoriented" (p. 196) for reading to occur. The brain's existing structures and functions must operate in new ways, all in concert, to allow reading to be possible. Dehaene (2009) further clarifies that this "neuronal recycling" is "the partial or total invasion of a cortical territory initially devoted to a different function, by a cultural invention" (p. 147). Maryanne Wolf emphasizes the complexity and dynamic plasticity of the brain and its "astonishing ability to rearrange itself ... its protean capacity to make new connections among structures and circuits originally devoted to other more basic brain processes ... such as vision and spoken language" (Wolf, 2007, p. 4).

The process of reading is extremely complex and requires coordination and cooperation between and among many systems in the brain. The process of reading begins with our eyes, and our eyes must constantly be in motion on a page in order to decipher the meaning of words in succession. Dehaene (2009) provides an understandable overview of the reading process:

> Our visual system progressively extracts graphemes, syllables, prefixes, suffixes, and word roots. Two major parallel processing routes eventually come into play: the phonological route, which converts letters into speech sounds, and the lexical route, which gives access to a mental dictionary of word meanings. (p. 11)

According to the model of reading acquisition introduced by Uta Frith (Frith, 1985), there are three major phases of reading acquisition: the pictorial phase, the phonological stage, and the orthographic phase. Although Frith's theory outlines three phases, Dehaene (2009) points out that these phases are not "rigidly partitioned" (p. 199), as sometimes thought. However, these phases do help to clarify details and provide a description of reading acquisition.

Around the age of five or six, children experience the *pictorial* stage of reading, in which they begin to recognize words as objects (similar perhaps to their earlier pattern-recognition ability to recognize faces). The pictorial phase, Dehaene (2009) explains, "relies on all the available visual features: shape, color, letter orientation, curvature" (p. 200). Children at this stage may recognize their name as a word and a few other words as objects. This recognition of words is not reading; in fact, Dehaene (2009) refers to it as "artificial reading," but argues that it is an important step towards learning to read. The brain attempts to connect words to meanings but without attention to pronunciation or separate letters of the alphabet (or other orthographic symbols).

The second or *phonological* phase involves an ability to decode words into their individual letters and to draw connections between letters and speech sounds (grapheme-phoneme correspondences). Children accomplish this by paying attention to individual letters and letter groups. As children receive reading instruction, they begin to understand different speech sounds as made up of phonemes which can be combined and recombined to form new words. This phonemic awareness does not usually come about automatically; explicit teaching of phonemes and the corresponding alphabetic code is needed. Dehaene (2009) explains that the brain's visual areas are changed when children learn that words can be broken down into graphemes (letters) and phonemic awareness is evident. The understanding of graphemes and phonemes are closely linked, and an understanding of one feeds the other. Dehaene (2009) expands on these connections: "The acquisition of letters draws attention to speech sounds, the analysis of speech sounds refines the understanding of letters, and so on in a never-ending spiral" (p. 203). An accomplished reader knows a wide range of word roots, prefixes, and suffixes, and is able to make connections between the meaning of a word and its pronunciation as well as combine roots and prefixes to make novel words. It is a generative process.

The *orthographic* stage represents an advance in reading ability, when the length of words comes to have little relevance for how difficult a reading passage is perceived to be. At this stage, the brain has the capacity for analysis of strings of words: meaning is more easily comprehended and pronunciation of written words more automatically accomplished.

Although the cerebral counterparts of the stages of reading acquisition and the different processes involved in reading in English and other languages are still not clearly understood, new research is making strides towards this understanding. With the help of modern brain imaging, researchers are now able to actually see areas of the brain which are activated when a person is reading. This is helping to clarify the "road map" in the brain for reading (Dehaene, 2009).

To add to the complexity of the reading process, the neuronal connections which are used for reading in one language may not be the same as when reading in another language. Wolf (2007) points out that "reading can be learned only because of the brain's plastic design, and when reading takes place, that individual brain is forever changed, both physiologically and intellectually" (p. 5). Reading in different languages demands acquisition of new knowledge and wiring in unique sets of brain pathways. Thus, for example, when a Chinese reader attempts to read English, the same neuronal connections that have been hardwired for Chinese are not wholly transferable. To read English, the Chinese reader must develop different neuronal architecture. This is yet another demonstration that language is a powerful extension of our consciousness into the environment and is an extension of the environment into our consciousness.

For us, the basic point is how expansive and complex the reading experience is and how profound its implications in the development of the human being. Human beings are now in danger of losing this remarkable ability, one that has shaped human knowledge and consciousness for many centuries, and one that has been the foundation for our belief in human civilization as we have come to understand it. Nicholas Carr suggests the implications for the past and the future:

> For the last five centuries, ever since Gutenberg's printing press made book reading a popular pursuit, the linear, literary mind has been at the center of art, science, and society. As supple as it is subtle, it's been the imaginative mind of the Renaissance, the rational mind of the Enlightenment, the inventive mind of the Industrial Revolution, even the subversive mind of Modernism. It may soon be yesterday's mind. (Carr, 2010, p. 10)

Like Carr, we worry about the challenges to deep reading in this new century (see Chapter Six). One cannot achieve deep reading with divided attention; deep reading demands focus and attentional capacities in an age which seems to be increasingly distracted. As we have emphasized throughout this book, deep reading makes us more human. It has allowed us to think intensely and to wisely contemplate and make meaning of our existence. Before we close this chapter, we want to offer a couple of practical examples of how teachers in the classroom can stem this tide of increased distraction.

CULTIVATING ATTENTION FOR LITERACY

The capacity to focus and develop one's attentional capacities is at risk in the 21st century. This is the effect of an overemphasis on the visual rather than the verbal, the image rather than language. One's attention becomes divided, and the ability to focus on one thing becomes continually more difficult. This is why we see the space in the classroom (our new neighborhood) as a potential safe haven from the distracting influences all around us. The space of the classroom provides a meaningful retreat from attention deficit and the distractions surrounding us. By focusing attention on a piece of good literature and placing it at the center of teaching and learning in a classroom context, participants make sense and make meaning of the narrative. Cultivating mindfulness, the ability to deeply enter into the state of moment-to-moment awareness as each moment opens itself to you, can be valuably utilized in the classroom in connection with literacy practices. Students can be asked to focus on a text using quiet time before discussion for reflective or contemplative writing. Mindfulness is just one way to bring the learners into the depth of the present moment and into a meaningful space created where all other distractions are put aside.

Kabat-Zinn's (2006) work has shown that mindfulness, which focuses attention on the mind, body, and context of the here and now, can reduce stress in people's everyday lives. His work at the University of Massachusetts at Worcester has shown that mindfulness-based-stress-reduction can reduce pain in people with chronic illnesses and improve their overall well-being and quality of life. We believe that "deep reading" can achieve similar effects for students. Literary narrative is often a way of focusing pain, and reading narrative can provide a way to shape that pain and create a space for reflection. Language shaped into narrative serves as an important human activity countering the silence of the world.

Alexander Astin has researched (Astin, 1985) the spiritual dimensions and needs of undergraduates and has clarified the kind of needs with which students arrive when entering higher education. Students come seeking meaning; they desire to learn; they want to know who they are. According to Astin (1985), despite the driving concern to learn skills that will make them good job applicants, students really want to know something more; they want to locate themselves in the world. They may be seeking practical everyday skills, but they also seek an adventure that will lead them to genuine knowledge—let's call it "wisdom." We believe that reading, writing, and discussing good literature can give them the opportunity to explore both these paths. The journey through language and literature holds promise for promoting learning, meaning-making, and life paths towards well-being—lives that can build "new neighborhoods" of citizens who serve their own interests and the interests of others. On such a journey, students learn the crucial skills of daily life, but they also learn the value of that life. They learn how to survive in a tough world, but they also learn why that life is worth living.

HOW CONTEMPLATIVE LITERACY PRACTICE CAN IMPACT THE CLASSROOM: A PRACTICAL RESEARCH STUDY

In research involving contemplative practice born out of an initiative from the Carnegie Foundation, two researchers (Maureen Hall and Olivia Archibald) created a project to investigate how contemplative practice in the classroom affected students' identities as writers and their perceptions of the value of writing. The project's emphasis was on "deep writing" as an aspect of contemplative practice:

> Our idea was to investigate how using reflective writing as contemplative practice affected our students' sense of who they are as writers and as teachers of writing. We

were also interested in finding out if writing at the beginning of each class affected our students' perspectives on the value of reflective writing as a tool for learning. (Hall & Archibald, 2008, p. 1)

Using sustained quiet writing activities connected to the assigned readings at the beginning of each class session, along with other writing assignments, the researchers investigated students' perceptions of contemplative practice in terms of how they experienced it and what was valuable or not.

Using Krathwohl's Affective Domain (Krathwohl, Bloom, & Masia, 1964) to assess students' affective learning, the researchers determined that a total of 30 of the 32 student teachers at the conclusion of the project valued a practice of reflective writing used at the beginning of a class. These 30 students had moved beyond Krathwohl's Level One category, *having an awareness* of reflective writing. They also had moved beyond Krathwohl's Level Two category: they did not just *respond* to the writing prompts, but in their responses indicated that they *valued* the experience, Level Three of Krathwohl's taxonomy. A total of 14 of the students indicated that they would like to *integrate* reflective writing into their lives after the course was over, Level Four in Krathwohl's taxonomy: they internalized the experience to the degree that they wanted to make it an ongoing part of their lives. What was unclear at the conclusion of the project was whether students would use reflective writing consistently in their lives and commit to it as a life practice, Krathwohl's Level Five (Hall & Archibald, 2008, p. 8). In addition, a qualitative analysis was conducted to identify emerging themes from student responses to the contemplative/reflective writing activities. Three themes emerged from student perceptions: (1) Preparing students' minds for focused work, (2) Writing as therapy/Writing as transformation, and (3) Sense of agency as writers/Building a writing community/Need for interconnectedness (for further details, see Hall & Archibald, 2008).

Although this study was practical research, not a scientific experiment, and the student teachers' responses may not have high reliability, the majority of those who participated benefited from learning about contemplative, reflective practices as applied to writing. More studies need to be conducted to measure student learning through transformative forms of pedagogy and approaches which will help build a history of practice in education, as advocated by former Carnegie Foundation President Lee Shulman (Shulman, 2004).

The Hall and Archibald (2008) findings are interesting, but there is more work to be done in order to provide additional empirical research on contemplative practices and on educating teachers about alternative pedagogical modes. In this way, the value of contemplative practices for facilitating "deep literacy," both writing and reading, and for improving student learning can be further explored.

PRACTICAL EXAMPLE: HOW COGNITIVE-AFFECTIVE LEARNING IS OPERATIONALIZED IN THE CLASSROOM

As we have suggested in previous chapters, through our work in urban alternative school settings, we have utilized service learning approaches with a focus on literacy and set up learning opportunities for both the high school students and preservice teacher education students involved in our projects. The larger goals, in terms of cognitive-affective learning, are the same for both groups of stakeholders; that is, to utilize literacy as a medium for the creation of community—a new neighborhood of educational opportunity. We believe that "literature can help students locate themselves, and through good discussion, provide opportunities for them to create community with others who are also looking for safe places to inhabit in their worlds" (Hall & Waxler, 2007, p. 124). The creation of community has a multitude of affective elements. Part of this community-building involves feeling safe and connected in a classroom where there are high expectations for student learning and engagement. For us, the larger cognitive-affective learning goals are the same for high schoolers and preservice teachers. But there are differing goals for each of these populations as well.

We want the high school students to engage with the literature and start to believe that they too can succeed in college. Many of these high school students do not believe they can be college students, and yet there is no sensible reason underpinning this belief. They are bright and higher learning could be an option for them—if only they can see themselves in that context. The college students, on the other hand, are role models for these high school students. One of our goals is to create empathy between the two groups through discussion so that the differences between them will diminish.

In one of our experiments, preservice teachers were involved in a service learning project and assigned to tutor a student at the alternative school for the duration of the semester. The tutoring, along with the discussion of several stories, was designed to give them real-world K-12 experiences, an experience where literacy was clearly central for learning.

For this project, the intention was for the college students to "serve" the high schoolers, and we emphasized the idea of preservice learning, as Balbir Gurm defines it:

> Service is engagement with another for the benefit of the other without expectation of reward. Learning is acquiring new understandings about a person or phenomena [sic]. Therefore, service learning is learning through engagement as you provide benefit to another. Service learning is about taking knowledge or theories learned in formal education and seeing if they work in the real world. (Gurm, 2009, p. 1)

In part, the theories that we talked about in the college classroom grew from Palmer's (1998) *The Courage to Teach.* One reflective assignment for the college students, due at the end of the semester, was to create a case study of their assigned tutees, who were individual high school students. The college students were asked to reflect on the connections between and among their tutoring experiences, Palmer's text, and their developing notions of what it means to be an effective educator. More specifically, we asked the students to write about an important theme from Palmer's text and to articulate that theme in connection with the learning gained from their interaction with the student whom they tutored and from their experiences with a literacy component in which they shared discussions about pieces of literature with the whole group of college students and high school students (Hall, 2009).

COGNITIVE-AFFECTIVE LEARNING OUTCOMES FOR PRESERVICE TEACHERS

The themes which the preservice teachers identified and wrote about from Palmer's (1998) text were: (1) fear, (2) identity and integrity, and (3) community. These reflective components demonstrated their deepened learning of important affective dimensions inherent in being a teacher. Through their case studies, they demonstrated new understandings through their meaning-making and articulation of the aforementioned themes.

Fear

They learned that not all fears are negative, and that teachers need to be aware of what is going on with their students, developing empathy and conducting themselves as positive role models. One student made connections between Palmer's (1998) notion that "Some fears can help us survive, even learn and grow—if we know how to decode them" (p. 39). This preservice teacher linked Palmer's notion to what she observed in the urban alternative school and reflected:

> Every student goes through the same type of fears, but chooses to deal with them differently, which is the case for the kids we are tutoring … . They put up a "tough front" but deep down I am sure that they fear many things, whether they might have to go home to a family fight, or how they may appear to their peers. This is something all kids go through as they are trying to create their own identity. They need positive influences in their lives who cannot give up on them because they need a strong support system to get through adolescence, which can be extremely scary and difficult.

This preservice teacher discovered a point where theory, in this case, Palmer's theory of fear, met practice. She realized how important the influence a teacher can be on a developing adolescent. Part of a teacher's professional responsibility is to create a supportive environment for all students. Students' concerns need to be articulated, as Palmer (1998) suggests, so that learning and self-reflection can occur. We believe that these points have implications for deep reading and deep writing in the classroom. Fears are identified, made known, and woven into a discussion which is a safe context, creating a community for all participants to share ideas and acknowledge their vulnerability.

Identity and Integrity

New understandings of Palmer's combined theme of identity and integrity were also explored; preservice teachers reinforced the value of the prior experiences that they and the high school students brought to the service learning experience. One student who wrote about this combined theme of identity and integrity reflected on earlier experiences with his own teachers. Palmer (1998) points out that a teacher's knowledge of subject matter is important—but that a teacher's knowledge of his or her self is also critical, as this preservice teacher remarked:

> The theme of identity and of knowing one's self is of particular importance to me because the best teachers I have ever had were ones who were wise in all areas of their lives, not just in their particular subject matters. As a student, the classes that have been my favorite and taught me the most were classes in which I was allowed to share a little bit of myself and the teacher was willing to do the same. I would hope that as a teacher, my students would be aware of my identity as well as their own, and I would also hope that our identities would play an important part in the learning process; our identities shape the way in which we learn best as well as the way in which we change as a result of what we've learned … Sometimes it is not only the content of learning that is important,

but the way you feel about learning in the first place; thus if the teacher who is attempting to educate you does not know how they feel about their material or even their life, their lack of identity and self will directly reflect on the learners.

This preservice teacher made a connection between the created classroom environment and Palmer's (1998) view on the self: "The self is not infinitely elastic—it has potentials and limits. If the work we do lacks integrity for us, then we, the work, and the people we do it with will suffer" (p. 16). Teaching, unlike some other professional work, is a vocation. A good teacher, as Palmer espouses, finds ways to weave together the self, the subject matter, and students into a dynamic learning mix.

Community

Students who wrote about this theme illuminated new ideas about community and how developing a trusting environment grows out of mutual respect between teachers and learners. More than one student reflected on Palmer's (1998) view of good teachers, as they "possess a capacity for connectedness" (p. 11). In order to highlight the importance of creating community, one preservice teacher wrote about how critical it is to know something about students' backgrounds. This preservice teacher reflected:

> I think it is extremely important to be a connected teacher. As a teacher one needs to understand the students you are teaching, the community they come from, and their individual strengths and weaknesses. To understand these things a teacher needs to be connected. According to Palmer to be connected means that you open your heart to your students. I agree with him. You cannot connect to your students if you yourself are not open. To open yourself to your students is to trust them; students will see this trust and respond in kind … . These (alternative school) students need to be in a safe and trusting environment to be able to learn.

Knowing one's students is a large part of being able to create a community of learners. This preservice teacher made reference to opening one's heart to students. Nothing in teaching replaces the willingness to get to know students. Schools are places where good teachers exhibit genuine interest in their students' lives; strong teacher–student interactions can provide the energy and openness needed in the best learning environments.

Through this reflective part of the project, preservice teachers (college students who were enrolled in this education course) were able to enlarge their understandings of the cognitive and affective dimensions of being a teaching professional. Through reflective writings on their experiences with high school students, these preservice teachers were able to apply theory to practice and also to understand theory from practice. The two-way street of service learning was paved: high school students got new role models for learning and participated in discussions about good literature, and college students deepened their understanding about the struggles and delights of being a teacher (Hall, 2009).

CONCLUDING THOUGHTS ON PROMOTING LITERACY AND CONTEMPLATION

In this chapter, we share the worries of Dehaene, Wolf, and others that reading is an activity that may be lost in the confusion and distractions of the 21st century. By keeping narrative at the center, valuing the reading process, and making sense and meaning though face-to-face discussions with others, we believe that reading can flourish. Cultivating student attention in the classroom must be a priority, and contemplative practices can facilitate the learning made possible through deep reading and deep writing. Various educational terms and concepts are linked to the idea of present moment learning; these approaches include Contemplative Education, Teaching to and from the Whole Person, Holistic Learning, and Integrative Learning. The main idea at the center of all of these terms is the cultivation of focused attention for deepened learning.

In this chapter, we have also considered the work of neuroscientists in terms of research on how the brain functions when learning. New understandings of mirror neurons, for example, reinforce the value of present moment learning. When people are fully focused and embodied in an interactive classroom moment (e.g., in a lively literature discussion about a character's actions and the ethical implications of those actions), the learning can pass from short-term to long-term memory. In this way, learning in the classroom can lead to deep and enduring knowledge. Deep reading and deep learning can be activated through the plastic nature of the brain; we see present moment learning in the classroom space as a way to unlock and engage human potential.

We also offer two different types of classroom examples. The first is a summary of a practical research study from a project utilizing contemplative writing as contemplative practice (Hall & Archibald, 2008), and the second is part of a service learning project we conducted with college students in an education course who were considering teaching as a profession. We wanted these college students to stop and reflect on the kinds of change they had experienced through contemplative writing.

In the next chapter, we turn to an exploration of language and the arts in the learning environment and continue to make our argument for deep reading, which we believe should be a central focus for the education and well-being of individuals and the larger society.

CHAPTER FIVE

LANGUAGE AND THE ARTS

As we have indicated in Chapter Four, there are many areas of research in neuroscience which underpin the ways in which people interact with and make meaning of literary narratives. Our argument so far is current and urgent but also traditional. It is current and urgent because the reading brain is threatened by the digital age, but it is traditional because for a long time scholars from a variety of disciplines have insisted that language is the fundamental marker separating human beings from all other species. Our argument privileges linguistic narrative—stories and natural language—more than other cultural inventions. The human ability to tell stories and to invent and participate in a complex language system makes humans different than other animals. Language allows humans to be self-reflective, the argument goes, providing them with a unique opportunity to create human meaning and to locate themselves in the world.

The bedrock foundation for human society is, by this reasoning, language. John Russo, for example, is clearly thinking along these lines when he claims: "Complex literary language penetrates the imagistic surfaces, probes into the furthest recesses of mind and feeling, breaks the force of habit, and draws patterns of coherence in order to deepen and empower a self-determining, continuously developing selfhood" (Russo, 2005, p. 35). For Russo, as for us, language is close to the origins of human consciousness. We consider language to be at the heart of the best learning; no other medium holds such potentialities for the reader and learner.

Dewey (1899/2009), in his description of what is needed for a child's education, captures this idea most succinctly:

> What is needed, in a word, is to afford occasion by which the child is moved to educe and exchange with others his store of experiences, his range of information, to make new observations correcting and extending them in order to keep his images moving, in order to find mental rest and satisfaction in definite and vivid realization of what is new and enlarging. (Dewey, 2009, p. 82)

Our argument has been right along that literary narrative offers what Dewey called for in the classroom ("What is needed ... is to afford occasion by which the child is moved to educe and exchange with others his store of experiences ... "). The best literacy learning requires direct student-to-student interaction, a genuine educational "exchange." Although other mediums, like music, dance, and film, may inspire people and help illuminate human meaning, no other medium can replace the literary text in terms of complexity and what it can offer experientially to the learner for developing and understanding the self.

THE VALUE OF LANGUAGE SHAKEN

We acknowledge that this belief in the unique power of language to enrich the human self and community has recently been shaken from a number of angles and for a variety of complex reasons, both theoretical and practical. For example, although it is generally agreed that speaking and listening have a strong biological basis in terms of human evolution, while reading and writing appear to be cultural in origin, the idea that spoken language, once established, developed and expanded for social and cultural reasons into writing systems is these days open to heated debate. This debate was first highlighted by the work of Jacques Derrida in *Writing Difference* (Derrida, 1978). Such a debate raises interesting and problematic questions about the relationship between speech and writing, and about the phonological and visual features of various writing systems, their graphic shapes and orthographic patterns of sound-spelling correspondences. It also leads to other intriguing questions, such as: does speech actually precede writing? Is it possible to imagine that writing precedes speech? Did writing actually develop to expand spoken language? Coulmas (1989), for example, maintains that writing began as recordings of events and transactions, and only later served as a way of recording speech. These questions, and many others, no doubt contribute to the current complexities involved in determining the importance of language and for understanding the origins of human consciousness itself.

For us, the dialogic nature of language and human consciousness, as well as of speech and writing, seems crucial and correct in its broad outlines. As Vygotsky (1986) has claimed: "Thought development is determined by language, i.e., by the linguistic tools of thought and by the sociocultural experience of the child" (p. 94). Our own experience in the classroom supports this view. Deep reading and the potentialities for engaged discussion remain the best hope to maintain and enhance the human sense of the world and of the self within that world. However, with the increasing seductive rhythms of different kinds of media drawing both teachers and students' attention in many different directions, we believe that deep reading and the art of discussion in the classroom are becoming devalued at a time when they are critically important for human learning. This is our concern.

LITERARY CONVERSATIONS IN THE SPACE OF THE CLASSROOM

Wheatley and Whyte (2006) make an important point about conversation. Human beings are constantly explaining themselves to others through conversation; in fact, *conversations with others shape the relationships we have with others*. Wheatley and Whyte (2006) identify a hunger in society for a sense of belonging in a complex world, and such a hunger is something we have felt and observed among students in the classroom as well. In part, that hunger seems to have intensified as one-on-one conversation and language, in general, have been devalued. As Wheatley and Whyte (2006) put it:

> I wish we could take our sense of love and need of vocation and avocation, our sense of strangeness, our sense of the future speaking through us and realize that we must simultaneously reclaim a language that has been devalued. It is this language that is so richly abundant in the academy but not honored any longer. (p. 16)

Educators must reclaim the value of language. Wheatley and Whyte (2006) ask the pertinent question, "What if part of our work (in the academy) is to be brave enough to realize that we are existing in a culture that cannot yet, and has not yet, provided us with processes for seeing things that we know are essential to us?" (p. 16). The classroom space is the right place for this conversation to happen. Keeping narrative texts at the center and utilizing deep reading and an analogously reflective form of deep writing to discover what is essential in human life, the classroom can become a space for just this kind of exploration, a journey to discover what has not yet been revealed, an adventure to discuss what has not yet been seen. No doubt technology can extend some of the conversations in the space of the classroom, but technologies can never substitute for the complex flow of language necessary for the courageous teaching and essential learning that Wheatley and White have in mind.

As Tomlinson and McTighe (2006) point out, "Classrooms are small universes. In those universes, we learn to accept and appreciate one another's variances—or we learn to resent and be suspicious of differences" (p. 43). Dialogic interaction within the classroom space creates the kind of embodied experience that enhances appreciation of the quest for knowledge and expands consciousness. Through conversation with others, human beings open themselves to others, work through blind spots, and make connections otherwise lost. Listening to others, humans hear their own deep voice, allowing them the possibility of overcoming resentment and suspicion through language. As Palmer (1998) puts it, "teaching and learning are always attempts to 'lead out' from within the self a core of wisdom that has the power to resist falsehood and live in the light of truth, not by external norms but by reasoned and reflective self-determination" (p. 31). Interaction with new technologies cannot replace the face-to-face encounter within the classroom, and as Palmer (1998) points out, "what we teach will never 'take' unless it connects with the inward, living core of our students' lives with our students' inward teachers" (p. 31). In order to create community with others, a teacher must first be in community with his or her teaching self, a community celebrating language and narrative, as we have insisted throughout this book.

FROM THE LINGUISTIC TO THE PICTORIAL

More broadly speaking, the issues related to natural language are especially complicated these days by what has recently been labeled as a turn from the linguistic to the pictorial (or visual), which suggests a heightened focus on images and immediate perception, as well as on the mass media in general. This focus has been brought about in part by what Walter Benjamin called "the culture industry," an industry that has substantially contributed to a collapse of boundaries between "high culture" and "popular culture" (Benjamin, 1968), and, according to many thinkers (e.g., Toffler & Toffler, 2006), has now, like a supersonic train (faster than the speed of light), ushered in the digital age. Miller (2007) reminds us how disrupted our lives have become as a consequence of this industry: "With television, Internet, and music at home or at work, we find our attention distracted. We often feel compelled to do two or three things at once" (p. 118).

We agree with Miller and worry that the accoutrements of the digital age devalue literary language, pushing it to the margins of consciousness. In contrast, we see literary language as the epicenter of human activity for making sense and making meaning, the hallmark of human existence. In the next chapter, we will develop more fully our notion that the digital technologies, for the most part, represent a medium without such a human message. But here we want simply to sound an initial warning: we see the heightened focus on the visual rather than the linguistic as a tragic mistake. The focus on the visual, we believe, has not only devalued language but reduced our human capability to acknowledge and appreciate the deepest dimensions of human identity. Such focus diminishes the human imagination and the complex and fluid sense of knowledge itself. Knowledge is dynamic and ever-changing, and we must remain open to all of its possibilities. Knowledge is complex, deriving from and linked to all of the senses and both affective and cognitive domains. The processing of information is crucial to learning and the building of information, but it is through the imaginative and shaping power of language that the deepest processing of information takes place. That kind of "deep processing" transforms information into knowledge. For us, the best learning is not finally about processing information, but about transforming information into human knowledge. That kind of imaginative transformation is the beginning of genuine human understanding, what we dare to call "wisdom." Such ongoing transformation through language and the imagination always suggests what cannot quite be measured or seen. It is singular and points to the human singularity and mystery at the heart of identity and community.

Tomlinson and McTighe (2006) approach the same idea from a slightly different angle: "Learning happens *within* students, not *to* them. Learning is a process of making meaning that happens one student at a time" (p. 22, emphasis in original). The intense focus on the visual often leads human beings too quickly away from that human mystery, the depth of self that cannot be made visible or be easily measured. Even neuroscientists are sensitive to the problem when they seem to be concentrating primarily on the visual system. As Semir Zeki, a leading brain researcher, declares:

> If I have concentrated more on the visual system than on other sensory systems it is not because I know more about it but because I know less about the other systems. And this is quite simply because we actually have a great deal more information on the visual system. (Zeki, 2009, p. 4)

THE CHANGING NATURE OF KNOWLEDGE AND THE NEED FOR COMMUNAL SPACES OF INQUIRY

With the use of a poetic example, Zajonc (2006b) illuminates how knowledge changes, is dynamic and not static, and how people, from birth, naturally desire to know more about themselves and their relationship to the world. They seek to know more than what they can see, the mystery that is never quite revealed no matter what the explanation. Zajonc (2006b) offers an example of a sunset viewed by a parent and child. The child asks the parent for an explanation of the sunset, especially its beauty. Using a metaphor of a journey through time, Zajonc (2006b) suggests that through the "increasingly scientific centuries" (p. 60), the explanations for the sublime beauty of the sunset have changed according to the new theories in science, but whether the sunset is explained by Newtonian principles, quantum mechanics, or other theories, the mystery of the sunset, especially its beauty, remains undefined. Human beings need something more than scientific explanation, in other words, something more than the visible to gain knowledge of the world.

Zajonc (2006b) also wants us to realize that "it is best to be modest in our pretensions to understanding the world" (p. 60). When reflecting on knowledge, Zajonc (2006b) warns about scientific pretensions and hubris. The quest for knowledge demands that human beings always acknowledge their mortal limitations and recognize that there might be more invisible than visible things in the world. Zajonc offers some advice for this quest; he says people should "accommodate the aesthetic, ethical and spiritual dimensions of our lives" (Zajonc, 2006b, p. 63). Those dimensions of human consciousness often explore what cannot be seen, what might, at times, be beyond immediate explanation or known evidence, but what are without doubt part of human experience. Zajonc's point underlines the dynamism of knowledge, an ongoing quest, which emphasizes the importance of questions rather than facts and fixed explanations, the seeking of knowledge rather than the often illusionary satisfaction of temporary information. On such a quest, the questions asked and the conversation that follows from those questions make life adventurous and worth living.

Much current neuroscience research seems to resonate with this view that information is not knowledge, that human life itself remains "a mystery," and that the human quest for understanding and knowledge is an ongoing and deeply felt experience extending out from the self to the world. We see this especially when brain researchers reach out to the philosophical tradition of phenomenology and embodiment theory (e.g., Ramachandran, 2004; Zeki, 2009). Such theories suggest that the human body is a medium that extends into the environment, which allows human beings to develop a deepened sense of identity in connection with the outer world and to experience and know that outer world through the senses. Our imaginative ability to create stories and other symbols of beauty can be considered a cultural process in this regard, a way of shaping our chaotic experience of the world, making it knowable to us in human terms. Such a process arouses the neural circuits and extends the senses, offering pleasure and momentary (sometimes profound) satisfaction and pleasure. In this context, it can be argued that different art forms provide different ways of experiencing this pleasure and satisfaction, appealing to different senses in various combinations. Each art form (music, painting, dance, film, and so on) makes an important contribution in different ways to heightening senses and increasing personal understanding of the self in the world. Nevertheless, as we have insisted, language remains singular in this regard, and it should not lose its privileged place among the different modes of expression. Language offers the most complex and vital expression of the human ability to know and to make meaning, through connecting all of the domains of human activity and the worlds of the past, the future, and the imagination with our ability to read other humans and their minds. When human beings engage at the deepest levels with the complexity and sensuous qualities of language, especially language shaped into narrative, they are, in our view, as close as they can venture into the "deep mystery" of the human world. Language calls to the body and the mind, helps to shape feeling and ideas. Most importantly, language, especially literary narrative, embodies the richest and most precise sense of that double perspective which is one of the significant marks of our humanity. Language contains within it both the sensuous experience and the interpretation of that experience. Literary language calls to the individual human being (the reader) in a personal way to experience the world and to become self-reflective and to move forward.

Our argument for the central importance of linguistic narrative, reading and writing, in the 21st century classroom is both radical and traditional. Although other media and technology can provide a medium for learning, they do not deserve the attention they currently receive. The medium is not (contra McLuhan) to be equated with the message. Literary language offers human beings the best opportunity to locate themselves in the past, to project themselves into the future, and to develop a sense of being in the world. Humans are in this world in the two senses, as phenomenologists put it, of *being a body*—that is, directly experiencing the world as an extension of their body—and *having a body*—that is, being able to reflect on that embodied experience. Humans are, like good readers, always experiencing the world, in the same way that they read a good story—both from the first-person perspective, that of experiencing the story (world) themselves, and the third-person perspective, that of experiencing the story (world) from a distance removed from their own personal experience yet linked to it by human connection and empathy. It is language that allows for the deepest experience of this dual-perspective phenomenon. In fact, language seems to embody this kind of "double vision" which allows for different views on the same matter, that is, from the perspective of the first person "I" and from the perspective of the third person "he/she/it" or "they." These two perspectives, the self and the other, help to deepen understanding and also provide the basis for the merged perspective of "we," which, we have been arguing, should be developed in education through deep reading and conversation about literature in the classroom.

This "double vision" or doubleness of perspective is, in a sense, always somewhat incomplete, an ongoing grammar of self, a process of sense-making. Such "double vision" continues to create desire and self-reflection in people's search for meaning and stimulates future possibilities for new meaning and understanding, as well as new possibilities for enlarged "we" perspectives. Granted, all art offers human beings this kind of multifaceted experience, but, in our view, "high art" trumps "popular art," and literary narrative especially calls to the deeper parts of our identities. It does not just touch the surface of our ego, nor does it only arouse our aesthetic sense and appreciation on an affective level: it arouses the living voice and the imagination at the deepest levels of our individual and collective consciousness. Richly textured language should be celebrated in the classroom for all these reasons. It cannot be replaced, nor should it be.

IMAGINATION AND ITS CONNECTION TO LANGUAGE AND MEANING-MAKING

As should be clear to our readers by now, our argument is tied to the notion that imagination and language are linked together, and that the creation of meaning in and through language is fundamental to our human identity. This belief in the fundamental importance of language and the imagination has a long history running through Coleridge and developed more recently by such modern thinkers as Paul Ricoeur (e.g., Ricoeur, 1991). In *Biographia Literaria*, Coleridge (1817/1983) claims: "The primary IMAGI-NATION I hold to be the living power and prime agent of all perception" (Coleridge, 1983, p. 306). Such belief is connected to the idea that the living voice is the spark of human life, the unseen power that can transform mere visual information into knowledge. In addition, such belief highlights the notion that human experience and literary narrative (poetic story) are inevitably connected. Ricoeur (1991) seems to be extending Coleridge's discussion in the *Biographia Literaria* when he comments on the relationship between fiction and life: "If it is true that fiction cannot be completed other than in life, and that life cannot be understood other than through stories we tell about it, then we are led to say that a life examined, in the sense borrowed from Socrates, is a life narrated" (Ricoeur, 1991, p. 435). For both Coleridge and Ricoeur, literary language, the imagination, and ordinary human experience intersect in ways that create the depth of human meaning, the narrative self in the world. For Coleridge, literary language, sparked by the imagination, brings human beings close to the origins of the self, the mystery of human life. For Ricoeur, a fresh and surprising metaphor can refer the reader back to the world and simultaneously open the mind to new meaning. For both thinkers, it is not the visual that makes us human—after all, we share this sense with all other animate beings; it is human language empowered by the human spark of imagination that gives us knowledge of the human self and the world. It is first and foremost through language and imagination that we gain the depth of understanding, the unified sense of identity, the continuity of the past, present, and future. As we will discuss shortly in this chapter, the other arts also help humans achieve a similar end, but not as fully or completely as literary narrative—language plus imagination—does.

L. William Countryman, in his *Poetic Imagination* (Countryman, 2000), identifies and describes the action of the poetic imagination in a context similar to Coleridge and Ricoeur. Countryman explains, for example, how poetry can contribute to the development of self and explains the action of poetry as:

> taking [one's] inner experience, externalising and concretising it in the form of a little poetic word that the reader/hearer could then relate analogically to her internal experience, and of doing this in a way that allowed for movement, for a shift, a turn, a transformation. (Countryman, 2000, p. 30)

Countryman makes the point that poetry works to transform both the internal self and its relation to the external world. It expands human understanding and depends upon human connectivity. With the constant distractions of a modern life, we worry that both literary language and the transforming quality of the imagination are in jeopardy as is the depth of human connectivity.

Wheatley and Whyte (2006) argue that the poetic imagination is in itself a common language, a language that can connect people across a myriad of divisions that too often separate people. For Wheatley and Whyte (2006), the imagination is a "kind of inborn faculty inside each human being whereby we are able to place ourselves in incredible environments without having to divide up the world in order to do it" (p. 10). The poetic or artistic imagination, in particular, transports people "beyond the horizon" (p. 10). The creative imagination allows us to "see" new ways of living and of finding meaning as individuals and as part of the human community. In this sense, as Wheatley and Whyte (2006) observe, the imagination is crucial to creation of the future—it "must enter you long before it happens" (p. 10).

THE LITERARY IMAGINATION REVISITED

Literary and expressive language, combining similarity with difference, the literal and the figurative, excites the active imagination, and so new meanings can emerge. New meanings are derived from the complex ambiguity of the language itself, which creates, in turn, a pressure on the reader to experience both the mental response and the sensuous experience of those ideas felt along the pulse, and simultaneously to become self-reflective about those thoughts and feelings. Literary language, through both its syntactic and semantic structures, can give people back a memory and portend a future, moving them both backward and forward in time and helping them to experience the meaning of that movement through time. In an interview conducted with Ricoeur (1991), he explains: "To rediscover meaning we must return to the multilayered sedimentations of language, to the complex plurality of its instances, which can preserve what is said from the destruction of oblivion" (p. 137). Deep reading (as described in Chapter Two) provides an access point or entry into these complex levels and layers of linguistic meaning.

This is not to deny the importance of the visual domain such as is emphasized in other art forms and media besides literature, but to encourage the traditional notion that the power of the human imagination is primarily connected to the verbal not the visual. As Geoff Madoc-Jones suggests, in commenting on the relation of Bachelard and Ricoeur and their common belief in the deep rapport between the imagination and language (Madoc-Jones, 2008), the imagination creates complex human meaning not as a result of objects seen but from the "reverberation" of those objects in the mind's network of associations. In this context, we would suggest that those "reverberations" are what set in motion the kind of linguistic imagination that creates human meaning. What humans see as "objects" are similar to the "facts" of the world. Those "objects" are given human meaning through the language used to shape and define what we consider to be the human world. The classroom should be a learning environment that emphasizes just such a process of knowing, and students should understand the long tradition that has established this kind of human knowing. As Madoc-Jones (2008) insists:

> A most important principle of language arts education is making sure that as the emergence of a student's personal creative use of language takes place, it is seen not merely as a subjective act but also as an instance of the re-emergence of the logos within a linguistic tradition. (p. 59)

The classroom should be the place where students are encouraged to make meaning and be uninhibited in their interpretations of texts. It should reverberate with the intelligent energy of human language shaped into meaning, and it should be a place where linguistic tradition is celebrated.

We are not attempting to denigrate the role of the visual, as people navigate the 21st century with all its options, gadgets, and distractions; nor are we suggesting that educators abandon pedagogical methods for multimedia or the related idea of multiple intelligences. Our approach may at first appear in opposition to educational progressives who have, at times, appealed to a sense of freedom and egalitarianism without boundaries or hierarchical values. (For example, the "open" classrooms of the 1970s provided freedom for student learning, but were possibly too unwieldy and shapeless for many students to attain success.) However, if we are not progressive in this regard, we are perhaps radical in attempting to maintain core values and a traditional appreciation of human accomplishment and human discrimination. For us, the shaping power of the imagination, expressed through the richly textured language of narrative and the discussions that such engagement with narrative then evokes, offers the most valuable way to expand human understanding and to advance the learning necessary to know thyself.

HUMAN BEINGS NEED ART

Denis Dutton, in his book, *The Art Instinct* (Dutton, 2009), continues in the tradition of preserving a hierarchy of human values, pitting "high art"—the art of the recognized classical masters, including great writers—against popular culture and arguing that human beings need great art in order to evolve and survive. He focuses on four primary properties that are persistent qualities of "art's most demanding top-end excellence: high complexity, serious thematic content, a sense of insistent or urgent purpose, and a distance from ordinary pleasures and desires" (Dutton, 2009, p. 236). For him, *kitsch*, by contrast, only pretends to such values, and in doing so presents us with material of lackluster quality. For Dutton (2009), as for us, "flashy media and buzzing gizmos of daily experience" (p. 243) do not touch the art instinct in us, but merely give us as consumers trite phrases which provide an easy way to avoid the necessary wrestling with the deeper self. Ultimately, such flashiness lacks purpose and forward movement and creates cynicism by creating the illusion that there is really no deeper self, no future with purpose. By contrast to the empty experience of much of the clichéd world of popular culture, "high art" challenges us emotionally and intellectually; it offers the pleasure of virtuosity and skill; it is playful, but unlike most games, it does not invite us to focus on becoming players in a battle of winning and losing, but rather asks us to become participants in the beauty and pleasure of the experience itself. It sets us free in the sense that there are many potential paths of meaning open to navigation.

For Dutton (2009), stories are particularly powerful types of art in this regard, helping individuals and groups expand and deepen their own understanding of human social and emotional experience. As Dutton (2009) insists:

> The teller of a story has, in the nature of the story-telling art, direct access to the inner mental experience of the story's characters. This access is impossible to develop in other arts—music, dance, painting, and sculpture. (p. 118)

We agree with Dutton that literary narrative allows entry into worlds not fully available via other arts. By portraying the "mundane imaginative structures of memory, immediate perception, planning, calculation, and decision-making, both as we experience them ourselves and as we understand others to be experiencing them" (Dutton, 2009, p. 119), the best literary narratives take us beyond the ordinary, giving us the gift of imaginative human expansion. Building on Dutton's point, we argue that reading and rereading allow human beings to give voice to the silent language of the narrative, to create an expanded text. As readers, we engage with the language of a narrative text and experience the common processes, the mundane structures, of other human beings—their memories, their perceptions, their planning, their calculations, their decision-making, as Dutton says—and then we map our own processes and structures onto those experiences. As readers we follow and then become the characters we read about, and those characters become us as well. We read and reread ourselves and others in just this way, and it is as if our own human life is extended in this process of reading and rereading. Then we continue that expansion through discussion of that ongoing text. Through this linguistic process, human beings continue to create their own narratives of their personal life stories.

MUSIC, FILM, AND DANCE

Other art forms strive for similar effects, but their achievement is less capacious and often more limited, we would suggest. Music, for example, can capture our attention, keep it focused, arouse desire and pleasure, and evoke memory and rhythmic movement as well as surprise. However, as Julia Kristeva and Anne M. Menke, in *Language: The Unknown* (Kristeva & Menke, 1989) suggest, although music has in common with other languages a system of differences (a *differential system*), it transmits only a *ludic*, that is, pleasurable, pattern, that only hints at meaning, and a broad emotive or affective message. There is no clear connection between musical elements, or combinations of these, and specific meanings. Thus, the sounds of music may be connected to the meaning which is intended by the composer or player of the music or which is perceived by the hearer of the music, but there is no direct and purposeful linkage between the two. Language, unlike music, involves semantics, which embodies complex patterns of connected meaning. And a painting, although it might be considered a "pictorial utterance" or a "text," usually lacks extended narrative. Though it may be rich in images and symbolic meaning, it is usually closer to a snapshot than an extended narrative, a moment in time or psychological space. We argue that it is only natural language shaped into narrative that fully pushes the limits of the human world and evokes the depths of the human experience.

What about film? In the world of the visual, cinema—and now video—appear to have taken on an extended sense of language and narrative. As Kristeva and Menke (1989) put it: "Since cinema is a system of differences that transmits a message, it can be christened a language" (p. 317). In addition, cinema incorporates language in spoken and narrative story forms. Here we enter the world of semiotics and visual literacy, a world which extends the possibilities of human expression. However, as Kristeva and Menke (1989) also note, there is nothing in the cinematographic system that can be compared to the phonological level of language; film is perhaps more like a form of hieroglyphic writing gaining its meaning through structure and procedure, through pattern recognition and signifying, but in our view it is at best *procedural literacy* and not primarily *verbal literacy*. It is, as Dutton (2009) explains, not the best way to open the imagination to its potential capacities for high-level cognition. Visual stimulation is an important human experience, no doubt, but it is not the main access route to nonverbal reasoning and to the full articulation of the sensuous body itself.

Dance as an art form, as Jack Miller explains, is designed to help students "deepen their perception of inner feelings by giving shape to them through physical activity" (Miller, 2007, p. 124). Dance, no doubt, allows the dancer an opportunity for expression through movement. Miller (2007) shares the example of children who may be exploring fear as a concept, offering a pathway for them through dance: "The students can first start with an unstructured visualization in which they let images of fear come into their minds. They then can articulate these images or draw them, and finally they can express their image of fear through movement" (Miller, 2007, p. 124). Like music, dance can provide a ludic pattern, a pleasurable path, but, for us, there is not a clear and identifiable connection between dance and emotional purpose and intention. In other words, a group may watch the same dance performance and not be able to come to consensus in terms of the meaning of the emotions expressed through the movement of the dancer's body. Language-based art, such as in poetry and novels, although open to different interpretations, provides much more precise, specific, and complex elements for conveying meaning than this. In the classroom where the literary narrative is at the center, students are able to connect to the emotional shape of the characters because written language has a distinct and discernible semantic structure that allows both in-depth and precise communication to other human beings.

ART AND HUMAN MYSTERY

How can we describe the depth and mystery found through linguistic narrative? In his essay, "The Storyteller," Walter Benjamin makes the point that the reader of a novel looks for human characters from whom he or she derives the "meaning of life"—a meaning that is revealed only in death (Benjamin, 1968). Therefore, the reader "must, no matter what, know in advance that he will share [the characters'] experience of death: if need be their figurative death—the end of the novel—but preferably their actual one" (Benjamin, 1968, p. 101). For Benjamin (1968), the remembrance of that mortal life, that stranger's fate, consumed by the flames of reading the story, "yields the warmth which we never draw from our own fate" (p. 101).

At its best, art always allows for this possibility; its beauty opens us to our mortality in relation to the plight of others, to pity and compassion, giving a glimpse of our finite condition—our vulnerable human identity. All great art provides visions of beauty, teaches and delights, moves the reader to self-reflection, and allows him or her to experience fear and hope, resonating with mystery and depth. But our argument continues to be that the richly textured literary narrative, drawing on the ambiguity and complexity of human language and experience, offers the best opportunity to effect such response and keep the self open to depth and self-reflection. Admittedly, these days the verbal and visual narrative of film seems also to keep such possibilities open, allowing a potential space for interpretation and reflection. As Alan Kirby puts it:

> To oversimplify, traditional cinema lay between two poles: at one extreme you could station a camera somewhere, record what happened in front of it, and relay the images via a projector on to a screen... . [A]t the other extreme, you could make films out of your imagination. These two poles can be defined as thought versus actuality, the mind against the world, invention versus fact. In practice all films blend the two. (Kirby, 2009, p. 183)

The blending consists of the subjectivity of the filmmaker and the objectively recorded world, moving images with human beings using language, which is both visual and auditory. Visual narrative in this context offers a gap or missing part—something that underlines our mortality. It offers both story and visual elements as well as human conversation—the intelligent energy of language exchange. One might argue that the filmmaker even takes the place of the narrator of a literary text. But no matter what its potential for symbolic representation, in our view, the visual narrative cannot offer the degree of complexity and ambiguity, depth and mystery, that verbal narrative evokes. The presence of the human voice in a literary narrator, we would argue, is always singular and personal in this regard; it calls to the invisible depth of the reader's self and evokes the meaning of the human mystery that Benjamin speaks about in a unique way. Visual images on the screen, unlike the voice of a literary narrator, limit the ability of the audience to exercise their full imaginative agency. Visual images, in other words, may create a dream space, but they also inhibit the dream space of the viewer.

Computer-generated images, including recent computer-generated images in films, create a more extreme version of this problem. Computer-generated images are created by digital devices; these images create a glossy look, a sense of polish and of a finished product. They lack the direct content of the

human mind, and, as a result, seem devoid of any idea or substance beyond
the surface sheen. They are images distant from their human origins,
spectacle without empathy or pity, as Kirby (2009) suggests, "beauty
without the trace of the mortal wound or the warmth of remembrance"
(p. 169). In an important sense, they are mere illusions, artificially clean and
perfect.

Video games can be placed in this category as well; they too suggest the
problem with computer-based, posthuman representation. Although many
media critics have argued that the interactive features of computer-
generated games provide users with an opportunity to participate actively
in the performance, often ludic and spectacular, these video games are often
brutal and continuously turn back upon themselves, creating, for the user, a
never-ending sense of being caught in an endless present moment, a
perpetual NOW. In addition, they lack pity or empathy for the characters,
and they always stress winning and losing as the primary value. As a result,
they short-circuit memory and the appreciation of the full human moment.

Literary narrative again emerges, in our estimation, as a center for the
21st century precisely because it embodies what the new media lacks. It
opens the human imagination to its full potential. It opens space for self-
reflection rather than narrowing that space. Neuroscientists, such as Semir
Zeki (e.g., Zeki, 2009) and V. S. Ramachandran (e.g., Ramachandran,
2004), are particularly sensitive to the way images can inhibit self-reflection,
realizing that visual stimulus and response times are nearly simultaneous
and automatic. Visual images leave little space for human choice; they often
refuse to allow humans to set their own pace.

In fact, 90 percent of a human being's body response to most stimuli
seems to be auto-controlled, and so unconscious and beyond awareness.
This suggests that, at best, only 10 percent of a person's attention and
potential response might still be considered free of such control. For us, it is
that 10 percent that teachers need to focus on. That 10 percent should be
considered as the internal workspace for learning, the space in students'
consciousness to develop creative acts, as the neuroscientists speculate. We
think of that space as the place of the "symbiotic imagination," as the poets
call it. To keep that space open and energized, it is not the visual system but
the linguistic system that needs to be activated.

Educators should not abandon the study of visual literacy and the other
arts in classrooms, especially given the intensified experience of the visual in
the 21st century, but it should not overshadow the central importance of
work on reading, writing, and discussion of linguistic narrative. Many
media critics disagree. Barbara Maria Stafford, for example, argues in "The

Remaining 10 Percent" for the importance of focusing on visual literacy (Stafford, 2008). As she puts it: "Creativity may well lie in escaping, not giving in to, our autopoetic machinery and focusing carefully on the world" (Stafford, 2008, p. 45). For Stafford, the focus on visual literacy can create a way of keeping humans open to the world and not being defeated by the autopoetic machinery—"the solipsistic cell phones, environment-screening Bose headsets, mobile microsized PDAs or removable MP3 players, and VCR gaming systems," (Stafford, 2008, p. 46)—that works to limit human imagination and choice. But, perhaps paradoxically, Stafford is also quick to sound the warning cry about the dangers of the digital age. As she says: "the proliferation of autopoetic devices and zombie media makes this escape from the autopoetic machinery increasingly difficult" (Stafford, 2008, p. 46). Unlike Stafford, we believe that rather than focusing further on visual literacy, a renewed focus on language and narrative remains the best hope for human creativity and free choice. If teachers are to help students find the workspace that allows them to reflect on themselves, their ideas and feelings, it makes sense to us that rather than focusing on the visual to escape the autopoetic machinery of the world, students should instead return to the literary texts and face-to-face conversation.

RESISTING COMMODIFICATION IN A WORLD OF IMAGE SATURATION

Our encouragement of a return to the literary includes a belief that the verbal text, the use of natural language, provides the best hope for resistance to the image-saturated culture that we currently live in. Visual systems, both internal and external, are clearly important dimensions of human existence and crucial to any pursuit of human identity. However, our argument is that the unyielding onslaught of the visual in today's world needs to be checked to prevent the commodification of the human, the loss of that mystery which has traditionally been considered the human. Luiz Costa-Lima explains it this way in *The Limits of Voice* (Costa-Lima, 1996):

> We cannot fully apprehend the impact of the world of images if we consider no more than the amount of time we spend exposed to its influence. Nor does the world of images have the relevance it seems to have now because the socialization of children takes place more through the electronic media than through reading. The point is that the socialization and legitimation of the forms of power necessarily take place through the medium of images. (p. 318)

For Costa-Lima, the popular media have become the equivalent of the public sphere in our time, a place in this time of hallucination controlled by corporate capital choking off any sense of human community or individual freedom. From a different perspective, Tony Schirato and Jen Webb, in *Understanding the Visual* (Schirato & Webb, 2004), make a similar point when they insist that the visual media, fueled and directed by corporate capitalism, reduce the human being to a desiring and consuming entity, seeking, but never finding, the satisfaction in the visible field, the shopping mall, the latest fashion, the glitter and spectacle of the speeding images circulating on thousands of screens (Schirato & Webb, 2004).

In such a world, the viewer connects best with the technology—the television, the computer screen, or the smaller devices which emulate and incorporate these technologies—and becomes isolated, convinced that the screen and the image are attentive only to him or her. In this kind of endless cycle of ego-fueling image and image-fueling ego, the only relief comes from mindless entertainment, the hallucination of happiness, the illusion of the images themselves. As Neil Postman warned a quarter century ago:

> [T]he television commercial has oriented business away from making products of value and towards making consumers feel valuable, which means that the business of business has now become pseudo-therapy. The consumer is a patient assured by psycho-dramas. (Postman, 1985, p. 128).

Even the classroom in this context becomes an entertainment center; for us, this kind of "infotainment" learning environment is unacceptable.

Twenty-five years later in a global economy, Postman would seem to be out of date, although his message still resonates for us. The visual media regime makes viewers into their symptoms and then markets the illusion of a cure. Students begin to believe they are customers, and no customer is ever wrong. Consistent with a business model, teachers are supposed to provide the product to satisfy the needs of these consumers of education, and the education system itself begins to privilege administrators over teachers, encouraging total quality management and standardization to trump creativity and serious critical thinking. Neither to standardize their education nor to saturate students' consciousness further through screens and images will cure what ails them. In fact, the domination of the visual regime argues for the necessity of shifting perspective, of focusing and of slowing down. Without realizing it, students are hungry for something other than what the media are feeding them, such as for the contemplation of deep reading, the sense of community gained by discussing that reading face-to-face around the table. We envision each student and teacher in this face-to-face context seeing the human before them, acknowledging and appreciating the relationship between the self and the other. We celebrate treating each other not as commodities or instruments, but as human beings—as ends not means to something else. When everything you can see in the world is for sale, it is time to make the classroom into a place where that kind of seeing is recognized for what it is. Once that kind of recognition of error occurs, then teachers can return to the important work, the quest to know the human self.

The best education remains free from commodification of all kinds. It is not a means to an end, but an end in itself. The reading and discussion of literary narrative offer just such an experience. That is, in a sense, its truth. As James Wood reminds us in *How Fiction Works* (Wood, 2008) when he discusses the experience of reading what he calls *truthful texts*: "This, we say to ourselves, is what it would feel like to be outcast from one's family, like an insect (Kafka), or a young madman (Hamsun) or an aged parent kept in a bin and fed pap (Beckett)" (pp. 238–239). Literature is not an illusion, but the truth. This is an old idea, as Wood (2008) indicates, when he quotes Dr. Samuel Johnson (from his "Preface to Shakespeare"): "Imitations produce pain or pleasure, not because they are mistaken for realities, but because they bring realities to mind" (p. 239). That "truth," evoked by the human voice, is personal and singular; it cannot be mistaken for the illusions created by the screen culture. Such "truth" does not fragment us or isolate us; instead, it brings us together.

USING LANGUAGE FOR METACOGNITIVE AWARENESS: WAYS TO DEEPEN LEARNING

To put the matter in different terms: reading and writing contribute to enhancing skills of cooperation (vs. zero-sum games of winning and losing). They stimulate an appreciation for the personal and so give credence to the universal capacity of the human heart. "It is only when an idea or thought is endowed with a voice and expressed as emanating from a personal position in relation to others that dialogical relations emerge" (Hermans & Kempen, 1993, p. 212). Personal meanings must be embodied, and human language, given voice through speech and writing, is one of the primary ways to embody that meaning and make sense of the world for ourselves and others. Human language moves us beyond mere surface perception and immediate response and is an important dimension in the process of evolution separating us from the other species. Part of the value of a 21st century education must include our drive not to lose the depth of our evolutionary brain by compromising our gains in a world of screens and distracting images that cut us off from our emotional core and deepest cognitive resources.

To highlight the importance of the personal and the verbal within the intensified visual world, we acknowledge that it is useful to consider pedagogical activity within the classroom that combines literary narrative with other media. Granted, not everyone learns in the same manner. Teachers must constantly look for media that enhance student learning in a range of ways. In fact, a crucial role of a teacher is to broaden students' notions of how people learn, and, we suggest, one important way of doing that is by creating activities in the learning environment which combine literary narrative with other media. Such activity can promote what is often called *metacognition*, which refers to thinking about one's thinking or learning process. When a student understands how he or she learns best, metacognitive abilities expand, and this reflection on the way one thinks and learns (both successfully and unsuccessfully) becomes a kind of enduring learning which can be transferred to unlimited other contexts. Tomlinson (2001) elaborates on the concept of metacognition in the classroom from the teacher's perspective: "Your 'metacognition,' or thinking aloud about your thinking helps students understand your expectations. It also helps them develop ownership in their classroom" (Tomlinson, 2001, p. 38). For a teacher, metacognition means making transparent to one's students why certain activities are conducted, what the learning goals of the activities are, and then making these dimensions clear to the students. For students, developing metacognition means learning how to do self-monitoring. Using reflective or contemplative writing assignments (see Chapters Four and Seven) can help students accurately gauge what they understand and what they still have to learn. Inherent in metacognition is a deepened level of awareness; we see promoting this awareness as a path towards self-knowledge. The desired learning outcome for metacognitive activities in the classroom is to provide students with a clearer view of themselves as self-reflective learners. In practice, for both teachers and students, metacognition implies a "double vision," being active in both constructing and monitoring one's own learning. This active engagement and awareness of one's progress as a learner always occurs reflectively through reading, writing, and discussion. When teachers promote metacognition for themselves and in their students, learning can be improved, deepened, and even transformed.

CONNECTING LITERATURE AND FILM IN THE CLASSROOM

As we have indicated, we believe that the visual system should be considered as part of classroom activities. We want to conclude this chapter with two examples of how this can be done. When teachers connect literature and film, for example, they might ask students to view, analyze, and critique the "visual language" of a filmmaker's version of a piece of literature, allowing for contrast and comparisons of verbal and visual media. Such a contrast between the media can enhance learning. Although we do not believe that a great book can be made into a better film (i.e., so that people will say the film is "deeper" than the original book), no doubt the comparison of a novel and a film can often provide expansive dialogue within the classroom. Reading Ken Kesey's *One Flew Over the Cuckoo's Nest* (Kesey, 1962), and then viewing the film version (Zaentz & Forman, 1975), for example, can offer a valuable learning experience and expand appreciation of the importance of literary narrative as well. In the novel, the voice of Chief Bromden, the Native American narrator, is clearly central to the story. The story itself is expressed through the consciousness of the Chief, emphasizing the troubled roots of American identity and providing endless depth to the struggle between the 1960s counterculture (represented by the character McMurphy) and the so-called Established Order (represented by Big Nurse). By contrast, the blockbuster film version of the novel marginalizes the Chief, all but silencing his significant voice by limiting the story to a stereotypical clash between McMurphy and Big Nurse, individual freedom against the rigid mainstream culture. To discuss this kind of contrast is not only to enhance the significance of literature, but also to sharpen the ability to make contrasts and comparisons. Most importantly, it is an intriguing way to stimulate metacognitive activity within the learning environment.

This is not to argue that visual literacy is unimportant. It is crucial to the 21st century; but it should be taught in the context of the central significance of expanding verbal literacy. As another example, we can use Russell Banks' novel, *The Sweet Hereafter* (Banks, 1991), and its "translation" into a film version by Canadian film director, Atom Egoyan (Egoyan, Hamori, Frieberg, Webb, & Lantos, 1998). Banks' story tells of a school bus accident in a small town and how this town is affected by the deaths of its many children. The story is told through four different narrators: the bus driver who survives the crash, a father whose two children died in the accident, a lawyer who represents parents suing for damages, and a young girl who survives the bus accident but becomes a paraplegic. Both the novel and the film present interesting complexities worthy of discussion. In the film version, for example, the director uses literary techniques to help "deepen" the visual representation. As Margarete Landwehr points out, Egoyan chooses to use Robert Browning's poem, "The Pied Piper of Hamlin," to represent the deaths metaphorically: "Reciting of 'The Pied Piper' replaces the elided images of the accident with an alternative (trauma) narrative that depicts death metaphorically" (Landwehr, 2008, p. 34). Landwehr (2008) goes on to develop the idea of how a metaphor "serves as one means with which a victim can confront the past, but also maintain a necessary distance from the trauma in order to transcend it" (p. 21). When translating a novel into a visual medium such as film, there needs to be some way of depicting the deeper meaning contained in the written story. Film provides a visual depiction of the story, but the visual system is inevitably limited. In the reading of a novel, the readers must help create the pictures themselves. If a filmmaker attempts to replicate the whole of a novel, the meaning of the work usually becomes blurred, hard to follow, and hard to decode. In a discussion between Banks and Egoyan (as a special feature of *The Sweet Hereafter* DVD), Banks remarks on how clever it was for Egoyan to have inserted the poem ("The Pied Piper") into the filmic version.

Overall, Banks seems pleased with Egoyan's "translation" of the novel into a cinematic equivalent of his story. The film utilizes the four narrators in the story, but we would argue that the film does not provide the imagined depths of the working of their minds, as the novel does.

A CLASSROOM EXPERIMENT WITH LITERATURE AND FILM

We conducted a classroom discussion of another Russell Banks' novel, *Affliction* (Banks, 1989), as a literacy component of a preservice teacher education course. The group consisted of college students who were paired with high school students from a local urban alternative high school. This was a part of the Changing Lives Through Literature (CLTL) program that we integrated into two different urban alternative high schools in Massachusetts. Before the class session, both college students and high school students had read the selected CLTL excerpt from Banks' novel. Before the discussion began, the group was shown a portion of the film version of *Affliction* (Reisman & Schrader, 1997), which was connected to the excerpt they had read. After the discussion ended, students were asked to compare and contrast the literary version to the same scene in the film version and asked which version (literature or film) they considered more valuable and why. The excerpt that they read was focused on when the main character Wade pulls his own tooth out with a pair of pliers.

Students responded to the prompt in different ways. One student's response to the prompt for comparing and contrasting the literary version to the film version included this reflection:

> I thought the video portrayed the emotions of the literature very well, but I still do not think that it entirely captured all of it. In the written version, I felt more of an intensity involved with Wade's violent behavior and I felt as though the description of the way he looked and what he said had a more complete feeling to it. I did think that the filmic version showed the scene very well, but I think there should have been more emphasis on Wade's crazed state of mind.... In the end though, the literature version of *Affliction* had more of an emotional affect on me than the filmic one. I think totally capturing the serious crazed state of Wade as a little more descriptive in the text and I enjoyed that aspect of it better than the film.

Although this student appreciated the created visual imagery provided by the film, she felt that the power of the story, the narrative voice, spawned more powerful imagery in her imagination than the imagery she saw on the screen.

Another student went into more depth and gave particular examples from Banks' text:

> What happens to you when you reach your breaking point? How do you let flow all your bottled-up emotions? In Chapter 20 of Russell Banks' novel *Affliction*, Wade progressively becomes angrier and angrier. His incessantly aching tooth combined with his other problems push him so far that he becomes quite disoriented. After shouting at his father, Wade heads to the woodshed where he is blinded by the darkness. This concept of darkness is significant to this passage. Wade is physically swallowed by darkness, obscuring his thought process. Then the darkness "softens to a gray haze," making it seem like his decision to take a pair of pliers from the shed was seen with little clarity. The haze that clouded his thinking is written so vividly that we, as readers, are stuck in the fog with Wade. We know how awful this tooth pain has been; Banks compels us to come as close to feeling such hurt as possible. We, too, want to rip out that rotten tooth and be one step closer to escaping the chaos, escaping the darkness.... While reading, we can sense that precise focus. Wade pulls "harder, steadily" at his tooth. The use of "steadily" illustrates the concentration. Through these descriptions, Banks allows us to momentarily step back as well, focusing with Wade as he pulls out his aching molar. Of course, a movie cannot make you feel such emotions the way a book can. A movie can certainly show the sensations and emotions, but it is never the same as what the book does. The movie shows Wade's frustration, but we may not be able to actually feel that irritation and disturbance, like we can while reading.... The film

version of this specific scene only slightly allows us to grasp the emotions, and does not at all let us feel them.

This student highlights how the intensity of the actual literary narrative comes through the words and images and how they affect the reader more deeply than the "surface" experience with the film version. This student's comments demonstrate what is possible in the classroom, what thinking and writing can accomplish when students are deeply engaged.

No doubt visual literacy, especially in the case of extending a literary narrative through an equivalent filmic "translation," can broaden literacy for viewers and readers in compelling and engaging ways. In fact, new meanings might be found in the film version, and these new meanings can scaffold new understandings or empathic visions of the story, expanding classroom discussion and a sense of communal learning. Film can have a broadening effect on the construction of identity and can provide new pathways for understanding the interplay between and among aesthetics, narrative, and genre. However, for the many reasons we have been discussing, we believe literary narrative can never wholly be replaced by any other medium, including film.

CONCLUDING THOUGHTS ON PRIVILEGING LANGUAGE OVER THE ARTS

As we have argued in this chapter and throughout this book, literary language should be at the center of teaching and learning in the classroom. Interacting with the narrative text, in terms of making sense and meaning of the text and of the self, is an important way to develop our capacities and abilities as human beings. We worry about the oversaturation of the visual in our modern society. As a result of this oversaturation, literary language often gets pushed to the margins. As we have continually argued, literary language enlarges our capacity to acknowledge and fathom the depth of human identity. It opens the individual self to the world. At its best, learning occurs when people actively engage with the complex semantic and sensuous qualities of language.

Arts such as dance, music, and film may enhance our capacity to be self-reflective and create meaning, but nothing can replace the literary text in terms of achieving these purposes. As humans continue to navigate the digital age with all of its gadgets and distractions, we believe that it is crucial to re-emphasize the power of narrative stories for keeping us fully human.

The power of stories and literary language underpin the development of thought in shaping who we are and who we will become. Even when we break the spell of our experience of a good film and begin to explore its meaning and implications, it is language that we turn to for further discovery. Being human is dependent on our use of language to shape our ideas and the ideas of others. The classroom, with its potentialities for community interchange, is the right place for deep reading, deep writing, and face-to-face discussion with others. Make no mistake about that.

CHAPTER SIX

THE CHALLENGE OF NEW TECHNOLOGIES

In the previous chapter, we explored the arts in relation to literature, making the point that like literature, the arts are cultural inventions that appeal to the human sensibility and often contribute to the expansion of human consciousness. Like literature, the arts should be central to classroom activity. At the same time, we maintained our insistence that language and narrative should remain central to education in the 21st century. In this chapter, we want to discuss more fully the so-called "new technologies." When Marshal McLuhan claimed that the medium was the message (McLuhan, 1964), he was obviously unaware of the advances that would be made in recent brain research, but his idea that it was not so much the content but the medium that shapes the way human beings perceive the world seems particularly relevant when we consider these "new technologies" in the context of what has been discovered about how the brain works. Each new cultural invention, McLuhan knew, was an extension of part of the human self—the radio an extension of the ear, television an extension of the eye—and each extension not only intensified human awareness, but also numbed the senses involved. That was the trade-off that McLuhan wanted to point out.

Each "new technology" had its advantages and disadvantages. McLuhan only glimpsed what has now become obvious: the dramatic change from a "book culture" to a "screen culture" which has occurred within the last 15 years or so through the blinding speed and overwhelming power of digital technology in its relentless march to engulf the entire human sensorium. It is that radical shift in human experience, especially how it has affected reading and writing, that we want to explore more fully in this chapter. Maryanne Wolf succinctly describes the relevant phenomenon:

> The next few decades will witness transformations in our ability to communicate, as we recruit new connections in the brain that will propel our intellectual development in new

and different ways. Knowing what reading demands of our brain and knowing how it contributes to our capacity to think, to feel, to infer, and to understand other human beings is especially important today as we make the transition from a reading brain to an increasingly digital one. (Wolf, 2007, p. 4)

By the "digital brain," Wolf (2007) means the human brain increasingly interacting with the new electronic technologies. Unlike the "reading brain" as it is shaped by its interaction with printed texts in the era of the book, the "digital brain" is shaped by its interaction with digital gadgets in the era of the screen.

On the positive side, the new digital technologies often seem to expand human ability, serving as extensions of human capacity and identity. On the negative side is the ever-present threat that these new technologies will actually reduce or hinder human capability as the brain adapts to these new technologies. Reading and writing are complicated human activities, developed over many centuries, which continue to change as the new technologies change. To what extent, do these new technologies positively or negatively impact our reading and writing capabilities, and the capabilities underlying and supporting them?

Critics such as Dennis Baron, in *A Better Pencil* (Baron, 2009), like to point out that the fear of new technologies has a long history. Plato, for example, was concerned that reading and writing would hinder memory and negatively affect human intelligence, so he urged that writers be banned from his utopian Republic, where orators would have a prominent place. In fact, as Baron (2009) points out, evidence suggests that people who can read and write are able to hold in memory more information than people who cannot read and write and that reading can calm the mind, allowing for thoughtful self-reflection. Gutenberg's printing press was also considered a threat to direct human interaction and the sense of community. But, as we know, the printing press eventually offered people access to reading matter that would help usher into the culture a significant new way of promoting and thinking about democratic interchange and citizenship. Even the inventions of the pencil and the typewriter, Baron (2009) notes, were initially causes for alarm.

Granted, from one angle, this is an old question: does the abundance of new digital devices (cell phones, iPods, video games, ATM touch screens, GPS guides, and the like) and the various activities related to these devices (e-mail, Instant Messaging, iTunes, Facebook pages, MySpace posts, rapid clicking, Google searches, Twittering, and so on) actually expand or contract human consciousness? We can certainly agree with Baron (2009) when he says:

Whether we embrace them or fear them, the technologies that we use to compose, disseminate, and archive our words—the machinery that ranges from pencils to pixels, from clay tablets to optical disks—not only make reading and writing possible, they have also affected our reading and writing processes. (p. 14)

The effect of the new technologies on reading and writing is not simply a matter of enabling or enhancing those capacities. In our view, there is a difference between the technologies that find a comfortable niche in the human world and those that put a strain on that world, for example, by overwhelming humans with their power and speed. Some would argue that these new digital devices initiate a new world order, one of dramatic cultural and technological change. These digital devices are reshaping the way humans think about their relationship to the world and the way they think about themselves. The magnitude and speed of the digital takeover of our world require a careful assessment of both its positive and negative effects.

For us, this kind of assessment is particularly important when considering the future of education and the growing consensus based on brain research indicating that we are moving from the reading brain to the digital brain and that all knowledge is, in an important sense, embodied knowledge. As we have been arguing, teaching and learning are always situated in a social frame—that is, in the local and specific practices of everyday experiences. The body, mind, and environment work together, and the advancement of knowledge, as human beings have come to understand it over the last five centuries, is due in no small part to the literary mind. As Nicholas Carr has reminded us (repeated here from Chapter Four):

> For the last five centuries, ever since Gutenberg's printing press made book reading a popular pursuit, the linear, literary mind has been at the center of art, science, and society. As supple as it is subtle, it's been the imaginative mind of the Renaissance, the rational mind of the Enlightenment, the inventive mind of the Industrial Revolution, even the subversive mind of Modernism. It may soon be yesterday's mind. (Carr, 2010, p. 10)

What then is *today's mind*, the kind of mind that the new technology is creating? And what does this new technology mean for reading and writing in the 21st century classroom? What is it about reading and writing as we have known it that is worth preserving? And what is the difference between reading from a book and reading on a screen?

WELCOME TO THE DIGITAL AGE

According to Will Richardson, Tim Berners-Lee, the originator of the Internet, had a vision of making a space or a "medium" where people could meet up to read and write (Richardson, 2008, p. 2). As Berners-Lee developed that vision, other new technologies emerged, changing people and the way things work and in the process also changing the use of the Internet. The rapid development of new technologies, in other words, even outstripped Berners-Lee's grand technological vision. For Richardson (2008), the development of the Internet was liberating: "We are no longer limited to being independent readers or consumers of information" (Richardson, 2008, p. 2). For Richardson (2008), every new technology is a new medium for learning. Perhaps so, but Samuel Greengard, who is a frequent writer about business and technology, is worried (and so are we). As Greengard (2009) warns:

> Computer technology complements—and often enhances—the human mind … . [T]here's increasing concern that the same technology is changing the way we approach complex problems and conundrums, and making it more difficult to really *think*. (p. 18)

Like us, Greengard does not vilify new technologies, but he insists that we need to "take a closer look at technology and understand the subtleties of how it affects thinking and analysis" (p. 19). Greengard (2009) joins many others in this regard (e.g., Birkerts, 1994; Carr, 2010; Wolf, 2007).

The digital revolution, at times, seems to threaten to explode the old world order of the book, a technology that, like the reading classroom and like human beings themselves, is bounded and bounding, finite yet seemingly infinite, in its possibilities. The technologies that are creating the digital brain seem to do away with boundaries, creating a sense of limitless time and space. They seem everywhere and nowhere, creating a sense of a perpetual present, a moment without a past or a future. At the same time, these technologies threaten to prune away the sense of "deep thinking" that the book has created, as unused neural circuits lose the habit of "deep reading."

If we are correct in our argument throughout this book, language is a way into the interior of the self, as well as a way out to the community that surrounds the self. Engaging with language and stories through books preserves a fundamental connection to the past, through memory which language embodies, and to the future, through the stirring of desire and imagination which language and stories help to create. Such access to language intensifies the location of the self in the world and deepens the sense of time. Through time and the story unfolding, books offer continuity and duration. Through their bounded existence in space, books offer a sense of place, identity, and home. In both their temporal and spatial nature, books help to *situate* people within the world. As the poets say, they help human beings create a habitation and a name.

Digital technology changes all of this—both the human sense of time and of space. It elevates procedural literacy rather than verbal literacy, fostering the celebration of speed and boundless exhilaration rather than duration and deep thinking. Intelligence itself is redefined as the acquisition of procedural skills enabling the use of new electronic devices: it becomes a matter of how fast the user can acquire information and respond to the electronic screen in front of him or her. Both time and space undergo radical reconfiguration, collapsing into an endless NOW, a perpetual present without boundaries or direction.

SPEED VS. MEMORY

Paul Virilio explores this radical change (Virilio, 2010), which he refers to as "emotional fusion" or "meltdown." In his view, the boundaries of the world are collapsing, intelligent energy has given way to emotional chaos, and the force of imagination has lost its shaping power:

> The whole world stage is turned upside down as a result, to the point where "representations" gradually lose their pertinence ... . What is promoted instead is "presentation," an untimely, out-of-place presentation that suppresses the depth of time for shared reflexion every bit as much as the depth of field of action and its displacement. (Virilio, 2010, p. 6)

In such a world, human beings outsource their memory (to the Internet), and they begin to manipulate those outsourced images. Memory becomes hallucination; procedure trumps "deep thinking"; self-reflection gives way to rapid performance; and the depth of human identity is flattened out. In such a world, human beings begin to believe that the distance of "social networking" brings us closer, into a global village. But, as Virilio (2010) aptly puts it: "The proximity of the far away greatly favors exteriority to the detriment of all conscious interiority" (p. 45). The world is thus turned upside down. In the book culture, "in deep is far out," implying that the farther humans journey into the interior self, the more they learn about the connections to the world that surrounds them. In the screen culture, out far is not in deep: rather, the farther humans journey from the depth of themselves to some faraway place, the more fragmented and disconnected they become.

For Virilio, what is lost in such an exchange is not balanced by the possible gains. Human beings lose the immediate sense of life unfolding, the narrative and historical sense of self rooted in the temporal, spatial, and tactile experience of mortal life. Instead, interfacing with the screen, the human being craves instant exposure; the private becomes public; the secrets of organic and vital life, the challenge of slow discovery, give way to the fight to win instant gratification. Losing the depth of perspective, individuals lose themselves in the rapid information fragmented on the screen. In the words of Virilio (2010), "When you manipulate things, you give up living in them" (p. 78). For Virilio, the intersubjective social body has become a Hobbesian Leviathan.

Alan Kirby, writing about how the new technologies are reconfiguring our culture (Kirby, 2009), puts the matter in slightly different terms, but he too is clearly sounding a loud warning. For Kirby (2009), the new technology ushers in what he calls "the death of competence" (p. 241), creating an environment in which self-reflection and knowledge give way to technical skill. In such an environment, people develop a blatant contempt for education, believing that knowledge and wisdom are pointless (if not grand illusions). Kirby argues that these new technologies (especially computers, the Internet, and video games):

> ... enable individuals to engage with "worlds" or reality systems without socially interacting; this systematic desocialization is subsequently extended to the "real world" in the form of diminished capacity to relate to or to "read" other people, a preference for solitude and a loss of empathy; such technologies also do little to stimulate language acquisition. (p. 230)

For us, there is little doubt that the digital culture tends to undervalue human beings, as Kirby seems to suggest. How could it be otherwise, when an increasing amount of time is spent interfacing with an electronic screen rather than with the human face (as Levinas, 1985, might put it). In fact, we might ask how the human being can engage in "the deep reading" of other human beings—the kind of activity that allows for empathy and arouses the depth of the imagination—when, at best, that person is distant and detached from immediate human expression. In this refashioned world, the screen absorbs all previous technology into itself, eliminating all sense of past knowledge. The screen does not become a book; the book itself is totally absorbed into the screen.

THE DIGITAL DIVIDE

We are already living in an age when those born after 1980, the *digital natives* (a term attributed to Marc Presque by Richardson, 2008, p. 6) seem to see the environment and behave in the world in a very different manner than those born before 1980, the *digital immigrants* who were not exposed to digital devices at an early age—those, in other words, who were often brought up in a book culture rather than a screen culture. The generation gap here is profound and also troubling for many.

The digital natives might argue that we digital immigrants are "cultural dinosaurs" unnecessarily worried, like Socrates, about the positive changes taking place in the culture as a result of the new technology. For the digital natives, speed in the digital age is a positive value; it makes people productive and efficient, a sign of success. Multitasking is also a positive value. The digital natives can read on one screen, write e-mail on another, listen to their iPod, and check their Facebook pages—all at the same time. The digital natives have expanded these new human skills and have the ability to do all this with ease.

We see this new behavior as problematic, however. Ease and comfort may always have been part of the suburban American dream. But the "user-friendly" world of the digital age suggests a deadly extension of the problems that social critics have recognized in that version of the dream, the lurking nightmare just beneath the surface of the well-cropped lawns of such suburban comfort. Where is the challenge and depth in such a "user-friendly" world? Where is the embrace of "the stranger" in the gated community? And where is the recognition of human vulnerability, the unpredictable and mysterious contingencies of mortal life? In such an environment, the digital natives seem to put their hope not in people but in gadgets (Lanier, 2010, p. 75), in speed rather than in contemplation, in the collapse of boundaries, rather than the bounding space of mortal identity.

MULTITASKING VS. FULL ATTENTION

The celebrated skill of multitasking is a good example of the problem, as we see it. Multitasking does not appear to accomplish what its advocates claim. Digital technology seems to fool us in this regard, claiming that it captures attention and makes people more efficient as well as smarter and able to accomplish several tasks simultaneously. Evidence suggests otherwise; the screen captures attention in order to distract people. Talking about the Google search engine, for example, Nicholas Carr makes the point this way:

> Every click we make on the Web marks a break in our concentration, a bottom-up disruption of our attention—and it's in Google's economic interest to make sure we click

as often as possible. The last thing the company wants is to encourage leisurely reading
or slow, concentrated thought. Google is, quite literally, in the business of distraction.
(Carr, 2010, p. 157)

Through such a bottom-up process, human beings speed along without time
to activate long-term memory, a top-down process. Human beings, unable
to think deeply or exercise their imaginations, become part of the
fragmented flow of the screen itself. They, too, become part of the NOW,
absorbed into the screen in front of them.

Patricia Greenfield observes that the digital culture causes divided
attention, and "divided attention is the precursor and prerequisite for
multitasking, defined as carrying out more than one task simultaneously"
(Greenfield, 2009, p. 54). For some, this behavior does have its positive
value. Linda Stone, for example, describing the way the digital natives often
use their energy, calls this behavior "continuous partial attention" (Stone,
2010). But for Stone (2010), there is a difference between multitasking and
continuous partial attention. Multitasking, Stone (2010) argues, happens
when "we are motivated by a desire to be more productive and more
efficient. We're often doing things that are automatic, that require very little
cognitive processing" (p. 1). Yet she too agrees that focus and attention is
the larger issue; the things we accomplish when multitasking oftentimes do
not require deep thought or insight. Fair enough, but the larger issue is the
issue of attention itself, and multitasking seems to short-circuit that
possibility. As Stone (2010) says:

Attention is the most powerful tool of the human spirit. We can enhance or augment our
attention with practices like meditation and exercise, diffuse it with technologies like
e-mail and Blackberries, or alter it with pharmaceuticals. In the end, though, we are fully
responsible for how we choose to use this extraordinary tool. (p. 1)

Multitasking and speed rarely lead to quality or productivity, but rather, at
times, to addiction, to sensation for its own sake, or to spectacle at the cost
of careful thinking. In our view, students do not need to learn how to speed
up, but how to slow down.

This is the new world order as we see it. The seductive power of digital
technology makes people feel that everything is just a click away, and so
feeds into the need for instant gratification—like fast food and fast
entertainment, like images wildly flickering across the electronic screen.
People receive information anytime, anywhere, but without any sense of
context or origins. Moving rapidly from one screen to the next, from one bit
of information to another, people are not fully attentive or fully engaged;

they rush to the next "now" moment. Fragmented and distributed, they are unable to be self-reflective or coherent in any obvious sense of the word.

Granted the new digital technology can allow humans to become ubiquitous in ways that have not been possible before: a person can interact via e-mail or Facebook with a friend, acquaintance, or a complete stranger, all in no time. But that sense of being everywhere might very well be a sense of being nowhere. When the user of the Internet joins a social networking site, for example, that user is no doubt responding to the very human desire to belong, to be part of something; but what is that connectivity other than the joining of a social or giant network, becoming just one more node in the pattern of that network?

THE BOOK VS. THE SCREEN

Clearly technology cannot satisfy all human desires and needs, and it can create problems that might be impossible to overcome. Technologies are extensions of ourselves, and both books and digital gadgets are technologies that can change us. But books have boundaries and a history just as a life has physical limits (birth and death, for example) and so does a story, a biography; and books privilege language and story, narrative and the human voice. In contrast, digital devices privilege algorithms, formulas, and binary bits over language and story, and they operate with the liquid flow of electrical currents and speed. Language and story are not technologies; they are alive, working within the body, the mind, and the environment; they have their own cultural and biological existence. When human beings engage with language and story, they engage with something alive; they experience the personal voice of the author, the biological and cultural sense of the language and the story, the boundless possibilities contained within the book itself. Language is part of our biology as well as our culture. Language can give the human being direction and purpose; it can help formulate goals. Language not only moves us, but, in so far as it is alive, it *is* movement. In a world increasingly aware of the dynamic relationship between body, mind, and environment, such knowledge demands that people think seriously about what language and story mean for the future of education and the meaning and purpose of "knowing thyself." Without language and story, the singular nature of human identity is lost.

It is ironic that Jaron Lanier, the father of virtual reality technology, raises this very issue, in asking, "What is a human being?" (Lanier, 2010, p. 5). Putting readers on guard against the new technology, his answer is telling: "Being a person is not a pat formula, but a quest, a mystery, a leap of faith" (Lanier, 2010, p. 5). As Lanier makes clear, Facebook, online dating services, YouTube, and all sorts of other social networks flatten people out, turning life into a database. As Lanier (2010) suggests, information on a social network is inevitably programmed, and so limited—a reduction in life. For the father of virtual reality, there is no mystery or "awe" in a digital image, no originality, no surprise: "A digital image captures a certain limited measurement of reality within a standardized system that removes any of the original source's unique qualities" (Lanier, 2010, p. 134). Measurement does not enrich the quality of the human experience. Teaching to the test doesn't either.

In the new scheme of the digital age, both friendship and education are at stake. Lanier (2010) puts it this way:

> Information systems need to have information in order to run, but information underrepresents reality ... . Under the No Child Left Behind Act of 2002, for example, U.S. teachers are forced to choose between teaching general knowledge and teaching to the test ... . What computerized analysis of all the country's school tests has done to education is exactly what Facebook has done to friendships. In both cases, life is turned into a database. (p. 69)

Lanier's commentary brings into question the reasoning and research behind the currently promoted modes of teaching and learning, which only serve to highlight the memorization of facts and information. Following Lanier's reasoning, we might also realize why the early studies of the television show *Sesame Street* revealed that preschoolers were not learning much about reading, despite the boasts from educational television. Jane Healy, in her book, *Endangered Minds* (Healy, 1990), made this point clear: "Studies showing how young children should be taught to read indicate that Sesame Street is going about the job the wrong way" (p. 222). Despite the claims of educational breakthrough, there was apparently little learning taking place on *Sesame Street*—partly because the images were moving too fast across the screen, creating sensation rather than engagement with a deeply felt human experience, and partly because there was no time for contemplation and the exercise of the imagination.

Healy (1990) worries that parents may be "fooled" about their children's reading skills:

> Tests which show that young children's scores are rising may simply be focusing on the "lower level" skills of word reading while neglecting the real heart of the matter: How well do they understand what they have read? Can they reason—and talk, and write—about it? (p. 26)

Reading without understanding is worthless; high reading scores are meaningless unless there is data showing a depth of understanding from reading, and that depth of understanding can only come from "active reading," alias "deep reading," the unmeasureable and unseen possibilities of engagement with language that leads to the reader's meaning-making. Such meaning-making is the way human beings know themselves in the world. It is the way they name themselves, create their identity, and understand their relationship with the environment around them. Without this ability to engage deeply with language, human beings are in danger of losing their ability to know themselves.

Recent studies seem to indicate similar problems with teaching through the screen. As previously mentioned, Patricia Kuhl's work (e.g., Kuhl, 2009) suggests that English-speaking babies between eight and ten months old have little trouble learning the basics of Mandarin Chinese when they are placed in a relationship with an adult human speaker, but they cannot learn Mandarin at all when placed before a screen displaying a similar human speaker. We believe that these studies might also indicate the importance in general of learning in a richly human environment. As Wolf and Barzillai (2009) found in another study, early reading done online "tends to require certain cognitive skills, such as multitasking, and habituates the learner to immediate information gathering and quick attention shifts, rather than deep reflection and original thought" (p. 118). Increasingly, education becomes training for the digital age much as education, for too long, was training for work in the industrial sector. Procedural literacy begins to trump verbal literacy in such a context.

NATURE VS. DIGITAL BITS

We believe that the rhythm of human life and the human heart is closer to the rhythm of nature than it is to the rhythm of the flow of electricity and digital bits on an electronic screen. The difference could be described as the difference between contemplation and calculation. Fortunately, experiencing nature and other natural surroundings cannot be completely replaced by new technologies—at least not yet. Even if a person watches a breathtaking video of a natural environment on a screen, the experience seems distant and mediated. Instead of feeling the cold air on one's face on a winter walk and hearing the crunching of leaves under one's hiking boots, the viewer undergoes what can only be felt as an artificial experience, a mediated moment—an experience of virtual reality perhaps, but rather different from the natural and direct experience of nature. The viewer looking at a screen becomes the algorithm, the calculation, in that the screen experience is always established by the original computational program no matter how many iterations it has gone through. There is a blind spot in the screen experience that refuses to allow the integration of all the human senses in this kind of experience; something incalculable and mysterious is missing.

Likewise, the experience of reading—a person sitting quietly with a book—is an experience that cannot easily be replaced by new technologies. We know people who own a Kindle (a reading screen that can be purchased through *amazon.com*), and so read books by downloading them onto the Kindle device. One woman, reflecting many others, explains that she feels something is "missing" by not holding an actual book in her hands. She has adjusted to a Kindle, but still claims that when she loses her place in the Kindle, it is almost impossible to find it again. Perhaps digital natives can adjust more quickly, but the difference in the experience is worth noting. To hold a printed book in your hands, to feel the pages as you turn them, structures a strikingly different biological experience than holding the Kindle and reading an e-book. The touch and feel of a printed book, the smell of the pages, the tactile nature of the experience, the distant voice emanating from the printed text (rather than the digital font)—all activate the senses in a special way; such experience often reminds the reader of childhood, reading with parents, being comforted at bedtime, and so on. It arouses memories that cannot be duplicated by the cold digital screen. Perhaps the experience is somewhat parallel to the example of hiking through nature. Feeling the cold air on one's face when walking in winter might be similar to feeling the paper in your hands as you turn the pages of a book. The leaves of nature become the leaves of the book, as Walt Whitman long ago suggested (Whitman, 2005). We can only wonder what Whitman would conclude about the new marketing strategies of e-book publishers now—strategies that include adding more and more images and other visual components such as color fonts and advertisements for so-called "readers" to access on their new electronic gadget.

THE HUMAN BODY: ROUND OR FLAT?

As we have continually insisted, it is the flattening out of human identity—the sense that the human self is, for example, simply a node in a network, or a flat screen—that, we believe, literary narrative appropriately counters.

Since the beginning of the industrial age, the relationship between the human body and mind and the increasingly machine-like technical environment has created debate and anxiety about the meaning of personhood, or *the human self*. But with the advent of the digital age, those anxieties have reached a new level of intensity. As intrinsic value has yielded to technical rationality, enchantment and imagination to instrumental thinking, print culture to screen culture, productivity to corporate consumerism, many people, it seems, have abandoned the traditional sense of "the human" for a new sense of personhood that can be termed the "posthuman." Some argue that this new world of electronic gadgets has freed us up, made us masters of nature and cyberspace. But, as John Ratey writes, in our "constantly connected civilization much of our life is spent sitting in front of one screen or another" (Ratey, 2009, p. 1). In his view, this may have "given us great advantages with our cyber slaves but has also left us enslaved" (p. 1).

We might resist such a radical reframing, but understand Ratey's (2009) dire warning. More powerful than the locomotive, or the old factory machines, the new digital devices can easily make us slaves to their own addictive processes. By contrast, literature is the best tool we have to promote freedom and preserve the human being as an individual and part of a community within this technological age. Every indication we have suggests that recent discoveries about the relationship between the brain, the body, and the environment is crucial to learning, and that the power of literature to change lives can make a significant difference in the classroom—providing, of course, that we still believe that education has to do with the human desire to learn, to "know thyself," and to belong to a community—in other words, to be a *social being* and to express complex feelings, emotions, and thoughts as well as to exercise empathetic imagination.

Electronic devices create social networks, but they also create intense anxiety because they create the illusion that the user is "hooked up," that he or she is part of a community, that he or she is in the loop, being seen. The result seems often to be that that user has to stay online all the time, in order to remain visible (even if only in cyberspace). To live this way is, at some deep level, to believe that you must be seen to be alive; that you are dead if you are not visible. The goal is to win celebrity status; you live as long as you believe your image is still in the social network (even if nobody is really watching). For us, there is something sad about all this. We recognize this preoccupation or obsession as, in a way, a rejection of the mortal self, a desperate attempt to avoid risk, a defense against human vulnerability. The user stays online to avoid feeling rejection. What is left out in this strategy of being through being online is the deep mystery and coherence of an embodied human existence. Such a sense of coherence and embodiment must be gained in other ways. As Mark William Roche argues:

> the technological age does not easily lend itself to a sense of coherence, but in reading literature and understanding the unfolding narrative of a human life and the developing whole of an artwork, we are encouraged to gain a deeper sense of coherence that may be transferable to reflection on our selves, on the hidden logic of our own development. (Roche, 2004, p. 211)

We could not agree more.

STILL AMUSING OURSELVES TO DEATH

In previous chapters, we have insisted that the most human of all our faculties is the telling of tales, the creation, in other words, of stories—an act which evokes imagination and offers an opportunity for ongoing coherence and connection. The intensification of visual culture—television and video, and now all screens—does not offer this opportunity, at least not as well as language shaped into narrative does. As a result, *the human being is reduced.* As we have suggested throughout this book, the visual culture does not activate the depths of the imagination the way language can, and this is especially true in an age heavily mediated by the onslaught of images endlessly appearing on screens. In such a culture, the emphasis on the visual diminishes the power of the imagination, the creative capacity of humans. We need to return literature to the center of classroom activity. Twenty-five years ago, Neil Postman put the issue this way: "Television educates by teaching children to do what television-viewing requires of them" (Postman, 1985, p. 144). Postman's point, in part, was that we were quickly becoming a culture that was "amusing itself to death." We preferred spectacle to deep thinking, simplicity and ease to complexity and paradox, superficial entertainment to a deep exploration of the human self. Although Postman didn't realize it at the time, he could have included the recent rapid acceleration of online courses, which can be accessed anywhere, anytime.

Comparing printed stories to televised stories, Wayne C. Booth made the same kind of point in his 1982 essay (Booth, 1982), later extended into a book called, *The Company We Keep* (Booth, 1989). In the essay, Booth (1982) suggested that television characters affect viewers differently than the characters accessed through print culture. For Booth, the action on the screen remains remote from the viewer, and the characters seem isolated in their own world, at a distance from the viewer. "[P]rinted stories are not like that. The action takes place in a country somehow in my head, yet freed to occur in a space not in my head, let alone confined to some box or screen" (Booth, 1982, p. 39). For Booth, viewers of television are tourists who might skim the surface of the screen culture, but always remain remote from its origins; in contrast, the printed word creates a context (or "a country" as Booth puts it—or "a new neighborhood" as we have envisioned the classroom throughout this book) that needs us to help shape it, to enrich its meaning. Through engagement with the print story, we are continually recreating that story, re-imagining it in ways denied to us by the visual medium. Like other early pioneers concerned about the growing influence of the screen culture, Booth was warning all of us of the limitations of the screen culture and the importance of verbal literacy in a world growing increasingly fascinated by the flickering images racing across the electronic grids.

BROWSING VS. DEEP THINKING

The digital revolution does not necessarily end, but it certainly problematizes, the traditional humanistic sense of identity, an identity that celebrates the human ability to think deeply, to create lasting human relationships, to appreciate and to acknowledge mortal vulnerability and compassion, an identity that we connect with the book culture. This old book culture identity implies a coherent sense of self existing through time and located in space. That self has a narrative shape to it, a temporal duration, a spatial depth. For the digital natives, the loss of this sense of human existence is not seen as a problem. In their world, it is not surprising that there is little distinction between online and offline identities. The digital natives accept the notion of fragmented selves, distributed identities, discontinuous and immediate. They are skimmers and browsers skating across the screens in the time of NOW.

Mark Nepo, in *The Book of Awakening* (Nepo, 2000), talks about how in Dante's *Divine Comedy* the only difference between the lovers in Hell and the ones in Paradise is that the ones in Hell have "no individual center, and so they spin in endless identification with each other" (Nepo, 2000, p. 135). For us, Nepo's insight has particular relevance in the current age of online living. New digital technologies may aid adolescents in discovering some sense of identity, but what that identity is and whether that identity offers the hope of individual understanding and self-reflection is questionable. As Nepo (2000) puts it, "Unless we work to be ourselves, we can never truly know others or the numinous world we live in" (p. 135). In this new digital world, Nepo believes, little space is given for reflection and assimilation of new understandings of self and others. Perhaps this is why many students today can only write short paragraphs and read short novels. They have entered the digital world of bits and tweets, unable or unwilling to shape their own long narrative story, their own substantial identity.

THE BOUNDED VS. THE BOUNDLESS

The digital natives might respond by saying "so what?" As Thomas de Zengotita claims, there is no natural human self, no unmediated natural experience. In *Mediated*, de Zengotita (2005) insists that all experiences are now mediated by new technologies. For him, the world has an "edgeless quality ... so the real world, dissolving into optionality, is reconstituting itself on a plane that transcends ancient solidities of nature and custom, craft and industry" (de Zengotita, 2005, p. 17). Unlike the rigid printed book with its bounded edges and hard printed borders, the new world is boundless and fluid, not focused and linear, but diverse and serial. If the digital world is without context, it has the virtue of freedom, writers like de Zengotita argue; humans now have the flexibility of boundless activity.

We agree that something like this is beginning to happen, that it is increasingly difficult to separate the natural from the virtual, the old human self from the cyborg self, the original from the copy, and that the conventional boundaries which we have taken for granted—including the distinction between private space and public space—are breaking down. This does not mean that literature or the book is dead, or should be forgotten; rather, it underlines the need for books (which are not simply rigid—as de Zengotita seems to believe). Language mediates human experience by making the world human. Narrative helps shape our identity. Like life itself, the book is bounded and bound. Like life itself, the book has a beginning and an end, but it offers endless surprises, the ongoing mystery of human existence. Deep reading and deep writing and thinking must be brought back to a central location in the classroom if humans are to preserve their depth, their memory, and their ability to think and to make choices and meaningful decisions.

LITERACY LEARNING IN THE DIGITAL AGE

Certainly, there is potential for developing literacy in young children using screens, but when screens become the all-purpose medium for the delivery of learning, then teachers are abandoning their primary responsibilities. Young children spend enormous amounts of time before the screens of the computer, the television, and the cell phone (Jennings, Hooker, & Linebarger, 2008). Such constant interaction with screens changes the brain (Wolf, 2007) and often demands that literacy itself be redefined. Verbal literacy gives way to television literacy, visual literacy, design literacy, computer literacy, procedural literacy, and so on, in the ever-expanding world of the digital revolution. For some time, critics have argued that the intense focus on visual literacy—television literacy, for example—is counterproductive and antithetical to traditional notions of reading and writing development. Granted, other critics have maintained that motivation for learning can be increased through screens, that "alternate forms of media may enhance and enliven conventional literacy" (Jennings et al., 2008, p. 230). We have no doubt that literacy development through new technologies will remain a contested territory as we all continue to try to sort out what the gains and what the losses might be as we move from the book culture to the digital age. What we do not want to do is to throw the baby out with the bathwater. What we do want to do is to keep verbal literacy at the center of attention.

Greenfield (2009) has studied the benefits and drawbacks of some of the new technologies in terms of how they affect learning. Visual literacy, Greenfield argues, is heightened and developed through the visual capabilities of the Internet, video games, and television. But what are the drawbacks? As she puts it: "The cost seems to be deep processing: mindful knowledge acquisition, inductive analysis, critical thinking, imagination, and reflection" (Greenfield, 2009, p. 71). As Greenfield (2009) further reports, there is evidence that "visual technology inhibits imaginative response" (p. 71). And so, although new technologies can expand visual intelligence, we believe, as Greenfield does, that nothing can replace the "work" of deep reading, especially the active reading and discussion of stories.

If the digital natives celebrate speed and multitasking, fast reading and timeless flights into spaceless non-locations, we want to celebrate slow reading, which allows for self-reflection and imaginative flights to deep and contextualized space where temporal duration and an enduring sense of deep identity preside. Narrative, we argue, offers an embodied sense of time and space, a sense of home through the richly sensuous and complex associations of language given to the reader in great books. Extended narratives demand that we slow down, that we experience the rich storehouse of language itself, language that carries the present and the past, language that hints through memory, at the future. Narrative excites the imagination through its auditory and visual power, as well as through the movement readers feel when they are engaged with the intensity of the unfolding and organic curve of the language experience. Narrative invites us into the interior of ourselves, unlike the digital social networks that flatten out the self in the name of speed and leave little room for empathy or self-reflection. John Paul Russo puts it well, in *The Future Without a Past*, when he says: "Complex literary language penetrates the imagistic surfaces, probes into the furthest recesses of mind and feeling, breaks the force of habit, and draws patterns of coherence in order to deepen and empower a self-determining, continuously developing selfhood" (Russo, 2005, p. 35). Literary language connects us to the past—personal, communal, and historical. Digital devices refuse entry into this kind of world.

DEEP READING REVISITED AS SHARED ATTENTION

In this context, we also believe that deep reading is "mindful" in the best sense of that term, and it offers pleasure precisely because it is difficult and complex. Deep reading is not mere entertainment. Entertainment is always easy and so not mindful, creating in its simplicity a temporary illusion of satisfaction, but always leaving the viewer empty once the sensation has worn off. By way of contrast, deep reading is like going to the gym, rigorously working out even if you at first do not want to. When you are finished, you feel it was worth it, and this is a satisfaction that makes you more alive and fulfilled. Deep reading is not mindless entertainment, but it offers substantial gratification. It therefore serves as a kind of counter-weight, and in a sense a "counterculture," to the easy hallucination of having leisure time all day every day, 24/7. As S. Craig Watkins says in *The Young and the Digital*:

> In today's technology-rich world, any place can be a leisure space—a place to download a video, watch a movie clip, listen to your favorite pop single, or take a quick peek at a friend's personal profile. Addiction is not the more common challenge in the digital

world; the ubiquitous presence of entertainment and the desire for constant gratification are. (Watkins, 2010, pp. 190–191)

Deep reading also works against the inevitable distraction and inattention of the screen culture. For this reason, we believe that at the center of 21st century education must be a clearly defined classroom devoted to building focus and imagination and creating what is best described as "shared attention." Recent brain research (Kuhl, 2009), indicates that very young children seem to learn language best when they share attention with a parent or teacher, when they look at an object and sound out the appropriate word for that object together with an adult in a dyadic relationship. "Shared attention" underscores the notion of learning within a social framework, and for us, that includes the central connection between language and the shared vision of a community within the classroom environment.

Deep reading of good narrative must be part of any significant classroom activity. Discussion of that narrative offers the possibility of "shared attention" as everyone in the environment, having read the same story, each in a different way, comes together through time to give their attention to the depth of the text in front of them.

Literary narrative, when it is working well, can draw readers into a new location, bring them into "deep space." In a classroom, teacher and students focus together on the same text, looking at the marks on the pages, turning those marks into language and meaning, moving with the characters in a setting that they imagine separately and together as a group. When students sit in a classroom in this way, they begin to exercise their imaginations, create individual identity, and build communal vision as they share attention to the book, the object before them. Such experience is, as we have suggested in earlier chapters, an adventure, a journey, the creation of a neighborhood for ongoing learning. The narrative in a book, bounded and bounding, absorbs the readers as they become the living book.

To embark on the adventure of becoming a living book is to expand human consciousness and enhance "shared attention" through a journey not available to those spending most of their time interfacing with electronic screens. Carr (2010) explains the implications in terms of the working of the brain itself:

The influx of competing messages that we receive whenever we go online not only overloads our working memory; it makes it harder for our frontal lobes to concentrate our attention on any one thing. The process of memory consolidation can't even get started. And, thanks once again to the plasticity of our neuronal pathways, the more we use the Web, the more we train our brain to be distracted—to process information very quickly and very efficiently but without sustained attention. That helps explain why many of us find it hard to concentrate even when we're away from our computers. Our brains become adept at forgetting, inept at remembering. (p. 194)

Such implications cry out for a return to the book. Through the reading of narrative, humans not only move through a succession of events, but reenact the struggle for meaning of those events, a challenge which the author has already undergone and internalized through the writing process, an engagement with the rhythm of language stirring desire to discover the ongoing secrets of human existence as they unfold within the narrative curve of the story.

In a recent article in *American Scholar*, Sven Birkerts argues that reading fiction matters even more in the digital age precisely because we need to step away from the screen and "bring sensation to life in the mind" (Birkerts, 2010, p. 43). For him, words, above all else, are capable of just such activity. "They are part of our own sense-making process, when their designations and connotations are intensified by rhythmic musicality, a receptivity can be created" (Birkerts, 2010, p. 39). Literary narrative offers an opportunity to slow the foreclosure on our ability to focus by arousing the imaginative process, and stimulating the beat of the human heart. As Birkerts (2010) insists: "Imagination must be quickened, and then it must be sustained—it must survive interruption and deflection" (p. 39). We turn to our classes and our stories, away from the screens and new electronic gadgets, to rejuvenate enchantment, the human imagination, a sense of shared attention and focus. In Birkerts' (2010) words: "To achieve deep focus nowadays is also to have struck a blow against the dissipation of self; it is to have strengthened one's essential position" (p. 44).

A PRACTICAL EXAMPLE FROM THE EMBODIED CLASSROOM

In our class, the students might be reading "Sonny's Blues" by James Baldwin (Baldwin, 1999), a story told by an unnamed older brother, a schoolteacher and a family man who has kept a convenient distance from his younger brother, Sonny, a jazz musician and blues player, who is a heroin addict as well. As readers, the students have moved deep into this story now, feeling the conflict between the brothers, the narrator's wish that his younger brother (Sonny) could be safe and secure despite his passion and struggle, the younger brother filled with the suffering and rage of the world, in love with his music, longing for his brother's understanding. The students have, in other words, engaged in the process of what

Birkerts (2010) has called "a double transposition" (p. 38), the kind of "deep process" which occurs when readers make "the inward plunge" and agree to the experience of the narrative (what Coleridge called "a willing suspension of disbelief") and then make a connection to the living voice of the story itself. For us, the students are doing something even more—"a third transposition," we might call it, one in which the classroom itself becomes part of the living story affecting "shared attention" from everyone in the embodied space.

At this moment, the unnamed narrator of the story looks out his apartment window and down to the Harlem streets and notices an old-fashioned revival meeting "carried on by three sisters in black, and a brother. All they had were their voices" (Baldwin, 1999, p. 279), the narrator tells us, "and their Bibles, and a tambourine" (*ibid.*). As readers, or shall we say writers, helping to create the story, the students move with the small crowd, pay witness, and watch.

As the singing on the street fills the air, the faces of those listening to the singing change, the area around the eyes attentive to something within; time itself, for a moment, seems to fall away, soothing the pain, transporting those on the street in Baldwin's story and the community of readers in the classroom, back to origins and forward to the source of their dreams. As a class the students are here in the classroom (Bachelard's, 1994, dream space, perhaps) and also there with the brothers, one looking through a window and one in the open street—both listening to the music. It is a moment of *embodied knowledge*, that is, knowledge rooted in Baldwin's story and in the immediate experience of the students in the classroom as they expand their consciousness, remembering their own past experiences, joining together through shared attention to imagine their futures.

"Then I saw Sonny," the narrator tells us, "standing on the edge of the crowd" (Baldwin, 1999, p. 280). The voice of the narrator is shaping the moment, as we in the classroom shape it, individually and collectively, a moment filled with revival music, a moment that will become "Sonny's Blues." As a class, each reader experiences the moment in his or her own way, while also remaining open to that experience and to each other. The community of readers are in an imaginative space that demands a response, that questions the reader, and that calls to the reader to listen and respond.

Sonny enters the house where his brother stands, and for a moment there is silence in the text, something unspoken between the brothers, just as there is something unspoken in each person in the classroom. The students all experience the emotion which is pulsating, and almost palpable, implicating them in each other's lives and in the lives of the brothers.

"You want to come some place with me tonight?" (Baldwin, 1999, p. 281), Sonny asks. It is a question that he has wanted to ask for many months, but he kept it locked up, repressed. Why does he ask this question now? We ask the class, anticipating that they will bring their whole world now, their fully embodied individual experience, to that question as they grapple with it, each in their own way. "He was afraid to ask before," one student says. "He didn't want to be rejected again," another claims. "It's the first time they feel close," a third chimes in. "Sonny feels he can trust his brother. He hasn't felt that way in a long time," another declares. "The narrator is finally listening to Sonny," someone else says. Each of those in the classroom brings a unique life and a singular experience to that one question and shapes that question through that individual life experience—not the personal details, but the universal truth of the moment as they know it. One line in a story allows such inquiry, such insight, such shared attention. Literature allows people to see that we are all brothers and sisters, ready for conversation, ready for the joy of language exchange. That is the hope that literature offers and that the classroom can evoke.

In another class, the students might be reading Walter Mosley's *Always Outnumbered, Always Outgunned* (Mosley, 1998). The main character, Socrates Fortlow, having spent half his life in prison, is now out on the main streets of South Central, struggling with anguish and rage to make his life right. He is mentoring a young boy, Darryl, who is involved with "gang bangers" who are now pursuing him, ready to do him considerable harm. In a public park, Darryl is approached by the gang leader, Philip, while Socrates watches at a distance as the two boys get into a fight. Darryl pulls a steak knife on Philip; but before long Philip has the upper hand: "With his left hand he was trying to force Darryl to turn over. In his right hand he held up a .45 automatic" (Mosley, 1998, p. 130). Socrates responds by knocking the gun from Philip's hand, and Darryl picks it up, as Philip falls to the ground. Darryl then holds the gun in both his hands as he staggers near the prone body of Philip. "The boy lurched from side to side as he approached, the pistol pointing anywhere and everywhere … . Philip's widely spaced small eyes came awake while he was staring at that gun" (Mosley, 1998, p. 131). Darryl is not sure what to do. His eyes dart back and forth between Philip and Socrates. And then, in the classroom, we read this line: "Don't look at me," Socrates says (*ibid.*).

We'd like everyone in the class to consider that line in the context we, as a community of readers, have been developing. We'd like each person reading the story with us to bring their experience, their own story, to that one line. What is the depth of that statement? What is Socrates feeling? What is he thinking? What does the line tell us about the relationship between Socrates and Darryl at this moment? What does the line tell us about ourselves? Have we been there before? The single line evokes multiple questions, invites inquiry, holds potential surprises, brings us together in the imaginative classroom.

"Socrates doesn't want the responsibility for what Darryl might do," one student declares. "No, I think he's telling Darryl he has to make his own decision," another says. "Imagine what it takes to say that to Darryl," a third student suggests. "It's courageous to make that kind of statement in this situation." "He must trust Darryl a lot," another student opines. "Socrates is empowering him—but it could be costly." The voices in the classroom mingle with the voices in the story, multiple voices and multiple perspectives, all worth careful attention, all worthy of consideration. Students listen to each other and build community together out of the reading and discussion of the story. They imagine their past and glimpse their future.

There is no safe place in this world, no long-term protection against suffering and death, as Baldwin and Mosley both know. It is our fate, our mortality that is always at stake. What we do with the knowledge of our mortal limitations is what gives meaning to our life; that is part of the power of language and literature, that shock of recognition of the boundaries that shape our identity, our place in the world. Literature provides hope precisely because it teaches us something important about our temporal and spatial experience, our vulnerability; it helps us read ourselves and understand each other. It reminds us of pain and suffering, of our bodily existence, of the environment that surrounds us and is always part of us, but it also allows us to glimpse another place, to dream about a place where the self could be, a place filled with meaning and purpose. We all have our stories and we all have the opportunity to make a story from the raw experiences of our life. That is the central task of education, we believe, now and for the future. We cannot back away from that commitment.

As Nicholas Carr reminds us, "neurons that fire together wire together" (Carr, 2010, p. 120), and the kind of old-fashioned classroom that we have just described seems to be just the kind of place to keep those neurons that allow for depth and identity, individual and communal, active. Human beings can continue to debate whether or not the new technology is just another device that will bring both positive and negative value to the species, but there seems to be more at stake than usual in this debate. As Carr (2010) puts it: "Our uses of the Internet involved many paradoxes, but the one that promises to have the greatest long-term influence over how we think is this one: The Net seizes our attention only to scatter it" (p. 118). By way of contrast, we would argue, literary narrative and class discussion about that narrative works in just the opposite way: it captures our attention to keep us focused on the journey to discover a deep and meaningful human life.

When we ask what the goal of a book is, we answer by saying that it is to inspire readers to search for the depth of human experience, to expand their knowledge about themselves and the human condition. We cannot measure such goals. The goal of most electronic devices seems very different. It seems much closer to the bottom line on economic spreadsheets, a nod to ratios as the best way to determine the meaning of life. To us, that is a very different goal than gaining understanding about the human condition. Of course, even the goal of electronic devices cannot really be measured. Such devices, with their endless speed, keep their users jumping to the next best thing. Which way do human beings want to go?

CONCLUDING THOUGHTS ON THE CHALLENGE OF NEW TECHNOLOGIES

We are far from convinced that new technologies enhance knowledge or strengthen our ability to better understand the complex mysteries of human identity. In Chapter Four, we talked about how contemplation and focused attention are needed for deep and enduring learning. In this chapter, we described how new technologies affect human beings, drawing their attention in many directions at once and often short-circuiting self-reflection. We worry about the reading brain and again emphasize how important deep reading is for students' learning and the quality of life in general. Digital technologies will continue to shape how people think about themselves and their relationship to the world, but, in our view, the incessant immersion in visual culture, with its breakneck speed and constant distractions, fragments creative focus and imaginative ability. We see deep reading, along with deep writing and discussion, as an important way to counter the fragmentation and inattention exacerbated by the digital age. Unlike the frenetic encounters with new electronic gadgets, deep reading creates a safe place to inhabit, one that provides the slower pace needed for self-reflection. Where digital natives put their trust in new technology, we put our trust in the engagement with language shaped into narrative. We believe that deep reading activates and exercises the human imagination, the human spark that inspires deep thought and meaning-making. We believe in the power of the word, the power of literature to change lives; it has been our argument all along. Reading and writing must be central to education if we are to counter some of the dangers and remedy some of the ills inherent in the digital age.

In Chapter Seven, we share an extended example of our continuing work with college students and high school students. Keeping language and meaning-making at the center of the learning environment, we facilitate a journey that these students take together. Through this adventure, both sets of students—college students and high school students—learn about their identity and build empathy and understanding of others. Through shared reading, writing, and discussion, they travel back and forth, from texts to their lives, from their past to their future, and, engaged in this process, they learn about themselves as individuals and about the new neighborhood they help to create.

CHAPTER SEVEN

WEST SIDE CLOSED BUT OUR WORK CONTINUED

As we suggested in the opening chapter, the experiment we tried in the New Bedford West Side school, inspired by the Changing Lives Through Literature program (Waxler & Trounstine, 1999), met with moderate success and helped us to form some of the ideas presented in this book. Because of budget cuts, the alternative school in New Bedford was closed in June of 2008. To continue our work, we established a new partnership with another high school in Fall River, a neighboring city to New Bedford. The Fall River school, like the one in New Bedford, was attended by at-risk students who had been expelled from their previous schools and who, in general, struggled with troubled family lives, poverty, and limited positive role models. Like those in New Bedford, these students often felt that they were powerless and without voice or hope. In short, they were vulnerable. These high schoolers offered an ongoing challenge, and we decided to give some of the college students at our university, those beginning to develop a career in teaching, a chance to develop teaching skills by working with these alternative school students to see if they could make a difference in the high schoolers' lives.

READING AND WRITING CAN CHANGE LIVES

The central focus of our work remained on literature and the belief that the Socratic notion of "know thyself" was as important to the modern world as it had been in ancient Greece. We also continued to be driven by a strong sense that the French philosopher Emmanuel Levinas was right in his view that human beings need first and foremost to acknowledge "the face," that is, the presence of another human being standing before them, to listen to that presence carefully, and to respond to its resonance and depth (Levinas, 1985). As Levinas says, when people see "the face" of the other before them, they always hear first the words: "Thou shalt not kill" emanating from that presence, reminding them that there is a human being in front of them and that they should do no harm to that person. For Levinas, the presence of another human being creates an ethical demand to respect and cherish that person, to acknowledge the other—an ethical demand that no human being should ignore. Levinas reminds us that we teachers also have an ethical obligation in the classroom, an obligation to acknowledge the vulnerability of each student and to respect it, to respond to it, and to make sure we do that student no harm. In the face of the other, we recognize our own fears and longings, our own contingent nature, the human condition which makes us, at times, strangers to ourselves but also members of a shared community.

In this new phase of our education project, we gave reading and writing assignments related to our work in Fall River to the University of Massachusetts at Dartmouth students enrolled in an education course. Our work with the college students who were prospective teachers was based on our previous findings in New Bedford and the theoretical assumptions about language and learning which we continue to embrace. Furthermore, we felt that the metaphors of "life as journey" and "the classroom as an adventure to create a new neighborhood" were particularly apt for what we were trying to accomplish.

The project included the work of what is often called "service learning" (see Chapter Four). Service learning consists of a two-fold process: first, identify the needs of the community, and then provide a community service with learning opportunities for the providers of the services. There should be a clear symbiotic relationship between the provided service or services and the student learning. As Jacoby (1996) conceptualizes it, service learning should encourage student engagement which:

> ... address[es] human and community needs together with structured opportunities intentionally designed to promote student learning and development. Reflection and reciprocity are key concepts of service learning. (p. 5)

In myriad ways, our work with Education students in the local alternative school provided structured and intentional experiential learning for the preparation of future teachers. We identified the community needs, which, in this case involved both the need to develop the reading and writing skills of alternative high school students and the need to encourage these students to believe in their ability to think, to be self-reflective, to learn about their identity and their belonging in the world. Simultaneously, we knew that our future teachers needed experiences in a classroom setting to interrogate their own assumptions about teaching and learning and to temper those assumptions with authentic experiences and interactions with students in a school setting. As in all service learning experiences, learning needs and opportunities have to be present on both sides of the relationship; that is, both the needs of the "servers" and the "served," the teacher and the student, the speaker and the listener, must be explored and identified in their full complexity. There is always a reciprocal relationship inherent in service learning, an assumption that the person standing before you is, in an important sense, part of you and worthy of your help and respect. Like Levinas, we believe that service learning is part of that ethical demand that insists on the need to serve and acknowledge the other. Service learning, like all good teaching, is a calling, an act inspired by the acknowledgment of the dignity of human identity and human community. We, too, were part of this exchange.

When we designed this project, we identified the needs of the high school students; we perceived that they had academic needs and would benefit from the guidance of good role models. The college students also needed live encounters with students in the classroom setting as well as exposure to language and literature, and they would later reflect in writing on their experiences within the context of the learning goals for which this project was assigned. We wanted both the high schoolers and the college students to engage with the literature that would be read and discussed in group settings, and we also planned to be involved in that interaction.

SAME PROJECT: DIFFERENT ALTERNATIVE SCHOOL

Although West Side, the initial place where our work had begun, had closed, we were continuing our work started there by partnering with a different alternative school. Though we were disheartened by the abrupt closing of West Side, we knew our project at West Side had affected positive change and learning in both college students and the high schoolers. When we first met with the new group of Education students at the University of Massachusetts at Dartmouth, a diverse group from all levels (elementary, middle school, and secondary) and subject areas, we explained to them what we had done in New Bedford and our idea about creating "a new neighborhood." We shared what we hoped to accomplish, using the metaphor of "life as a journey," and suggesting that we were all on a path together, attempting to reach this new place, this new neighborhood. We then asked them to read and discuss with us the Robert Frost poem, "The Road Not Taken" (Frost, 1969d). We want to close this book with an account of that adventure, one that we have written about before (Hall & Waxler, 2010) and that we think is ongoing and representative, and one that highlights some of the central ideas we have been fostering throughout this book.

POETRY AS A JOURNEYING VEHICLE FOR DEVELOPING METACOGNITION

We believed that Frost's poem could prove useful as a pathway to explore the metaphor of "life as a journey," and more specifically, as a way of exploring through language (text and discussion) how these college students were on a journey as they began their service learning work in tutoring roles at the Fall River Alternative School. Unlike Coleridge's "Ancient Mariner," with its sublime imaginative vision (see Chapter Three), the Frost poem seemed closer to the ordinary and everyday experiences of life and its contingency and unpredictability, a way of sensing and making sense of the singularity—the individual uniqueness—of human choice through language which appears simple and common, yet surprises the reader with its depth and complex implications.

Through reading and discussing the poem together with the college students, we began to investigate how meaning is made in the interaction between our lives and texts such as stories and poems. Through this engagement with poetic language, we also enriched the learning environment by helping to create the imaginative space that we have been calling "the new neighborhood." We believed that poems often give the reader an intense sense of duration, allowing the experience of time to unfold directly through the complexity of the language and rhythm of the poem. In addition, a short poem like "The Road Not Taken" lends itself to reading and rereading, allowing everyone to understand that rereading is not simply repetition, but rather a way of "deepening understanding," consolidating memory, and strengthening and creating the pathways of the neural patterns of human experience. It is a powerful impetus to stimulate self-reflection and metacognitive processes, and it can lead to "deep learning." As Eva-Wood (2008) argues:

> [P]oetry can offer its readers opportunities to stretch their awareness, adapt their perspectives, and construct new knowledge in a way that many expository texts cannot. Poetry, as a bridge to self-understanding, can complement and build on the self-knowledge inherent in metacognitive practices. (p. 565)

In the college classroom, we read the Frost poem out loud several times with different student voices, each time:

Two roads diverged in a yellow wood,
And sorry I could not travel both
And be one traveler, long I stood
And looked down one as far as I could
To where it bent in the undergrowth;

Then took the other, as just as fair,
And having perhaps the better claim,
Because it was grassy and wanted wear;
Though as for that the passing there
Had worn them really about the same,

And both that morning equally lay
In leaves no step had trodden black.
Oh, I kept the first for another day!
Yet knowing how way leads on to way,
I doubted if I should ever come back.

I shall be telling this with a sigh
Somewhere ages and ages hence:
Two roads diverged in a wood, and I—
I took the one less traveled by,
And that has made all the difference. (Frost, 1969d, p. 105)[1]

Listening to the poem resonate several times through the classroom, the college students were exercising their auditory imagination, deepening their focus and awareness, and expanding their learning space. As they listened, they were also encouraged to reflect on how they were launching a life journey towards their future, and how they were making meaning of that life journey by weaving together life and literature—their experience and language—an experience that included not only their own past stories and their feelings and thoughts in the present, but also a glimpse of their future. The language of the poem, in other words, as it echoed through the classroom, was helping them to shape their own lives as story and, by experiencing the creative power of language, they were engaged in an important human activity which could affect other lives (e.g., the high schoolers at the alternative school and ours as writers of this book). We also knew the poem possessed a proven power, because of its openness, to inspire a range of meanings which readers construct for themselves. It was as if Frost had written the poem as an invitation for readers to participate in the movement of the language, to experience its jolts and surprises, to open themselves to its shocks, and then to bring new interpretation to bear. Peskin, Allen, and Wells-Jopling (2010) highlight this kind of reading in terms of teaching adolescents to make meaning. These researchers argue that in poetry, in particular, there is a "fluidity of interpretation [which] reduces the tendency for students to try to pin down the specific meaning of any symbolic construct—and to feel the frustration of failure to do so. It rather encourages them (students) to look for a range of possible meaning, thus increasing their sensed level of competence and the feeling of success and enjoyment that go along with that" (Peskin et al., 2010, p. 503). Through such reading and discussion, vulnerability gives way to competence, frustration gives way to playfulness, stubborn defensiveness and fear gives way to openness and the joy of multiple voices and perspectives. Readers then become active and engaged meaning-makers, both within the classroom and within their lives.

We reminded the students that Frost's "The Road Not Taken" was the primary focus on this educational journey. "Two roads diverged in a yellow wood, / And sorry I could not travel both / And be one traveler, long I stood" (Frost, 1969d, l. 1–3, p. 105). The voice of the speaker connects with the human breath circulating in the classroom: through engagement with voice and language, everyone makes a choice between the two roads. That choice is individual for each reader, but communal for the class. In the initial reading and discussion of the poem, we were following the journey with the college students, getting them ready for discussion with the high schoolers, and sensing an expanding learning environment.

To give additional meaning to our pedagogy, we also drew on the conceptual framework of Lev Vygotsky (e.g., Vygotsky, 1978), John Dewey (e.g., Dewey, 1899/2009), and Jean Piaget (e.g., Piaget, 1954), whose theories of learning and language place the student at the center of the learning experience and give the teacher the opportunity to create an interactive space for students to make meaning. In addition, we drew again on the work of the Changing Lives Through Literature (CLTL) program (Waxler & Trounstine, 1999), the literature experiment that has fueled much of our work and thinking throughout this book. (We continue to refer to this CLTL program and our individual applications of it by the term "experiment" in order to emphasize its novelty and challenge to current classroom practice.)

We wanted these college students and future teachers to consider from the start that by connecting the reading and writing of a poem (or story) to the reading and making of life narratives, learners can enhance both reading and life experiences; they can, in other words, make meaning by reading and writing the body, mind, and world they inhabit. The challenge was to allow them to recognize that their lives, like the texts they read and write, are in part constructed from the choices they make. The meaning of their lives, like the meaning of a text, can be shaped and reshaped by the journey they choose. For us, this process, learner-centered and language-based, bridges reading, writing, and making meaning, as it also builds competency in the midst of vulnerability.

Of central importance was our insistence on the significance of language in this process. As we explained to the students:

> Reading is direct and immediate engagement with language. Discussing what we read intensifies this engagement, giving us an increased sense of authority and self-confidence. We believe that as we build language skills, we also build life skills. Humans learn our place within the world of language. In an important sense, by reading and discussing what we read, we all create our own place in the world. (Waxler, 1997, p. 3)

For us, this quote also served as a springboard to explain why learning is an embodied experience and why language is so central to that experience. In an important sense, we wanted to impress on the students our notion that human beings are always reading and writing their lives and that reading and writing in the classroom is good exercise for that larger kind of experience.

Words and phrases create sentences and paragraphs, or poetic stanzas of verse, which, in turn, deepen the way human beings shape their thinking, their emotions, and their connections to the world. The author's choice of language reminds readers where they are headed as well as what they have left behind, what they have said and what they have not said, what they have done and what they have not done. Reading and writing is no different than walking on the paths of life and learning to understand the marks along those trails. Making your way through language is similar in this context to making your way through the world. Our bodies take us ahead; language gives us direction and purpose.

When human beings read a text deeply, that text is inscribed in them but human beings also help to create the meaning of that inscription. In a sense, they help to write the meaning of the text. In other words, when human beings are reading deeply, they too are always making choices, mapping their life experiences onto the experiences the text offers, and creating meaning from the richness of the language before them. In a similar sense, when reading the world, humans need the courage to write their lives from the inscriptions they experience. Reading and writing, experiencing the world and acting in it, humans continue to make choices and so construct the meaning of their lives. We wanted the students to think about these ideas.

We have repeated this kind of thinking so many times in this book that it might very well be a cliché for the reader by now, but we need to say it once again in this last chapter: Reading, discussion, and writing help students to locate themselves and build identity. However, it is not simply an individual identity that emerges in this complex process. To recall Wheatley and Whyte (2006): "The identity of individual human beings is predicated, ironically enough, on belonging" (p. 11). The tensions of both solitary and communal work are significant in identity construction. The activities of reading, discussion, and writing help build a community, a new neighborhood, for everyone participating in the flow and shaping of the language. Individuals learn to make a home in the language, and that contributes to individual and community identity. As Wheatley and Whyte (2006) put it: "What brings a human being alive is a sense of participation in the conversation with others, with the great things of the world, with the trees or landscapes or skies or cityscapes, and ... this conversation is the way by which a human being comes to understand the particularity of their own gifts in the world" (p. 11). Reading and writing are both individual and social acts connecting us all to the world of experience. Through engagement with language, human beings enter into a conversation which allows them to transcend their own egos, to transcend the boundaries of their own skin.

In this sense, reading, discussing texts, and writing about them is a social activity with ethical implications. The richly textured language of good literature, filled with ambiguity, always calls to the readers, encourages interpretation and response, and demands that they participate in the making of its ongoing meaning. Reading this way, we believe, calls for response through discussion and writing, allowing everyone in this learning process to recognize what they have in common and also to acknowledge what is unique and should be honored and appreciated in each individual, the "face" (Levinas, 1985) standing before others. In the classroom, our challenge, as teachers, was to create a community of learners (a new neighborhood) which would inspire these future teachers, themselves college students, and which would also include the disaffected high schoolers in Fall River.

To create this kind of "new neighborhood," we also decided to encourage students to slow down, to resist the distractions of the overstimulated visual world that they know so well. We wanted the students to understand that deep reading (unlike their fevered encounters with electronic gadgets) could be an act of meditation, an act of resistance to the speed and turmoil of contemporary life, a way to regain a place for self-reflection. We were reminded of what David L. Ulin said in his book, *The Lost Art of Reading* (Ulin, 2010):

> Reading, after all, is an act of resistance in a landscape of distraction, a matter of engagement in a society that seems to want nothing more than for us to disengage. It connects us at the deepest levels; it is slow, rather than fast. That is its beauty and its challenge: in a culture of instant information, it requires us to pace ourselves ... . Even

more, we are reminded of all we need to savor—this instant, this scene, this line. We regain the world by withdrawing from it just a little, by stepping back from the noise, the tumult, to discover our reflections in another mind. As we do, we join a broader conversation, by which we both transcend ourselves and are enlarged. (Ulin, 2010, pp. 150–151)

To help students appreciate this process of slowing down and to enhance their ability to be self-reflective, we drew on the process of contemplative writing (as a type of contemplative practice) and integrated that into our project as well. (See Chapter Four for further information about contemplative practice as a method to resist the digital onslaught.) We wanted to create a space free from distractions, a space where students could practice and enhance their attentional skills. At the beginning of each class in the semester, we would ring a meditation bell three times. Students were encouraged to breathe in and out slowly with each ringing of the bell and think about how that breath was connected to the depth of the human voice. The ringing of the bell acted as a kind of ritual to frame the writing session, much as Stephen Batchelor suggests when he explains the meditative process: "Breathing is a self-regulating motor function of the body. For the most part we draw and exhale breath as effortlessly as a plant turns towards the light of the sun. This natural process happens of its own accord" (Batchelor, 2004, p. 107). The breath is naturally connected to the rhythm of nature and to the natural voice; it is the beginning of all human possibilities. But in a world dominated by the distractions of electronic devices and the noise of gadgetry, it has become, as we have suggested throughout this book, increasingly difficult to get close to the origins of those human possibilities. So we began with the sound of the bell, meant to serve as a call to the students, a way of creating an intentional, secular space for focusing through breathing and for deepening learning. Next, students would be given a prompt related to various aspects of language and learning on which they were currently working. At the end of the time allotted for the writing, the bell would ring again three times, adding a bounded quality to this new space.

The ritual of starting class in a quiet and focused way provided a reprieve from the constant distractions and overstimulation that we all experience. As we outlined in Chapter Four, this kind of reflective activity, in helping students disconnect from the many distractions surrounding them, centers them both psychologically and physically in the learning space of the classroom. It therefore helps them focus on the depth of the present moment and on the task at hand. Such reflective activity moreover helps them relax, and reduces stress, and so enhances mental and physical health (Hall & Archibald, 2008). After the students finished their writing, discussion began.

We also set up a luncheon so that the college students could meet the high schoolers with whom they would be working during the semester. We knew that many of the high school students had never ventured to our university campus—or any university campus, for that matter. We believed that visits to the college campus were an important part of the learning experience for the high schoolers. We wanted to craft a vision together—college students in partnership with high school students, both groups thinking about their futures by interacting in a learning environment. As we were creating a new neighborhood together, we started in the existing "neighborhood" of the college students, and we wanted the high schoolers to feel welcome.

We met at Woodland Commons, a new and inviting communal space on campus and a perfect place for the students from two different environments to begin their new journey together. There, all wearing nametags, the future teachers and high schoolers would have their first meeting, eat lunch together, and start to get to know one another. The nametags were used in part to encourage everyone to feel included and also for a very practical and organizational purpose—to start to match up tutors with tutees. We designed the seating plans at each table to be composed of alternating college students and high schoolers. As they enjoyed their lunches, all of the students engaged in dialogue. When someone made a connection or found someone with whom they would like to work, we asked them to write that person's name on the back of his or her nametag so that a preliminary connection could be made, in part by choice, in part by chance. Their journey together had begun.

At the luncheon, we also read "The Road Not Taken" (Frost, 1969d) aloud to the whole group. After that reading, we asked for some individuals, both college students and high schoolers, to also recite the poem aloud. Following the read-alouds, we began a discussion on the poem's various meanings and how these meanings could be applied to their life situations.

The high schoolers and the college students seemed genuinely excited, as they shared many interpretations and perspectives on the poem. They talked about how the narrator had made figurative meaning of his life experiences through the description of the literal experience of walking in the woods. Others shared their views of how the narrator, arriving at the crossroads, was confronted with a choice and a decision, similar to what we all go through on the journey of life. Still others made personal connections to their own life experiences as they wondered about the meaning of the two roads in the poem; what did it mean to take the road "less traveled"—why did that choice "make all the difference"? All of the students, high schoolers and college students alike, were especially struck by the last three lines of the poem: "Two roads diverged in a wood, and I- / I took the one less traveled by, / And that has made all the difference" (Frost, 1969d, l. 18,

p. 105). As we both facilitated and made observations of the discussion, we heard students share personal accounts of decisions they had made in their lives. There was palpable energy in the room, substantial evidence of engagement with the language and ideas of the poem, and, as teachers, we became aware of the variety of thinking involved in this engagement. The poem had transported all of us to a new place as the energized conversation enacted the meaning-making of language, opening new possibilities where we could view both past decisions and future aspirations.

This luncheon and literacy discussion was the start to an ongoing schedule for tutorial meetings between the college students and their respective tutees at the alternative school. We also joined together as a large group for the three planned literature discussions of the semester for these three stories: T. Coraghessan Boyle's "Greasy Lake" (Boyle, 1999), Joyce Carol Oates' "Where Are You Going, Where have You Been?" (Oates, 1999), and Ursula Leguin's "The Wife's Story" (Leguin, 1999)—(all from Waxler and Trounstine, 1999). These literature discussions proved to be passionate and full of energy. Many controversial issues about the relationships between males and females were at the center of these discussions, provoked by the complexities inherent in the richly textured language of the stories. The discussions reinforced our beliefs about the way literature can change lives. In particular, how it can: (1) deepen understanding of the difficult relationships between young men and women, and (2) act as a mirror for individuals on a journey seeking identity and a sense of belonging.

The Oates story stirred the most energy and controversy. In that story, a young female character named Connie is tormented by Arnold Friend, a sinister older male (for a detailed analysis and discussion of this story, see Chapter Three). The high school students were split in their feelings about Connie, in particular, and commented extensively about the often thorny relationship between girls and boys. By contrast, the college students seemed to be holding back in the discussion, and appeared to be uncomfortable with the high schoolers' responses. The college students told us later that they were concerned with the emotional level of the discussion, at times, judging it to be almost out of control. The fact that the future teachers were uncomfortable with the younger students' highly emotional discussion suggested to us an area of needed attention and expansion of their perspective. As experienced teachers, we viewed the free-flowing and often high-key discussion in a positive light. For us, the students' engagement with the controversial issues presented—to which there are no easy or pat answers—was a sign of a successful learning experience. Even after the discussion ended in the classroom, students continued talking about the story, exchanging points of view, grappling with ideas and consequences, as they walked down the hallways of the school.

After this very passionate discussion, we decided that it might be a good idea to have a debriefing session with the Education students and emphasize the notion that engagement with language, with reading and writing, is almost inseparable from life experiences. We also wanted to explore more fully with the college students, en route to becoming teachers themselves, the meaning and implications of what they had actually experienced in this impassioned classroom exchange. It was an opportunity, we saw, to mirror a metacognitive activity for these future teachers and also to deepen the learning about this hot discussion in the new neighborhood. As future teachers, some were insistent that the high school students needed to read the story more carefully and pay better attention to details; others argued that the discussion of the Oates story needed more discipline and boundaries; still others suggested that what was most important was not what the high school students said about the details of the story, but that the high schoolers *had something to say* about the story, and that they were interested and involved, sharing a multitude of interesting points about the ways in which they thought real life intersected with the story. We listened to their views and then talked about how giving respect to all students' voices—just like we were doing with them in this debriefing session—was extremely important in any learning environment. We wanted them to understand that our vision of a fruitful discussion did not necessarily progress in a calm and orderly way, nor end with everyone necessarily coming to consensus about the issues at hand. Rather the best classroom discussion might be determined by both how *genuine* the responses were, that is, how free and safe people felt to express their true thoughts and feelings, and how much *respect and dignity* each position is given within the exchange itself. The learning environment should be a place of safety for sharing a wide range of ideas and concerns, but it should also encourage risk-taking. That environment should be a place where all voices are welcome and deep listening is honored. The people involved in a successful classroom discussion about literature might leave with a few temporary answers but, more importantly, with a variety of new questions to further contemplate on their quest to know themselves.

For the end of the semester, we created a self-reflective writing assignment for the college students. This assignment was designed to encourage these future teachers to think more deeply about what they had learned over the course of the semester, what new ideas they had about teaching, and what they had learned about themselves. The writing assignment asked them to provide a culminating assessment of their service learning activities at the alternative school—an assessment of both their individual student tutees and the group literature discussions. It also allowed the students to consider again the Socratic dictum—"Know thyself."

We designed a plan to again use the Frost poem as a lens through which these future teachers might further reflect on the power of language and how meaning is created through particular choices and decisions. We wanted to highlight the never-ending engagement and learning about the self and the other that takes places through language as a shaping power, and we wanted them again to consider the activities of reading and rereading, thinking and rethinking. In particular, we were interested to know how the literature discussions had impacted the thinking of these future teachers, how their ideas about reading and writing had been affected, and what their views might be on our approach to creating a new neighborhood. We knew that our own teaching and thinking might be changed or affected by their feedback, and we welcomed their voices and ideas.

To begin this reflective piece, the college students were given a single question to consider: "How did the reading and discussion of the Oates story and the debriefing of that discussion impact your view of reading and writing? In your response, utilize the theme of 'being on a journey' from the Frost poem, 'The Road Not Taken'." Each student was again given a copy of the Frost poem and told that the poem would be read aloud several times before they would be asked to start their 8–10 minute contemplative writing session at the beginning of the next class. The chime of the meditation bell signaled the time to begin their written response. A few examples from their responses are indicative of what members of this group had been thinking. One of the college students reflected on the intersection between reading and learning in these terms:

> Reading allows people to participate in the human experience in every form and fashion. In the case of the teenagers we are working with, my hope is that they take these lessons taught to them by each story and use them in such a way that they use more discretion when deciding which road to travel down … . [T]here are points in your life when you must decide alone, where you are going. There are some choices that, once made, cannot be undone. These students are at that point in their lives right now.

As this college student realized, the discussion of the reading evoked real-life dilemmas and connected to the high school students' current concerns. She made clear that for her, life is a journey. She also understood how that journey relates to the idea that people make meaning out of both life and texts in terms of the decisions they make; each decision they make is a choice, drawing them in particular directions for the future. In her response, she emphasized how important a teacher's influence can be. She mentioned how literature can teach important lessons about life experience and that teachers can help students comprehend how decisions made now will later impact their lives.

Another student made clear that by taking part in this project she had seen how important it was to make sure all students in a classroom have a voice and that all are treated with dignity. This experience in the literature classroom, a created space where students could find themselves in the stories and participate in a community for learning, had been unforgettable. She had witnessed high school students who were at high risk overcome their feelings of vulnerability and willingly participate in the ongoing conversation. She saw students take on the challenge of reading and rereading a narrative text and begin to make meaning of the text in their own lives. Through the discussion, she realized students were able to find themselves in the narrative. For us, this student's feedback offered support for our vision of the classroom as a "new neighborhood." As she put it:

> After going to the Fall River Resiliency School for a semester, I got to experience something new. I got to interact with students who struggle in school and need help. These students want to learn deep down inside ... . So when my class came to have a discussion about the readings, these kids now had a chance to talk and have an opinion ... . I got to see ambitious students who had very strong opinions about the story, and they were sticking to them.

This student could see great potential for learning in these high schoolers and was beginning to understand that every human being has an innate desire to learn. She commented on the high schoolers' ambition and strong wills, recognizing how discussion could open a space for student voices to be heard and respected. Her ideas, and others articulated by her fellow college students, also carried with them implications for the larger society. When students read a good story, they read themselves and others, and, in turn, become good citizens who are able to be active participants and contribute to building a fairer and more egalitarian society.

This same student went on to further comment about the heated discussion of the Oates story:

> As I observed the whole debate, I noticed that these certain kids who act like they don't like school and do not want to read and write, deep down enjoyed participating in the discussion. Seeing their faces as they discussed the story truly showed this.

For this future teacher, the project had given her an insider's view on how students can be energized about learning and start to develop both confidence in themselves and a renewed belief in their own capabilities. Many students feel that to engage in school is not "cool." However, the engagement in the reading, writing, and discussion of the stories had given these high schoolers a voice and got them excited about the adventure of thinking. It served as a testament to the belief that every human being desires to learn, but that desire needs, at times, to be stimulated by teachers. Finding a voice gives us all hope for the future. Learning can be exciting; thinking can inspire gratitude.

Another college student, through this final assignment, experienced a moment of metacognitive thinking. He imagined himself in the role of a teacher and started to consider the kinds of boundaries he would need to establish in his own classroom, bounding boundaries that would not prevent students from missing out on anything in their learning journeys or negatively affect the creation of the classroom as a new neighborhood. He reflected:

> As teachers, we will have to learn to monitor and mediate the classroom discussions; some may cross a line of being quite personal while others may deal with broad topics. The discussions in Fall River acted as a demonstration of a passionate conversation. The debriefing allowed us to brainstorm ways to keep students engaged in a lively discussion with boundaries; for example, having them always go back to the text allows for text-based arguments instead of opinions being thrown across the room. The goal of reading is to take you on a journey; you begin by reading, ways of thinking of the material emerge, and by talking about it, new ideas are born. As a teacher, you do not want to hinder this journey.

This student had imagined himself in his future classroom. He clearly identified with the notion of a teacher as a "journey facilitator" and understood that teachers help students give birth to new ideas and perspectives on their journeys. He also understood that the relationship between the text and life includes the rhythm of moving from the text to life experience and then back to the text. The narrative inspires thinking about life and life inspires further thinking about the narrative. As members of a classroom neighborhood, we were all engaged in the quest of making meaning, individually and mutually, through the discussion. Using contemplative writing as a tool further reinforced this learning. Our new neighborhood supported the processes for evolving new meaning in our own lives as well as in our identity as a growing community.

Yet another college student depicted his experience in the literacy and tutoring project as a journey and started to imagine how other journeys could be facilitated through similar reading and writing projects:

> The way in which the reading, discussion and debriefing impacted my view on reading and writing is that now I understand how much interpretation factors into reading and writing. I further realized that it truly is not the idea that everyone comes to that is important, but rather it is the journey there.

This student's commentary on the importance of the process of the journey itself resonated with one of the core beliefs in our book: the best measure of any successful learning process is not by the number of voices excluded, but by the number of voices that are included in the conversation, not by the number of answers offered, but by the questions raised through the ongoing energy and shape of the quest itself. Reading this student's comments, we felt some success in our efforts to show that reading and writing can make a significant difference in a person's journey through life; we had renewed hope for the future of education itself. The creation of a new neighborhood of interpretative voices, evidencing a "community of truth," as Parker Palmer had explained it (Palmer, 1998), stood as a fine example of participatory education. Through narrative and discussion, we had witnessed learning as a genuine engagement in education, a learning environment for everyone.

What had we accomplished in this educational experiment? We had helped a group of future teachers take an important journey, an adventure in learning. This journey was designed to deepen their understanding of the profound relationship between reading, writing, and creating meaning in their own lives and in those of the high school students as well. We used the Frost poem, as well as the reading and discussion of various other stories, as a pathway to shape a community of truth. On this journey, we promoted learning for both the college students and urban high schoolers. We wanted them to connect with the literature and see how meaning of self and of the larger group could be made through engagement with language shaped into narrative. This journey had offered assignments and activities (checkpoints) throughout the semester. These included: the opening discussion of Frost's poem, the individual tutoring sessions with the high schoolers, the group reading and discussion of the stories, and a self-reflective written piece on the discussion of those stories and on the debriefing session for one of the discussions. The last assignment, the self-reflective piece, was linked with other important cognitive and affective moments through the exposure to language in the poem, the stories, and the discussion—all of which served to deepen further the future teachers' understanding of the profound relationship between reading, writing, and creating meaning in their own lives and in those of the high school students. In educating both the future teachers and the high school students, we hoped to affect some change—change their minds and perhaps their lives. These changes, we hoped, might ripple through the education system to others as both sets of students carry this knowledge to other classrooms and neighborhoods as their journey continues.

The written assignment also helped the future teachers to understand that the journey which they started with the Frost poem and ended with their own writing mirrored in many ways a journey that they had taken in their own lives. By helping these college students, who were preparing to become teachers, realize the power of written language to make a difference in other people's lives, we were also demonstrating that reading and writing can stand as a model for bringing students and educators together—that reading and writing, in other words, can help create a community for learning. In a sense, we were all contextualized by the reading and writing process and were able to locate ourselves within that context. We were able to see what we shared and where we stood in relation to others within the patterns of language which we had helped to create. We were all members of the new neighborhood.

CONNECTIONS TO TEACHER EDUCATION AND ON-SITE LEARNING

Clift and Brady (2005) conducted a retrospective review of the literature of teacher education, investigating ways in which preservice teachers are prepared for their future classrooms through both methods courses and field experiences. In their review of research from the period 1995–2001, they noted that teacher preparation programs were working on changing or modifying the thought processes of preservice teachers. This focus was based on an understanding that "one's beliefs, intentions, knowledge frames, and skills interact continuously in classroom teaching" (Clift & Brady, 2005, p. 313). As Clift and Brady (2005) well understood, learning is always ongoing and embodied, grounded in what human beings bring to the complex learning environment. And teachers' beliefs, intentions, knowledge, and skills both influence and are influenced by their teaching in classroom settings. In the education of teachers, nothing replaces classroom experience. Preservice teachers certainly can practice and refine their pedagogical vision in such a dynamic setting. Our work with preservice teachers provided just this kind of opportunity; the college students in our project gained authentic classroom experience and were then asked to reflect on their experiences. Our activities designed around the Frost poem put literature at the center, as a way to bring preservice teachers and high school students together. We were able to stimulate future teachers to think about the complexities inherent in the interaction within the classroom and how this kind of engagement is always part of an ongoing learning experience.

Clift and Brady's (2005) work further underpins our efforts to educate future teachers for the reading and writing classroom. When they investigated "the impact of structured and sustained interactions with children or adolescents during early field experiences" (Clift & Brady, 2005, p. 315), they found that these structured interactions provided an "experiential base for prospective teachers through course-based concepts and theories" (p. 315), and they concluded that preservice teachers' early field experiences and interactions with students promoted changes in ways these prospective teachers thought about teaching and learning. Through early field experiences, preservice teachers "became more accepting of students' ideas and more aware of their strengths and how those strengths interact with literacy development" (p. 316). Our own experiment seems to confirm what Cliff and Brady discovered. Preservice teachers must be given structured opportunities to work with students in schools and thereby bridge the theories they learn with actual classroom practice.

LEARNING THROUGH REFLECTIVE PRACTICE

As we have indicated, the reflective practices which we designed for this course included focused discussion with high schoolers and college students after readings, debriefing sessions with only the college students after these discussions, and self-reflective writing assignments for the college students to make sense of what each had learned. We, too, learned much from this one service learning experiment.

Starting with the discussion of "The Road Not Taken," a group of preservice teachers had made choices during the semester in their reading and writing, and in their discussions and interactions with others. They had, in this sense, created meaning in their lives as they had helped to re-create the meaning of the poem and stories in the lives of the high schoolers with whom they worked. As a result of these experiences, many of these college students, who were eager to be teachers, seemed to realize that they have the ability to speak and write, that they have a genuine voice and identity, and that the choices they make through language are similar to other choices they make in their own lives. Our work with preservice teachers highlights the importance of shifting the focus in teacher education from "the traditional teacher-centered approach to a more learner-centered approach" (p. 158), as Magno and Sembrano (2009) point out. The high school students, interacting with these college students, also acknowledged that participating in education through the discussions of the readings could be empowering. Their voices were heard and considered important. Similarly, the preservice teachers' realizations connected to those of the high schoolers. The preservice teachers gained a new view on the potentials for their future students and for themselves as dynamic teachers. Everyone was treated with respect; everyone gained a new sense of competency and dignity.

We believe that the experiences we all gained in the classroom will serve to inform the ways in which we continue to craft our future as people. From the crossroads, we chose a road that allowed all of us to become better learners and better citizens, significant members of a classroom and larger human neighborhood. Through reading and writing, discussion and self-reflection, we created new possibilities together in the ongoing effort to understand our individual selves and build strong communities for the future.

CONCLUDING THOUGHTS ON OUR EVOLVING NEW NEIGHBORHOOD

Throughout this book, we have offered a vision of our new neighborhood, providing theoretical underpinnings and practical classroom examples. We believe deeply in the human potential and capacity for learning— as individuals and as members of a community of learners. For us, the engagement with language—reading, writing, and discussion of good literature—must remain central to the learning process. In the first chapter, we discussed our initial experiments as the Urban Literacy Group, which brought together future teachers and students from an alternative school setting. In Chapter Two, we investigated the concept of *deep reading*, especially its importance in inspiring individuals to explore their own identity and their location in the world. When practicing the activity of deep reading, one's attention becomes focused on making sense of the narrative and making meaning of the text in one's own life. The act and quality of deep reading differs from most other kinds of reading people do in modern society (e.g., skimming a print or online newspaper, interacting with Facebook friends, or reading and sending text messages); deep reading requires the full power of one's attentional skills. For us, deep reading is a journey which moves back and forth from the narrative itself to life experience, and then back to the narrative. It helps create a new neighborhood, an adventurous learning environment.

In Chapter Three, we explored the qualities of the classroom environment and highlighted the elements of good teaching which we believe are necessary for creating the new neighborhood. We emphasized the importance of creating an imaginative space for learning and how the shaping power of language can contribute to the excitement and support of the learning experience.

Chapter Four explored the significance of developing the full range of students' capacities so that they could become successful members of the new literacy neighborhood. Different educational terms such as *holistic learning*, *integrative education*, and *contemplative practice* all support the notion of teaching to the whole person and of finding ways to bring learners to the present moment through different kinds of pedagogical practices. Drawing on some of the recent work in neuroscience (e.g., on how mirror neurons operate), we also made connections between current knowledge of how the brain works, how the best learning happens, and what some of the implications are for improving existing educational practices through language and story. In Chapter Five, we considered how other arts, such as music and film, can enhance the conversation about learning and enrich the understanding of literary narrative. We emphasized that these other arts, as important as they are, can never take the place of the literary narrative itself; that kind of narrative, remains central to learning in the new neighborhood we envision.

Chapter Six took up many of the new technologies which currently challenge the attentional capacities (as discussed in Chapter Four) needed for the skills of deep reading and deep learning. We argued that the contemporary screen culture, with its emphasis on visual images rather than verbal literacy, jeopardizes the quest to discover human identity and to create a genuine human community. Though many "digital natives" believe that they are successful in multitasking, we question this success and worry about the general drift into a posthuman world. In Chapter Seven, we concluded with another example of our experiments in creating the new neighborhood with college students, teachers, and high schoolers and again emphasized the essence and power of the concept of the new neighborhood.

Our work with college students and high schoolers continues, and we hope that, with the help of this book, others will join us to envision and create their own new, literacy-centered neighborhoods. We hope that this book serves as an invitation and hospitality call to readers. We have offered both theory and practical examples related to our concept of a new neighborhood for learning in the 21st century. We trust that, as readers, you will expand our vision, creating new imaginative spaces where teachers and students can journey together towards finding the meaning of literary texts and the deeper meanings of self.

NOTE

1. "The Road Not Taken," from the book, THE POETRY OF ROBERT FROST edited by Edward Connery Lathem. Copyright 1916, 1969 by Henry Holt and Company. Copyright 1944 by Robert Frost. **Reprinted by permission of Henry Holt and Company, LLC.** "A Winter Evening" by George Trakl, translated by Graham Harman. Reprinted by permission of Open Court Publishing Company, a division of Carus Publishing Company (Chicago, IL), from the book, *Heidegger Explained*, by Graham Harmon, Copyright 2007.

REFERENCES

Astin, A. (1985). *Achieving educational excellence.* San Francisco, CA: Jossey-Bass.

Attridge, D. (2004). *The singularity of literature.* New York, NY: Routledge.

Bachelard, G. (1994). *The poetics of space* (Original work published 1958). Boston, MA: Beacon Press.

Bakhtin, M. M. (1984). *Problems of Dostoevsky's poetics* (C. Emerson, Ed. and Trans.). Minneapolis, MN: University of Minnesota Press.

Baldwin, J. (1999). Sonny's blues. In: R. P. Waxler & J. Trounstine (Eds), *Changing lives through literature.* Notre: Notre Dame Press.

Banks, R. (1989). *Affliction.* New York, NY: HarperCollins.

Banks, R. (1991). *The sweet hereafter.* New York, NY: HarperCollins.

Baron, D. (2009). *A better pencil: Reader, writers, and the digital revolution.* New York, NY: Oxford University Press.

Batchelor, S. (2004). *Living with the devil: A meditation on good and evil.* New York, NY: Riverhead Books.

Bauman, Z. (2008). *Does ethics have a chance in a world of consumers?* Cambridge, MA: Harvard University Press.

Benjamin, W. (1968). The storyteller. In: *Illuminations: Essays and reflections* (pp. 83–111). New York, NY: Harcourt, Brace & World.

Bickerton, D. (1992). *Language and species.* Chicago, IL: University of Chicago Press.

Birkerts, S. (1994). *The Gutenberg elegies: The fate of reading in an electronic age.* Boston, MA: Faber and Faber.

Birkerts, S. (2010). Reading in a digital age. Available at http://www.theamericanscholar.org/reading-in-a-digital-age/. Retrieved on December 20, 2010.

Booth, W. C. (1982). The company we keep: Self-making in imaginative art, old and new. *Daedalus, 3,* 33–61.

Booth, W. C. (1989). *The company we keep: An ethics of fiction.* Los Angeles, CA: University of California Press.

Boyd, B. (2009). *On the origin of stories: Evolution, cognition, and fiction.* Cambridge, MA: Harvard University Press.

Boyle, T. C. (1999). Greasy lake. In: R. P. Waxler & J. Trounstine (Eds), *Changing lives through literature* (pp. 15–24). Notre Dame, IN: Notre Dame Press.

Call, J., & Tomasello, M. (1998). Distinguishing intentional from accidental actions in orangutans (*Pongo pygmaeus*), chimpanzees (*Pan troglodytes*), and human children (*Homo sapiens*). *Journal of Comparative Psychology, 112,* 192–206.

Carr, N. (2010). *The shallows: What the internet is doing to our brains.* New York, NY: W. W. Norton & Company.

Chickering, A. (2006). Strengthening spirituality and civic engagement in higher education. *Journal of College and Character, 8*(1). Available at http://www.collegevalues.opdfsrg//Chickering%20remarks.pdf. Retrieved on March 2, 2010.

Chopra, J. (1985). *Smooth talk* [motion picture]. USA: American Playhouse Goldcrest Films.

Cixous, H. (1988). Conversation with Helene Cixous and members of the centre d'etudes femininines. In: S. Sellers (Ed.), *Writing differences: Readings from the seminar of Helene Cixous* (pp. 141–154). Buckinghamshire, UK: Open University Press.

Clark, A. (1997). *Being there: Putting brain, body, and world together again.* Cambridge, MA: MIT Press.

Clift, R. T., & Brady, P. (2005). Research on methods courses and field experiences. In: M. Cochran-Smith & K. M. Zeichner (Eds), *Studying teacher education: The report of the AERA panel on research and teacher education* (pp. 301–320). Mahwah, NJ: Lawrence Erlbaum Associates.

Coleridge, S. T. (1969). The rime of the ancient mariner. In: H. E. Coleridge (Ed.), *Coleridge poetical works* (pp. 186–209). London, UK: Oxford University Press.

Coleridge, S. T. (1817/1983). Biographia literaria. In: J. Engell & W. J. Bate (Eds), *The collected works of Samuel Taylor Coleridge* (pp. 300–309). (Original work published in 1817). Princeton, NJ: Princeton University Press.

Costa-Lima, L. (1996). *The limits of voice: Montaigne, Schlegel, Kafka.* Palo Alto, CA: Stanford University Press.

Coulmas, F. (1989). *The writing systems of the world.* Oxford, UK: Blackwell.

Countryman, L. W. (2000). *Poetic imagination: An Anglican tradition.* Maryknoll, NY: Orbis Books.

Cover, R. (1995). Narrative, violence, and the law: The essays of Robert Cover. In: M. Minow, M. Ryan & A. Sarat (Eds), Ann Arbor, MI: University of Michigan Press.

Cunningham, A. E., & Stanovich, K. E. (2001). What reading does for the mind. *Journal of Direct Instruction, 1*(2), 137–149.

Deacon, T. W. (1998). *The symbolic species: The co-evolution of language and the brain.* New York, NY: W. W. Norton & Company.

Dehaene, S. (2009). *Reading in the brain: The science and evolution of a human invention.* New York, NY: Viking.

Derrida, J. (1978). *Writing and difference* (A. Bass, Trans.). Chicago, IL: University of Chicago Press.

Dewey, J. (2009). *The school and the society and the child and the curriculum* (Original work published in 1899 as The school and society: Being three lectures by John Dewey, supplemented by a statement of the university elementary school. Cambridge, UK: Cambridge University Press). Mineola, NY: Dover Publications.

de Zengotita, T. (2005). *Mediated: How the media shapes your world and the way you live in it.* New York, NY: Bloomsbury USA.

Dickey, J. (1970). *Deliverance.* Boston, MA: Houghton Mifflin Harcourt.

Donoghue, D. (2000). *The practice of reading.* New Haven, CT: Yale University Press.

Dustin, C. A., & Ziegler, J. E. (2005). *Practicing mortality: Art, philosophy, and contemplative seeing.* New York, NY: Palgrave MacMillan.

Dutton, D. (2009). *The art instinct: Beauty, pleasure, and human evolution.* London, UK: Bloomsbury Press.

Eagleton, T. (2008). *Literary theory: An introduction.* Minneapolis, MN: University of Minnesota Press.

Egoyan, A., Hamori, A, Frieberg, Webb, D., and Lantos, R. (producers) and Egoyan, A. (director). (1998). *The sweet hereafter* [motion picture]. USA: New Line Home Video.

Eva-Wood, A. L. (2008). Does feeling come first? How poetry can help readers broaden their understanding of metacognition. *Journal of Adolescent & Adult Literacy, 5*(7), 564–576.

Fiumara, G. C. (1995). *The metaphoric process: Connections between language and life.* New York, NY: Routledge.

Flaherty, A. (2005). *The midnight disease: The drive to write, writer's block, and the creative brain.* New York, NY: Mariner Press.

Fludernik, M. (2007). Identity/alterity. In: D. Herman (Ed.), *The Cambridge companion to narrative* (pp. 260–273). Cambridge, UK: Cambridge University Press.

Freire, P., & Macedo, D. (1987). *Literacy: Reading the word and the world.* Westport, CT: Bergin & Garvey.

Fried, R. L. (2001). *The passionate learner: How teachers and parents can help children reclaim the joy of discovery.* Boston, MA: Beacon Press.

Frith, U. (1985). Beneath the surface of developmental dyslexia. In: K. Patterson, J. Marshall & M. Coltheart (Eds), *Surface dyslexia, neuropsychological and cognitive studies of phonological reading* (pp. 301–330). London, UK: Erlbaum.

Frost, R. (1969a). Dust of snow. In: E. C. Lathem (Ed.), *The poetry of Robert Frost: The collected poems* (p. 221). New York, NY: Holt and Company.

Frost, R. (1969b). Neither out far nor in deep. In: E. C. Lathem (Ed.), *The poetry of Robert Frost: The collected poems* (p. 301). New York, NY: Holt and Company.

Frost, R. (1969c). One step backward taken. In: E. C. Lathem (Ed.), *The poetry of Robert Frost: The collected poems* (p. 376). New York, NY: Holt and Company.

Frost, R. (1969d). The road not taken. In: E. C. Lathem (Ed.), *The poetry of Robert Frost: The collected poems* (p. 105). New York, NY: Holt and Company.

Gadamer, H. G. (1975). *Truth and method.* London, UK: Sheed & Ward.

Gilligan, J. (1996). *Violence.* New York, NY: Vintage.

Glasser, W. (1985). *Control theory in the classroom.* New York, NY: HarperCollins.

Greene, M. (2007). Imagination, oppression and culture/creating authentic openings. Self-published essay. Available at www.maxinegreene.org/pdf/articles/downloader.php?file...oc.pdf. Retrieved on March 21, 2010.

Greenfield, P. (2009). Technology and informal education: What is taught, what is learned. Retrieved from http://www.sciencemag.org. *323*, 53–55.

Greengard, S. (2009). Are we losing our ability to think critically? *Communications of the ACM, 52*(7), 18–19.

Gurm, B. (2009). Service learning in the post-secondary system. *Transformative Dialogues: Teaching and Learning Journal, 2*(3). Available at http://kwantlen.ca/TD/TD.2.3/TD.2.2_Editorial_Service_Learning.pdf. Retrieved on July 1, 2010.

Hakemulder, J. (2000). *The moral laboratory: Experiments examining the effects of reading literature on social perception and moral self-concept.* Philadelphia, PA: John Benjamins Publishing Company.

Hall, M. P. (2005). Bridging the heart and mind: Community as a device for linking cognitive and affective learning. *Journal of Cognitive Affective Learning, 1*(2), 8–12.

Hall, M. P. (2009). Service learning in urban alternative schools: Investigating affective development in preservice teacher education. *Transformative Dialogues: Teaching and Learning Journal, 2*(3). Available at http://kwantlen.ca/TD/TD.2.3/TD.2.3_Hall_Service_Learning.pdf. Retrieved on February 11, 2010.

Hall, M. P., & Archibald, O. Y. (2008). Investigating contemplative practice in creative writing and education classes: A play (of practice and theory) in three acts. *International Journal for the Scholarship of Teaching and Learning, 2*(1), 1–18.

Hall, M. P., & Waxler, R. P. (2007). It worked for criminals: It will work for middle schoolers. *The Journal of Urban Education, 4*(1), 122–132.

Hall, M. P., & Waxler, R. P. (2010). Engaging future teachers to reflect on how reading and writing can change lives. *Writing and Pedagogy*, *2*(1), 91–101.

Harman, G. (2007). *Heidegger explained: From phenomenon to thing.* Chicago, IL: Open Court.

Hart, T. (2007). Reciprocal revelation: Toward a pedagogy of interiority. *Journal of Cognitive Affective Learning*, *3*(2), 1–10.

Healy, J. M. (1990). *Endangered minds: Why children don't think and what we can do about it.* New York, NY: Simon & Schuster.

Hedges, C. (2009). *Empire of illusion: The end of literacy and the triumph of spectacle.* New York, NY: Nation Books.

Heidegger, M. (1947). Letter on humanism. In: W. Barrett & H. D. Aiken (Eds), *Philosophy in the twentieth century: An anthology.* New York, NY: Harper & Row.

Hemingway, E. (1952). *Old man and the sea.* New York, NY: Charles Scribner's Sons.

Hermans, H. J. M., & Kempen, H. J. G. (1993). *The dialogical self: Meaning as movement.* New York, NY: Academic Press.

Holzer, N. (1994). *A walk between heaven and earth: A personal journal on writing and the creative process.* New York, NY: Three Rivers Press.

hooks, b. (2003). *Teaching community: A pedagogy of hope.* New York, NY: Routledge.

hooks, b. (2010). *Teaching critical thinking: Practical wisdom.* New York, NY: Routledge.

Huston, N. (2008). *The tale tellers: A short study of mankind.* Toronto, ON: McArthur & Company.

Iacoboni, M. (2009). *Mirroring people: The science of empathy and how we connect with others.* New York, NY: Picador.

Immordino-Yang, M. H. (2008). The smoke around mirror neurons: Goals as sociocultural and emotional organizers of perception and action in learning. *Mind, Brain and Education*, *2*(2), 67–73.

Immordino-Yang, M. H., & Damasio, A. R. (2007). We feel, therefore we learn: The relevance of affective and social neuroscience to education. *Mind, Brain and Education*, *1*(1), 3–10.

Jacoby, B. (1996). *Service-learning in higher education: Concepts and practices.* San Francisco, CA: Jossey-Bass.

Jennings, N., Hooker, S. & Linebarger, D. L. (2008). Observing the "ins" and "outs" of between the lions: Educational television and emergent literacy in preschoolers. A final report prepared for Corporation for Public Broadcasting. Philadelphia, PA: Annenberg School for Communication, University of Pennsylvania.

Johnson, M. (1987). *The body in the mind: The bodily basis of meaning, imagination, and reason.* Chicago, IL: University of Chicago Press.

Johnson, S. (2010, June 19). Yes, people still read, but now it is social. *New York Times*, p. BU3.

Kabat-Zinn, J. (2005). *Coming to our senses: Healing ourselves and the world through mindfulness.* New York, NY: Hyperion.

Kabat-Zinn, J. (2006). Wherever you go, there you are: Living your life as if it really matters. In: S. Awbrey, D. Dana, V. Miller, P. Robinson, M. Ryan & D. Scott (Eds), *Integrative learning and action: A call to wholeness* (pp. 129–141). New York, NY: Peter Lang.

Kenneally, C. (2007). *The first word: The search for the origins of language.* New York, NY: Penguin.

Kesey, K. (1962). *One flew over the cuckoo's nest.* New York, NY: Penguin.

Kirby, A. (2009). *Digimodernism: How new technologies dismantle the postmodern and reconfigure our culture.* New York, NY: Continuum.

Krathwohl, D. R., Bloom, B. S., & Masia, B. B. (1964). *Taxonomy of educational objectives: Handbook II: Affective domain.* New York, NY: David McKay.

Kristeva, J., & Menke, A. M. (1989). *Language: The unknown*. New York, NY: Columbia University Press.

Kuhl, P. K. (2009). Early language acquisition: Neural substrates and theoretical models. In: M. S. Gazzaniga (Ed.), *The cognitive neurosciences* (4th Ed., pp. 837–854). Cambridge, MA: MIT Press.

Kutz, E., & Roskelly, H. (1991). *An unquiet pedagogy: Transforming practice in the English classroom*. Portsmouth, NH: Boynton/Cook.

Landwehr, M. J. (2008). Egoyan's film adaptation of Banks' *The Sweet Hereafter*: "The pied piper" as trauma narrative and *mise-en-abyme*. *Literature-Film Quarterly*, *36*(2), 20–36.

Lanier, J. (2010). *You are not a gadget: A manifesto*. New York, NY: Knopf.

Lee, H. (1960). *To kill a mockingbird*. Philadelphia, PA: Lippincott.

Leguin, U. K. (1999). The wife's story. In: R. P. Waxler & J. Trounstine (Eds), *Changing lives through literature* (pp. 149–152). Notre Dame, IN: Notre Dame Press.

Levinas, E. (1985). *Ethics and infinity: Conversations with Philippe Nemo*. Pittsburgh, PA: Duquesne University Press.

Lewin, P. (1997). The ethical self in the play of affect and voice. Presentation at the "After Post Modernism" conference. University of Chicago. Available at http://www.focusing.org/apm.htm. Retrieved on January 20, 2009.

Littau, K. (2006). *Theories of reading: Books, bodies, and bibliomania*. Oxford, UK: Polity Press.

London, J. (1963). *The sea wolf*. New York, NY: Bantam Books.

Longinus. (1973). On the sublime. In: D. A. Russell & M. Winterbottom (Eds), *Ancient literary criticism: The principal texts in new translations* (pp. 46–78). Oxford, UK: Clarendon Press.

MacIntyre, A. (1981). *After virtue: A study in moral theory*. Notre Dame, IN: University of Notre Dame Press.

Madison, G. (1996). Being and speaking. In: J. Stewart (Ed.), *Beyond the symbol model: Reflections on the representational nature of language* (pp. 69–102). Albany, NY: SUNY Press.

Madoc-Jones, G. (2008). On Bachelard and Ricoeur. In: C. Coreil (Ed.), *Imagination, cognition, and language acquisition: A unified approach to theory and practice* (pp. 35–59). Woodside, NY: Bastos Educational Books.

Magno, C., & Sembrano, J. (2009). Integrating learner centeredness and teacher performance. *International Journal of Teaching and Learning in Higher Education*, *21*(2), 252–257.

Magolda, M. B. (Ed.) (2000). *Teaching to promote intellectual and personal maturity: Incorporating students' worldviews and identities into the learning process* (pp. 1–4). San Francisco, CA: Jossey-Bass.

Mailer, N. (1965). *An American dream*. New York, NY: Vintage.

Manguel, A. (1997). *A history of reading*. New York, NY: Penguin Group.

Mar, R. A., Oatley, K., Hirsh, J., dela Paz, J., & Peterson, J. B. (2006). Bookworms versus nerds: Exposure to fiction versus non-fiction, divergent associations with social ability, and the simulation of fictional social worlds. *Journal of Research in Personality*, *40*(5), 694–712.

McLuhan, M. (1964). *Understanding media: Extensions of Man*. New York, NY: Mentor Books.

Merton, T. (1979). *Love and living*. New York, NY: Mariner Books.

Miller, J. P. (2007). *The holistic curriculum: Second edition*. Toronto, ON: University of Toronto Press.

Milner, J. O., & Milner, L. F. (1999). *Bridging English*. Upper Saddle River, NJ: Prentice-Hall.

Moje, E. (2002). Re-framing adolescent literacy research for new times: Studying youth as a resource. *Reading Research and Instruction*, *41*(3), 211–228.

Mookerji, R. K. (2003). *Ancient Indian education: Brahmanical and Buddhist* (Original work published 1947). New Delhi, India: Motilal Barnarsidass.

Morrison, T. (1970). *The bluest eye.* New York, NY: Holt, Rinehart & Winston.

Mosley, W. (1998). *Always outnumbered, always outgunned.* New York, NY: Washington Square Press.

Murray, D. (1982). *Learning by teaching.* Portsmouth, NH: Boynton/Cook.

Nepo, M. (2000). *The book of awakening: Having the life you want by being present to the life you have.* San Francisco, CA: Conari Press.

Noddings, N. (1996). Stories and affect in teacher education. *Cambridge Journal of Education, 26*(3), 435–647.

Noe, A. (2009). *Out of our heads: Why you are not your brain, and other lessons from the biology of consciousness.* New York, NY: Hill & Wang.

Nussbaum, M. C. (2010). *Not for profit: Why democracy needs the humanities.* Princeton, NJ: Princeton University Press.

Oates, J. C. (1999). Where are you going, where have you been? In: R. P. Waxler & J. Trounstine (Eds), *Changing lives through literature.* Notre: Notre Dame Press.

Ong, W. (1968). *The barbarian within and other fugitive essays and studies.* London, UK: Macmillan.

O'Reilley, M. R. (1998). *Radical presence: Teaching as contemplative practice.* Portsmouth, NH: Heinemann.

O'Reilley, M. R. (2005). *The garden at night: Burnout and breakdown in the teaching life.* Portsmouth, NH: Heinemann.

Owen-Smith, P. (2004). What is cognitive-affective learning? *Journal of Cognitive Affective Learning, 1*(1). Available at http://www.jcal.emory.edu/viewarticle.php?id=31&layout=html. Retrieved on May 7, 2010.

Palmer, P. J. (1998). *The courage to teach: Exploring the inner landscape of a teacher's life.* San Francisco, CA: Jossey-Bass.

Palmer, P. J., & Zajonc, A. (2010). *The heart of higher education: A call to renewal—Transforming the academy through collegial conversations.* San Francisco, CA: Jossey-Bass.

Peskin, J., Allen, G., & Wells-Jopling, R. (2010). "The educated imagination": Applying instructional research to the teaching of symbolic interpretation of poetry. *Journal of Adolescent & Adult Literacy, 53*(6), 498–507.

Piaget, J. (1954). *Construction of reality in the child.* London, UK: Routledge & Kegan Paul.

Poe, E. A. (1984). *Complete stories and poems of Edgar Allen Poe* (Original work published 1843). New York, NY: Doubleday.

Postman, N. (1985). *Amusing ourselves to death: Public discourse in the age of show business.* New York, NY: Penguin.

Ramachandran, V. S. (2004). *A brief tour of human consciousness: From imposter poodles to purple numbers.* New York, NY: Pi Press.

Ramachandran, V. S., & Blakeslee, S. (1998). *Phantoms in the brain: Probing the mysteries of the human mind.* New York, NY: Harper Perennial.

Ratey, J. J. (2009, November). *Countering the cyber life: Getting in touch with our hunter-gatherer genes.* From the Mind and Brain conference proceedings at MIT in Cambridge, MA.

Reisman, L. (producer) & Schrader, P. (director). (1997). *Affliction* [motion picture]. USA: Lions Gate Films.

Richardson, A. (2010). *The neural sublime: Cognitive theories and romantic texts.* Baltimore, MD: John Hopkins University Press.

Richardson, W. (2008). *Blogs, wikis, podcasts, and other powerful web tools for classrooms.* Thousand Oaks, CA: Corwin Press.

Ricoeur, P. (1991). Interview with Paul Ricoeur. In: M. J. Valdes (Ed.), *A Ricoeur reader: Reflections and imagination* (pp. 15–30). Toronto, ON, Canada: University of Toronto Press.

Rizzolatti, G., Fogassi, L., & Vittorio, G. (2008). Mirrors in the mind. In: *The brain and learning* (pp. 12–20). San Francisco, CA: Jossey-Bass.

Roche, M. W. (2004). *Why literature matters in the 21st century.* New Haven, CT: Yale University Press.

Roeser, R. W., & Peck, S. C. (2009). An education in awareness: Self, motivation, and self-regulated learning in contemplative perspective. *Educational Psychologist, 44*(2), 119–136.

Rosenblatt, L. (1981). Aesthetics as the basic model of the reading process. *Bucknell Review, 26*(1), 21–22, 24–25. Cited from Donoghue (2000, p. 13).

Russo, J. (2005). *The future without a past: The humanities in a technological society.* Columbia, MO: University of Missouri Press.

Schirato, T., & Webb, J. (2004). *Understanding the visual.* Thousand Oaks, CA: Sage.

Searle, J. R. (2010). *Making the social world: The structure of human civilization.* New York, NY: Oxford University Press.

Shakespeare, W. (1937). A midsummer's night dream. *The complete works of William Shakespeare.* New York, NY: Walter J. Black.

Shelley, M. W. (1967). *Frankenstein.* New York, NY: Pyramid Books.

Shulman, L. (2004). *Teaching as community property: Essays on higher education.* San Francisco, CA: Jossey-Bass.

Stafford, B. M. (2008). The remaining 10 percent. In: J. Elkins (Ed.), *Visual literacy* (pp. 31–58). New York, NY: Routledge.

Steinbeck, J. (1937). *Of mice and men.* New York, NY: Covici, Friede.

Stewart, J. (1996). The symbol model vs. language as constitutive articulate contact. In: J. Stewart (Ed.), *Beyond the symbol model: Reflections on the representational nature of language* (pp. 9–68). Albany, NY: SUNY Press.

Stevens, W. (1921). Tea at the palaz of hoon. *Harmonium,* p. 97.

Stone, L. (2010). Continuous partial attention. Available at http://lindastone.net/2009/11/30/beyond-simple-multi-tasking-continuous-partial-attention/. Retrieved on December 24, 2010.

Tagore, R. (1988). The spirit of unity. In: *Creative unity* (pp. 125–140). New Delhi, India: Macmillan Pocket Tagore Editions.

Thomas-El, S. (2004). *I choose to stay: A black teacher refuses to desert the inner city.* New York, NY: Kensington.

Thurman, R. A. F. (2006). Meditation and education: India, Tibet and modern America. *Teachers College Record, 108,* 1765–1774.

Toffler, A., & Toffler, H. (2006). *Revolutionary wealth: How it will be created and how it will change our lives.* New York, NY: Random House.

Tomasello, M., & Call, J. (1997). *Primate cognition.* New York, NY: Oxford University Press.

Tomlinson, C. (2001). *How to differentiate instruction in mixed-ability classrooms.* Alexandria, VA: Association for Supervision and Curriculum Development.

Tomlinson, C., & McTighe, J. (2006). *Integrating differentiated instruction and understanding by design.* Alexandria, VA: Association for Supervision and Curriculum Development.

Trounstine, J., & Waxler, R. P. (2004). *Finding a voice: The practice of changing lives through literature*. Ann Arbor, MI: University of Michigan Press.

Turner, M. (1996). *The literary mind: The origins of thought and language*. New York, NY: Oxford University Press.

Ulin, D. L. (2010). *The lost art of reading: Why books matter in a distracted time*. Seattle, WA: Sasquatch Books.

Virilio, P. (2010). *University of disaster* (R. Julie, Trans.). Cambridge, UK: Polity Press.

Vygotsky, L. S. (1978). *Mind in society: The development of higher psychological processes*. Cambridge, MA: Harvard University Press.

Vygotsky, L. S. (1986). Thought and language. In: A. Kozulin (Ed.), Cambridge, MA: MIT Press.

Watkins, S. C. (2010). *The young and the digital: What the migration to social network sites, games, and anytime, anywhere media means for our future*. Boston, MA: Beacon Press.

Waxler, R. P. (1997). *Success stories: Life skills through literature*. Washington, DC: U. S. Department of Education.

Waxler, R. P. (2007). In honor of Rassias: What literature and language mean to me. In: M. B. Yoken (Ed.), *Breakthrough: Essays and vignettes in honor of John A. Rassias* (pp. 125–130). New York, NY: Peter Lang.

Waxler, R. P. (2008). Changing lives through literature. *Publication of the Modern Language Association (PMLA)*, *123*(3), 678–682.

Waxler, R. P. (2010). *Courage to walk*. New Bedford, MA: Spinner Publication.

Waxler, R. P., & Trounstine, J. (Eds). (1999). *Changing lives through literature*. Notre Dame, IN: Notre Dame Press.

Wheatley, M. J., & Whyte, D. (2006). A conversation on spirituality. In: S. Awbrey, D. Dana, V. Miller, P. Robinson, M. Ryan & D. Scott (Eds), *Integrative learning and action: A call to wholeness* (pp. 9–29). New York, NY: Peter Lang.

Whitman, W. (2005). Song of myself. In: F. Murphy (Ed.), *The complete poems* (pp. 63–125). New York, NY: Penguin.

Winnicot, D. (1986). *Holding and interpretation: Fragments of an analysis*. New York, NY: Grove Press.

Wood, J. (2008). *How fiction works*. New York, NY: Farrar, Straus and Giroux.

Wolf, M. (2007). *Proust and the squid: The story and science of the reading brain*. New York, NY: HarperCollins.

Wolf, M., & Barzillai, M. (2009). The importance of deep reading. *Educational Leadership*, *66*(6), 32–37.

Zaentz, S. (Producer) & Forman, M. (Director). (1975). *One flew over the cuckoo's nest*. [motion picture]. USA: United Artists.

Zajonc, A. (2006a). Love and knowledge: Recovering the heart of learning through contemplation. *Teachers College Record*, *108*(9), 1742–1759. Available at http://www.tcrecord.org. Retrieved on September 30, 2009.

Zajonc, A. (2006b). Science and spirituality—Finding the right map. In: S. Awbrey, D. Dana, V. Miller, P. Robinson, M. Ryan & D. Scott (Eds), *Integrative learning and action: A call to wholeness* (pp. 57–81). New York, NY: Peter Lang.

Zeki, S. (2009). *Splendors and miseries of the brain: Love, creativity, and the quest for human happiness*. Hoboken, NJ: Wiley-Blackwell.

Zull, J. E. (2002). *The art of changing the brain: Enriching the practice of teaching by exploring the biology of learning*. Sterling, VA: Stylus Publishing.

Printed in the United States
By Bookmasters